T0215272

Lecture Notes in Artificial Intelligence 12640

Subseries of Lecture Notes in Computer Science

More information about this subseries at http://www.springer.com/series/1244

Michael Cochez · Madalina Croitoru ·
Pierre Marquis · Sebastian Rudolph (Eds.)

Graph Structures
for Knowledge Representation
and Reasoning

6th International Workshop, GKR 2020
Virtual Event, September 5, 2020
Revised Selected Papers

 Springer

Editors
Michael Cochez
Computer Science Department
Vrije Universiteit Amsterdam
Amsterdam, The Netherlands

Pierre Marquis
Institut Universitaire de France
CRIL, Univ. Artois & CNRS
Lens, France

Madalina Croitoru
LIRMM
Montpellier, France

Sebastian Rudolph
Fakultät Informatik
TU Dresden
Dresden, Germany

ISSN 0302-9743   ISSN 1611-3349   (electronic)
Lecture Notes in Artificial Intelligence
ISBN 978-3-030-72307-1   ISBN 978-3-030-72308-8   (eBook)
https://doi.org/10.1007/978-3-030-72308-8

LNCS Sublibrary: SL7 – Artificial Intelligence

This Springer imprint is published by the registered company Springer Nature Switzerland AG
The registered company address is: Gewerbestrasse 11, 6330 Cham, Switzerland

Preface

The development of effective techniques for knowledge representation and reasoning (KRR) is a crucial aspect of successful intelligent systems. Different representation paradigms, as well as their use in dedicated reasoning systems, have been extensively studied in the past. Nevertheless, new challenges, problems, and issues have emerged in the context of knowledge representation in Artificial Intelligence (AI), involving the logical manipulation of increasingly large information sets (see for example Semantic Web, BioInformatics, and so on). Improvements in storage capacity and performance of computing infrastructure have also affected the nature of KRR systems, shifting their focus towards representational power and execution performance. Therefore, KRR research is faced with the challenge of developing knowledge representation structures optimized for large-scale reasoning. This new generation of KRR systems includes graph-based knowledge representation formalisms such as Constraint Networks (CNs), Bayesian Networks (BNs), Semantic Networks (SNs), Conceptual Graphs (CGs), Formal Concept Analysis (FCA), CP-nets, GAI-nets, and Argumentation Frameworks, all of which have been successfully used in a number of applications. The goal of the workshop series on Graph Structures for Knowledge Representation and Reasoning (GKR) is to bring together researchers involved in the development and application of graph-based knowledge representation formalisms and reasoning techniques.

This volume contains extended and revised selected papers of the sixth edition of GKR, under the auspices of ScaDS.AI – Center for Scalable Data Analytics and Artificial Intelligence Dresden/Leipzig, which took place jointly with ECAI 2020, the 24th European Conference on Artificial Intelligence, which was supposed to be held in Santiago de Compostela, Spain. Like ECAI, GKR had to be re-shaped into a virtual edition, given the global pandemic. This was a first, compared to previous editions of GKR held in Pasadena, USA (2009), Barcelona, Spain (2011), Beijing, China (2013), Buenos Aires, Argentina (2015), and Melbourne, Australia (2017). Still, like before, thanks to the association with a major international AI conference, the workshop provided the perfect venue for a rich and valuable exchange. As usual, the workshop submissions underwent single-blind reviewing by the program committee, each receiving between two and three reviews. On top of the extended workshop papers, this volume also contains two invited additional contributions from core GKR community members.

The scientific program of this workshop included many topics related to graph-based knowledge representation and reasoning, from sub-disciplines as diverse as conceptual graphs, formal concept analysis, graphical models, graph neural networks, concept diagrams, and others. Application areas included Smart Homes, Education, Team Formation, Enterprise Architectures, and Usage Pattern Analysis, demonstrating the wide applicability of graph-based KR methods. All in all, the sixth edition of the GKR workshop was very successful despite the unusual circumstances. The papers coming from diverse fields all addressed various issues for knowledge representation and reasoning and the common graph-theoretic background helped to bridge the gap between the different communities. This made it possible for the participants to gain new insights and inspiration.

The organizers are very grateful for the support of ECAI and we would also like to thank the program committee of the workshop for their hard work in reviewing papers and providing valuable guidance to the contributors. But, of course, GKR 2020 would not have been possible without the dedicated involvement of the contributing authors and participants.

February 2021

Michael Cochez
Madalina Croitoru
Pierre Marquis
Sebastian Rudolph

Organization

Workshop Chairs

Michael Cochez — Vrije Universiteit Amsterdam, The Netherlands
Madalina Croitoru — LIRMM & Inria, Université de Montpellier, France
Pierre Marquis — CRIL, Université d'Artois & CNRS, Institut Universitaire de France, France
Sebastian Rudolph — Technische Universität Dresden, Germany

Program Committee

Galia Angelova — Bulgarian Academy of Sciences, Bulgaria
Manuel Atencia — Université Grenoble Alpes & Inria, France
Pierre Bisquert — INRA & IATE, France
Zied Bouraoui — CRIL, Université d'Artois & CNRS, France
Dan Corbett — OptimodalTechnologies, USA
Olivier Corby — INRIA, Université Côte d'Azur, France
Dragan Doder — Utrecht University, The Netherlands
Nathalie Hernandez — IRIT, Université de Toulouse, France
Robert Jäschke — Humboldt-Universität zu Berlin, Germany
Mary Keeler — VivoMind, Inc., USA
Bernard Moulin — Université Laval, Canada
Uta Priss — Ostfalia University, Germany
Ricardo Oscar Rodriguez — Universidad de Buenos Aires, Argentina
Karim Tabia — Université d'Artois & CNRS, France
Wamberto Vasconcelos — University of Aberdeen, UK
Srdjan Vesic — CRIL, CNRS & Université d'Artois, France
Nic Wilson — Insight & University College Cork, Ireland
Bruno Yun — University of Aberdeen, UK

Organizing Body

Center for Scalable Data Analytics and
Artificial Intelligence Dresden/Leipzig
www.scads.de
@scads

Contents

Extended Workshop Papers

Active Semantic Relations in Layered Enterprise Architecture Development

Matt Baxter[1], Simon Polovina[1]([⊠]), Wim Laurier[2],
and Mark von Rosing[3]

[1] Conceptual Structures Research Group, Sheffield Hallam University, Sheffield, UK
a7033771@my.shu.ac.uk, S.Polovina@shu.ac.uk
[2] Université Saint-Louis, Brussels, Belgium
wim.laurier@usaintlouis.be
[3] LEADing Practice, Dronningmølle, Denmark
mvr@leadingpractice.com

Abstract. Enterprise Architecture (EA) metamodels align an organisation's business, information and technology resources so that these assets best meet the organisation's purpose. The Layered EA Development (LEAD) Ontology enhances EA practices by a metamodel with layered metaobjects as its building blocks interconnected by semantic relations. Each metaobject connects to another metaobject by two semantic relations in opposing directions, thus highlighting how each metaobject views other metaobjects from its perspective. While the resulting two directed graphs reveal all the multiple pathways in the metamodel, more desirable would be to have one directed graph that focusses on the dependencies in the pathways. Towards this aim, using CG-FCA (where CG refers to Conceptual Graph and FCA to Formal Concept Analysis) and a LEAD case study, we determine an algorithm that elicits the active as opposed to the passive semantic relations between the metaobjects resulting in one directed graph metamodel. We also identified the general applicability of our algorithm to any metamodel that consists of triples of objects with active and passive relations.

Keywords: Enterprise architecture frameworks · Layered enterprise architecture development · Business-IT alignment · Ontology · Semantics and reasoning · Conceptual structures · Model verification and validation

1 Introduction

Enterprise Architecture (EA) is a comprehensive approach to the documentation and understanding of organisational composition to promote alignment of its business, information and technology assets [9]. The Layered Enterprise Architecture Development (LEAD) Ontology includes a metamodel that is underpinned by building blocks consisting of 91 metaobjects organised in layers and sub-layers [7,14]. Semantic relations link the metaobjects thereby integrating

© The Author(s) 2021
M. Cochez et al. (Eds.): GKR 2020, LNAI 12640, pp. 3–16, 2021.
https://doi.org/10.1007/978-3-030-72308-8_1

all aspects of business, information, and technology for any organisation. These multiple relations highlight the inbuilt interconnections and the interdependencies between the elements in an enterprise. Conceptual Graphs (CG) are a formalised method of knowledge representation based on concepts and their relations [11,12]. Formal Concept Analysis (FCA) is a principled approach to determining a conceptual hierarchy of objects and their attributes [15]. FCA interrelates objects through their related attributes, thus enabling FCA to determine and visualise a conceptual hierarchy [3]. A CG can visually display LEAD's metaobjects and their semantic relations by linking each concept to another via these relations; however, validation can be difficult due to the manual nature of the task [1]. Subsequently, processing these 'triples' (metaobject–relation–metaobject) via FCA can highlight gaps in the model, revealing an organisational gap or human error in the modelling process. Thus, while a manual review of the LEAD artefacts can identify organisational gaps, an element of mathematical rigour can be applied to the process thereby complementing LEAD through the application of CG and FCA [6,8].

2   The Metamodel Diagram

To illustrate the contribution of CG and FCA, Fig. 1 acts as our starting point. This figure represents the metamodel of a warehouse pick pack process of a UK manufacturer, based on the LEAD Enterprise Ontology referred to earlier (i.e. LEAD ID#-ES20001ALL) [13]. The metamodel was created using the Enterprise Plus (E+) software (www.enterpriseplus.tools) from LEADing Practice, a not-for-profit body of LEAD industry practitioners (www.leadingpractice.com). E+ is a comprehensive repository of LEAD reference content, including its artefacts, metaobjects, and semantic relations. The semantic relations in Fig. 1 go in two directions between each metaobject. This duality is intended in many EA metamodels, including LEAD. That is because it reveals how each metaobject views itself in relation to each other directly, and indirectly through intermediate metaobjects; hence LEAD metamodels are two-way directed graphs [9].

3   Activating the Metamodel

The *CGtoFCA* algorithm converts the inherent ternary relations of CGs to the binary relations required for FCA [1]. This algorithm can also apply to other directed graph triples, including LEAD metamodels as illustrated by Fig. 1 [9]. The formal concepts can then appear in a Formal Concept Lattice (FCL). The CG-FCA software based on *CGtoFCA* thus facilitates an improved understanding of LEAD metamodels in tandem with highlighting human errors in the manual modelling process [1,9]. Further to that previous work, and in search of the metaobjects' dependence on each other, the proposed algorithm shown in Fig. 2 distinguishes the active and passive semantic relations. An active relation depicts a situation whereby a metaobject directs another, with the latter metaobject dependent on it, i.e. the passive relation. Following the identification

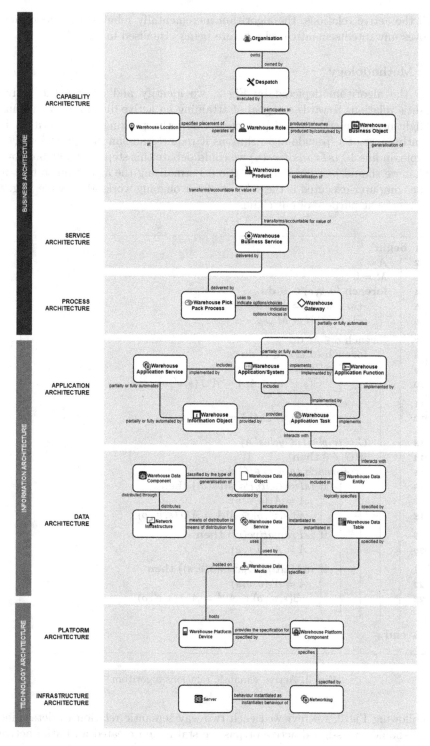

Fig. 1. Warehouse pick pack metamodel (from LEAD ID#-ES20001ALL)

of all the active relations, the algorithm incrementally rebuilds the model and removes unwanted semantic cycles before being visualised in an FCL.

3.1 Methodology

Using the algorithm depicted by Fig. 2, we identify and analyse the active semantic relations towards our goal of attaining an active direction graph, thus highlighting the metaobject dependencies. Strictly-speaking, our algorithm is presently more of a 'pseudo-algorithm' as it requires human interpretation. For example, in line 19 $isTransitive(v)$ we could debate this step, with one possibility that we should just invert the relation. Formalising the algorithm so that it can be computer-executed is the subject of our ongoing work. Meanwhile, Fig. 2 fits the present purpose of our claims.

```
 1 begin
 2     A = ∅
 3     M = ∅
 4     foreach (o, v, s) ∈ B do
 5         ¬∃o ∈ M|M = M ∪ o
 6         ¬∃s ∈ M|M = M ∪ s
 7     foreach o ∈ M do
 8         foreach (o, v, s) ∈ B do
 9             if isPassive(v) then
10                 ¬∃(s, v', o) ∈ A|A = A ∪ (s, v', o)
11             else
12                 ¬∃(o, v, s) ∈ A|A = A ∪ (o, v, s)
13     C = triplesInCycles(A)
14     if C ≠ ∅ then
15         foreach (o, v, s) ∈ C do
16             if isImplicityPassive(v)) then
17                 A = A\(o, v, s)
18                 ¬∃(s, v', o) ∈ A|A = A ∪ (s, v', o)
19             if isTransitive(v)) then
20                 A = A\(o, v, s)
21             if inMultipleCycles(o, v, s)) then
22                 A = A\(o, v, s)
23                 ¬∃(s, v', o) ∈ A|A = A ∪ (s, v', o)
24 end
```

Fig. 2. Active semantic relations algorithm

Following Fig. 2, we reviewed each two-way semantic relation to determine which should be assigned active or passive status and created an initial active model. We examined the semantics in the narrative of the relations and identified which metaobject was directing the other and vice versa. We then rebuilt the model by reviewing each concept in turn to remove semantic cycles [9]. Where both a direct and indirect pathway exists between two metaobjects, we removed the former, as the latter illustrates the mediating metaobjects. This step enabled a deeper understanding of the interdependencies. The ternary relations were compiled as 3-column CSV files and processed by the CG-FCA application to create the binary concepts. The operations and outcomes for each metaobject CSV file were recorded in a table to document the steps taken. After successfully refactoring each concept, we generated the FCL.

3.2   Findings

Following the selection of the active semantic relations in the one hundred forty-seven pairs of relations, the 00ActiveAll.csv file was unable to be processed by the CG-FCA application despite multiple attempts. The final attempt was aborted with the '00ActiveAll_report' file having amassed a size of over 10 GB after nearly eighty-eight hours of processing time. This first experiment prevented the creation of an FCL for the initial active model.

Table 1. Refactoring the Capability sublayer of the metamodel – Active Organisation, Role, and Organisational Function.

File	Operation & Outcomes
01ActiveOrganisation.csv	**Operation:** Adding all active (o, v, s) ε 00ActiveAll.csv with o or s = Organisation to empty file **Outcome:** No semantic cycles in 01ActiveOrganisation_report.txt
02ActiveRole.csv	**Operation:** Adding all active (o, v, s) ε 00ActiveAll.csv with o or s = Role to 01ActiveOrganisation.csv **Outcome:** No semantic cycles in 02ActiveRole_report.txt
03ActiveOrganisationalFunction.csv	**Operation:** Adding all active (o, v, s) ε 00ActiveAll.csv with o or s = Organisational Function to 02ActiveRole.csv **Outcome:** No semantic cycles in 03ActiveOrganisationalFunction_report.txt

Identifying the source of this seemingly infinite processing run was therefore attempted by employing an iterative approach and gradually increasing the number of triples included in 00ActiveAll.csv; however, we then encountered further issues. For example, in the case of 00ActiveAllDataObject1.csv (comprised of all 00ActiveAll triples up to and including the first instance of a Data Object triple), the processing time totalled just over twelve hours. Hence, there exists an issue of practicality in attempting to identify the triple that is causing the seemingly infinite compilation. We thus judged when to abort the processing due to uncertainty surrounding whether the processing run will not complete or whether it is only taking longer than expected compared to the previous iteration. The difficulty of the decision became exacerbated as processing time appears dependent on both the triple inserted and existing triples in the file, in the sense that one triple could cause a minimal increase in processing time while the impact of another could be significant. This intractability could reflect a combinatorial explosion: the number of input values increases exponentially with the number of potential outputs [2]. Nonetheless, and in light of the above experiences, we were able to proceed.

Table 2. Refactoring the data sublayer of the metamodel – Active Data Object.

File	Operation & Outcomes
16ActiveDataObject.csv	**Operation:** Adding all active (o, v, s) ϵ 00ActiveAll.csv with o or s = Data Object to 15ActiveDataComponent.csv **Outcome:** Two hundred thirty-five semantic cycles in 16ActiveDataObject_report.txt
16v2ActiveDataObject.csv	**Operation:** Deletion of transitive relation 'Data Object - influences the design of - Application Service' **Outcome:** One hundred twelve semantic cycles in 16v2ActiveDataObject_report.txt
16v3ActiveDataObject.csv	**Operation:** Deletion of transitive relation 'Data Service – encapsulates – Data Object' **Outcome:** Three semantic cycles in 16v3ActiveDataObject_report.txt
16v4ActiveDataObject.csv	**Operation:** Deletion of transitive relation 'Data Object - influences the design of - Application Task' **Operation:** Deletion of transitive relation 'Data Object - assumes or specifies - Platform Component' **Outcome:** No semantic cycles in 16v4ActiveDataObject_report.txt

The first five metaobject CSV files contained no cycles, three of which are detailed in Table 1. Subsequently, five cycles appeared in 06ActiveLocation.csv. The decision to replace 'Product - at - Location' with 'Location - at - Product' resolved all cycles[1].

We also encountered cycles in the LEAD Data sublayer, with cycles ranging from one to two hundred and seventy-nine. Table 2 shows the three iterations

---

[1] Not all the metaobjects and semantic relations appear in Fig. 1, including these two-way metaobjects and semantic relations, to maintain the figure's readability.

required to resolve all cycles initially presented in 16ActiveDataObject.csv. Due to space considerations, we do not list these cycles. We identified 'Platform Component – serves – Location' as a common triple across cycles; however, an alternative pathway remained undiscovered. 'Location –has – Process – produces/consumes – Data Object' exists as a more indirect pathway. However, we deleted it as part of an operation for 08v2ActiveProcess.csv, which highlights the cumulative effect of the decisions made at each stage of refactoring. Consequently, we made alternative choices. Considering the vast number of initial cycles presented (two hundred and thirty-five) and the manual nature of the activity, it is possible that a more indirect pathway does exist but overlooked by a human modeller.

3.3 Formal Concept Lattice

To visualise the output of CG-FCA, we created the FCL for 25ActiveInfrastructureService.csv, displayed in Fig. 3. The FCL lucidly exhibits the dependencies and driving metaobjects. A salient example is Product illustrated as being dependent on Process, which in turn is dependent on Role. In the context of the warehouse pick pack process, this dependency suggests that the product that is picked and packed is dependent on the process for doing so, which in turn is dependent on the employee that executes the process. Perhaps the most initially striking element of the FCL is the presence of Platform Component within the top-most formal concept, implying all objects below it in the diagram, i.e. its extent, are in some way dependent on it. While we might expect that technology ought to be driven by business, technology can drive business. For example, in recent years, the rise of cloud computing (a Platform Component) has driven a proliferation of decentralised business models. Accordingly, remote working is the norm and the presence of physical business components (Business Object, Location) is either minimised or eschewed entirely dependent on the industry.

A further interesting element elucidated in the FCL is 'Platform Device – hosts – Application/System', which implies that an Application/System is dependent on a Platform Device. This active pathway suggests that Platform Devices are the starting points, with the Application/System developed based on the specifications, constraints, and existence of the Platform Devices. While this makes sense, so does the opposing view, whereby Platform Device should be dependent upon Application/System because without an application to run, for what purpose does the device exist?

The presence of an empty formal concept close to the top of the lattice is also notable, and several potential explanations exist. Firstly, it could merely be a mistake in the modelling process, a probability which is heightened by the vast number of cycles encountered at some stages of the refactoring. Secondly, it could also be that the empty formal concept is irrelevant, as it exists purely as a vehicle for the facilitation of human understanding. Thirdly, and most speculatively, it could be pointing to a hitherto unnamed formal concept object, which in turn could potentially indicate a new metaobject arising from the other metaobjects and semantic relations, already validated by the LEADing Practice community.

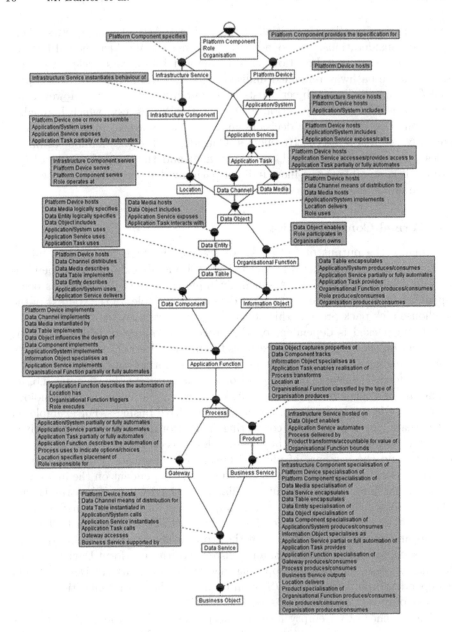

Fig. 3. 25ActiveInfrastructureService lattice

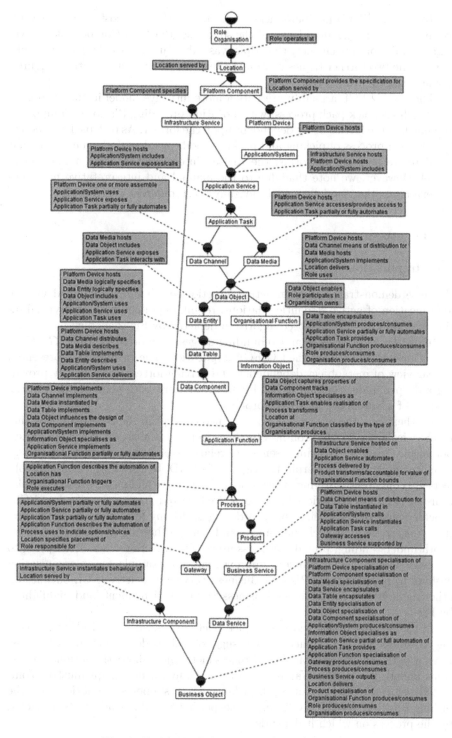

Fig. 4. 25v2ActiveInfrastructureService lattice

To remedy Platform Component's presence in the top-most formal concept, we reviewed the FCL and identified the source as 'Platform Component – serves – Location'. For convenience, the triple was substituted with the passive triple, as were the two further triples containing the 'serves' semantic relation. Figure 4 displays the resultant FCL.

The revised FCL arguably presents a more intuitive model in the context of the warehouse pick pack process, with Location preceding Platform Component and much of the lattice being dependent upon the former. As pick pack represents the physical process of picking and packing goods at a location – a concept that pre-dates technology platforms, the revised interpretation offers a more lucid model. However, we note that due to the manual and interpretative nature of the exercise, other modellers could feasibly reach different conclusions.

4   Discussion

4.1   Implications

We have demonstrated that an active direction graph can be attained via the identification of active semantic relations, rebuilding of concepts, and visualisation via an FCL. The proposed algorithm depicted by Fig. 2 enabled us to elaborate on the identification and rebuilding stages, supported by the $CGtoFCA$ algorithm implemented in the CG-FCA application. The ensuing FCL presented a clear view of metaobject dependency and driving forces, consequently providing a deeper understanding of the LEAD framework both generally and in the context of a warehouse pick pack process.

Furthermore, the presence of an unnamed concept in the 25ActiveInfrastructureService lattice could prompt a further, deeper examination of the semantics, potentially leading to refined semantic relations or a new metaobject. These enhancements would underpin the rigour of LEAD, by revealing which metaobjects are consistently driving others due to their active and passive semantic relations. It is in this scenario where the active-directed graphs visualised as FCLs provide value, due to their explicit ordering of driving forces and dependencies. It is conceivable that such diagrams could, due to their facilitation of more in-depth understanding, provide business users with direction when attempting to resolve issues or enact continuous improvement. For example, for an organisation wishing to improve the KPIs of a Business Service, the active FCL outlines all other metaobjects on which the Business Service is dependent, and highlighted by Fig. 5.

In the context of the warehouse pick pack process, if we consider the 'picking' Business Service, the active FCL suggests this is dependent upon Process. Review of the decomposition of the Process metaobject shows the various process steps undertaken by the Warehouse Admin. Many of these steps must be completed before the Picker can begin picking, which supports the notion that the picking Business Service's KPIs, e.g. picks per hour, could be adversely impacted by the process on which it depends.

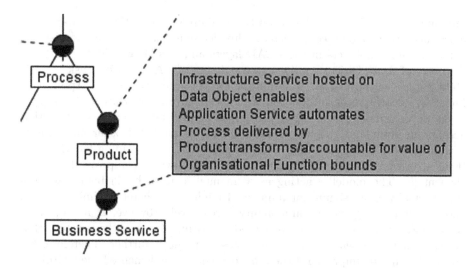

Fig. 5. Activated Business Service object and attributes

4.2   Current Limitations

We are aware that our choice of semantic relations from E+ might question the external validity of the work. From our experiments, we can quantify the scale of absent semantic relations as fifty-four out of two hundred ninety-four for the selected metaobjects. However, the number of incorrectly identified semantic relations (e.g. process – delivered by – Business Service) is unknown at this time. Both issues affect the selection process, as potentially erroneous assumptions for the former and the latter are uncertain by nature. These considerations are pertinent as they influence the active vs. passive selection, which in turn impacts all pathways associated with the triple. Inclusion of a triple from all one hundred forty-seven pairs of semantic relations potentially contributed to the issues with the CG-FCA application, reflecting the combinatorial explosion.

Similarly, the inclusion of triples with identical two-way semantic relations, e.g. Application Task and Data Table, increased the complexity of the task, subsequently increasing the likelihood of errors. While we based our approach on the proposed algorithm and selecting the TDV relation in these instances based on sound logic, alternative methods may exist. The omission of all identical two-way semantic relations would provide consistency but also prevent the explication of all pathways containing those triples. The manual nature of the exercise should also be considered, especially in the case of where many cycles occur. Determining which triple is most common across cycles by eye is imprecise when reviewing such a substantial data set.

Furthermore, we chose pathways based upon our intuitive knowledge of the LEAD framework. For example, during refactoring of 08ActiveProcess.csv, three triples were deleted ('Process – produces/consumes – Data Object', 'Process – produces/consumes – Information Object', and 'Application Task – partially or fully automates – Process') based on the assumption that other pathways with more mediating metaobjects existed. This decision was based on the distance between the metaobjects in the LEAD layers and was later validated with the discovery of 'Data Object – influences the design of – Application Task – uses – Data Table – encapsulates – Information Object – specialises as – Application Function – describes the automation of – Process' in 16ActiveDataObject_report.

However a more precise approach might be preferable, such as a tool that accepts an input and output metaobject in addition to all other metaobjects within the set, before returning a list of pathways in descending length order. If an algorithm comprises both logic and control, we can improve its control element [5]. The modeller acting as a 'manual' control by 1) being aware of the effect of a more significant number of triples and therefore limiting them, and 2) determining triple commonality across cycles by eye, is not optimal. As we have demonstrated, the proposed algorithm significantly assisted, thus based on our experiences, there are routes to refine it further. Therefore, the approach could be improved if the refined version complemented the CGtoFCA algorithm implemented in the CG-FCA application. Hence, the refined version duly implemented alongside CG-FCA can account for one or both these issues.

4.3   Future Research

We started with a(n) (ontology-based) metamodel, composed of concepts that were related by two-way, or bidirectional, relationships. The large majority of these bidirectional relationships seemed to be active in one direction and passive in the other. The LEAD metamodel reveals which aspects of business (the concepts) act upon or impact on others. In the context of change management (but also of the day-to-day management of a company) it is important to be able distinguish between the causes (active) and the effects (passive) of management issues (in day-to-day management) and identify the levers (active) needed to "pull" in order to realise the wanted change, while accounting for the passive effects that pulling the levers might have.

In case semantic relationships were two-way active or two-way passive, we needed to evaluate whether they could be reformulated as active-passive couples, i.e. the presently pseudo-algorithm (Fig. 2) into one that can be computer-implemented. With help from software libraries or web services that for example allow us to identify and rephrase passive and active relationships—e.g. Grammarly (www.grammarly.com) or DeepL (www.deepl.com)—the pseudo-algorithm could be automated as real executable code.

Our formal analysis of the metamodel has two main objectives. First, optimising the hands-on nature of the metamodel as a management tool: by separating the active from the passive semantics it is easier to find causes of a management issue and the levers that act upon this problem (that needs to be addressed) using the active semantics. Additionally, the passive semantics allow for identifying the effects of this management issue (and building the business case for the change). Moreover, the passive semantics will allow for identifying the (positive and negative) side-effects of the change, as the levers that are chosen or pulled will have an impact on the change goal, but also on other aspects of management that are actively affected. As such this clear "chain of command" is expected to both help identify the levers to obtain a desired change and minimise its adverse effects. Second, in ontology engineering there is an expectation that directed graphs with active and passive semantic relations should be isomorphic, i.e. a passive directed graph is the flip side of an active one. However, where they are not, there needs to be an elaboration. Is the "chain of command" thus asymmetric, and why, or are there missing concepts? As such this formal approach could be combined with OntoClean, METHONTOLOGY or other ontology engineering approaches [4, 10].

5   Conclusion

We have shown that by distinguishing the active semantic relations in bidirectional (two-way directed) graphs that we can identify the dependencies in metamodels from their metaobject and semantic relation building blocks. Furthermore, we outlined how our approach provides value to industry practice, thus promoting a deeper and more widespread understanding of Layered Enterprise Architecture Development (LEAD) and the LEAD Enterprise Ontology.

References

1. Andrews, S., Polovina, S.: Exploring, reasoning with and validating directed graphs by applying formal concept analysis to conceptual graphs. In: Croitoru, M., Marquis, P., Rudolph, S., Stapleton, G. (eds.) GKR 2017. LNCS (LNAI), vol. 10775, pp. 3–28. Springer, Cham (2018). https://doi.org/10.1007/978-3-319-78102-0_1
2. Butterfield, A., Ngondi, G.E., Kerr, A. (eds.): A Dictionary of Computer Science, 7th edn. Oxford Quick Reference. Oxford University Press, Oxford, England (2016)
3. Formica, A.: Ontology-based concept similarity in formal concept analysis. Inform. Sci. **176**(18), 2624–2641 (2006)
4. Guarino, N., Welty, C.A.: An Overview of OntoClean, pp. 151–171. Springer, Berlin Heidelberg, Berlin, Heidelberg (2004)
5. Kowalski, R.: Algorithm = logic + control. Commun. ACM **22**(7), 424–436 (1979)
6. Polovina, S., Scheruhn, H., Weidner, S., Von Rosing, M.: Highlighting the gaps in enterprise systems models by interoperating CGS and FCA. In: Andrews, S., Polovina, S., (eds.), 22nd International Conference on Conceptual Structures (ICCS 2016), 5th-7th July, pp. 46–54. Tilburg University, 12 Jul 2016
7. Polovina, S., von Rosing, M., Etzel, G.: Leading the practice in layered enterprise architecture. CEUR Workshop Proc. **2574**, 62–69 (2020)
8. Polovina, S., von Rosing, M., Laurier, W.: Conceptual structures in LEADing and best enterprise practices. In: Hernandez, N., Jäschke, R., Croitoru, M. (eds.) ICCS 2014. LNCS (LNAI), vol. 8577, pp. 293–298. Springer, Cham (2014). https://doi.org/10.1007/978-3-319-08389-6_25
9. Polovina, S., von Rosing, M., Laurier, W., Etzel, G.: Enhancing layered enterprise architecture development through conceptual structures. In: Endres, D., Alam, M., Şotropa, D. (eds.) ICCS 2019. LNCS (LNAI), vol. 11530, pp. 146–159. Springer, Cham (2019). https://doi.org/10.1007/978-3-030-23182-8_11

10. Sawsaa, A., Lu, J.: Building information science ontology (OIS) with methontology and protégé. J. Internet Technol. Secur. Trans. (JITST) **1**(3/4) (2012)
11. Sowa, J.F.: Conceptual graphs for a data base interface. IBM J. Res. Develop. **20**(4), 336–357 (1976)
12. Sowa, J.F.: Conceptual graphs. Found. Artif. Intell. **3**, 213–237 (2008)
13. von Rosing, M., Laurier, W.: An introduction to the business ontology. Int. J. Concept. Struct. Smart Appl. (IJCSSA) **3**(1), 20–41 (2015)
14. von Rosing, M., von Scheel, H.: Using the business ontology to develop enterprise standards. Int. J. Concept. Struct. Smart Appl. (IJCSSA) **4**(1), 48–70 (2016)
15. Wille, R.: Restructuring lattice theory: an approach based on hierarchies of concepts Ordered Sets. In: Proceedings of the NATO Advanced Study Institute held at Banff, Vol. 83, Canada, August 28 to September 12, 1981, pp. 445–470 (1982)

A Belief Update System Using an Event Model for Location of People in a Smart Home

Marie Bernert and Fano Ramparany(✉)

Orange Labs, 28 Chemin du Vieux Chêne, 38240 Meylan, France
fano.ramparany@orange.com

Abstract. Artificial Intelligence applications often require to maintain a knowledge base about the observed environment. In particular, when the current knowledge is inconsistent with new information, it has to be updated. Such inconsistency can be due to erroneous assumptions or to changes in the environment. Here we considered the second case, and develop a knowledge update algorithm based on event logic that takes into account constraints according to which the environment can evolve. These constraints take the form of events that modify the environment in a well-defined manner. The belief update triggered by a new observation is thus explained by a sequence of events. We then apply this algorithm to the problem of locating people in a smart home and show that taking into account past information and move's constraints improves location inference.

Keywords: Belief revision · Event logic · Semantic reasoning · Smart home · IoT

1 Introduction

A smart home should provide adapted services to its inhabitants. Indeed, the users' needs strongly depend on who is present in the house, where are the people located, what they are doing, at which time of the day and which day of the week, and so on. It is thus crucial to infer this context from the data provided by the house equipment. For example, concerning the "where" part of the context, the precise location of an occupant in the house can be used, among other, to chose a device to communicate with this occupant, or to suggest activities linked to this location. However, sensors' location information are often sparse and imprecise, due to the cost of equipping a house with numerous devices, and the rejection of too intrusive devices such as cameras. As an example of an easily available but vague information, a motion detector provides the information that at least one person is present in a room. Similarly, a smartphone WiFi connection provides the information that its owner is near or in the house. In spite of this vagueness, useful information can be inferred by tracking location information over time and taking into account the house topology. More generally, in many cases a knowledge about an environment is inferred from only sparse information. However, knowing the evolution constraints of the environment and accumulating information over time can lead to a substantial knowledge about the environment, as we do in our everyday life. Our goal is to implement an algorithm that takes location information

© The Author(s) 2021
M. Cochez et al. (Eds.): GKR 2020, LNAI 12640, pp. 17–32, 2021.
https://doi.org/10.1007/978-3-030-72308-8_2

from sensors of a smart home, and infer people location from this information, taking into account constraints on moves. More generally, we propose an algorithm able to revise knowledge taking into account well defined evolution constraints.

2   Use Case Example

In this section we present a use case scenario, defined as a main test case to design and test our location algorithm. In this scenario, we consider a simple house composed of four rooms and inhabited by two people: Alice and Bob. The four rooms are the entrance connected with the outside, the kitchen connected to the entrance, the living-room also connected to the entrance and the bedroom connected to the living-room (see Fig. 1). The home is equipped with some sensors that can give us information about people location:

- The entrance and living room are both equipped with a presence detector informing us whether some people are present in the room or not.
- The kitchen is equipped with a smart fridge informing us if someone is opening the fridge's door and is thus present in the kitchen.
- Bob is carrying a smart device informing us whether Bob is inside or outside the house.

Given the house topology and its sensor equipment, we consider the following seven-step scenario:

- step 1: Alice and Bob are both outdoor.
- step 2: Alice enters the house and is now in the entrance
- step 3: Alice goes in the living room.
- step 4: Bob then enters the house and is now in the entrance
- step 5: Bob goes in the kitchen.
- step 6: Alice then goes in the bedroom.
- step 7: Bob opens the fridge, notifying a presence in the kitchen.

When considering only the last step of the scenario, the location devices inform us that somebody is in the kitchen, nobody is in the entrance nor the living room and Bob is somewhere in the house. We infer from this information that Alice or Bob is in the kitchen, Bob is in the kitchen or the bedroom, and Alice is in the kitchen or in the bedroom or outdoor. However, when considering all the sensor information from the beginning of the scenario together with the room adjacency constraints, one can easily infer that Alice is in the bedroom and Bob is in the kitchen. This simple example shows that it is possible to infer much more information by taking into account the house's topology and past information. This use case can be used to discriminate an algorithm that uses such a strategy from one that does not.

3   Related Work

3.1   Logical Formalism

To address our problem, we need a logical formalism to deal about events and evolving facts. Many logical systems have been defined for this purpose. Here we present some of them.

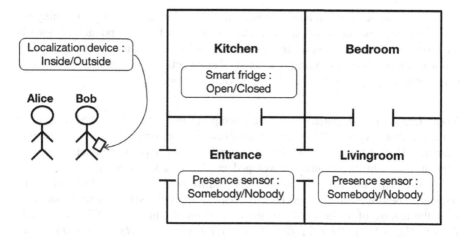

Fig. 1. Example of a smart home, equipped with simple location devices

Dynamic Logic. Dynamic logic was originally developed to reason about computer program, in particular to verify their correctness. Hoare's logic constitute a well known example of programming logic [6]. It was later realized that such logic could be used for other applications and it was then generalized to dynamic logic. Meyer gives a review of different dynamic logic applications [7]. In the context of our problem, we are interested by dynamic logic used as a logic of action.

Dynamic logic of action is build on a logical language $\mathcal{L}_{DL}$ and an action language $\mathcal{L}_{ACT}$. $\mathcal{L}_{DL}$ includes a set of propositional atoms P and is closed under the usual syntactic rules. $\mathcal{L}_{ACT}$ includes a set of atomic actions A and is closed under rules such as sequential composition of action $(\alpha; \beta)$, choice of action $(\alpha + \beta)$, arbitrary finite repetition of action (α^*), with $\alpha, \beta \in A$. In addition to the usual syntactic rules, $\mathcal{L}_{DL}$ is closed under the following rule: if $\phi \in \mathcal{L}_{DL}$ and $\alpha \in \mathcal{L}_{ACT}$ then $[\alpha]\phi$ and $\langle \alpha \rangle \phi$ are in $\mathcal{L}_{DL}$.

An interpretation for $\mathcal{L}_{DL}$ is a structure $\mathcal{M}$ of the form (S, π, r) where S is a non-empty set of states, $\pi : S \times P \to BOOL$ is a truth assignment function that associates a truth value to each couple of state and atomic proposition, and $r : \mathcal{L} \to \mathcal{P}(S \times S)$ a function that associates a state transition relation to each action. Given an interpretation $\mathcal{M} = (S, \pi, r)$ and a state $s \in S$, the truth value of a formula $\phi \in \mathcal{L}_{DL}$ is defined by:

- $\mathcal{M}, s \models p$ iff $\pi(s, p) = true$, for $p \in P$.
- $\mathcal{M}, s \models \neg\phi$ iff not $\mathcal{M}, s \models \phi$.
- $\mathcal{M}, s \models \phi \wedge \psi$ iff $\mathcal{M}, s \models \phi$ and $\mathcal{M}, s \models \psi$.
- $\mathcal{M}, s \models \phi \vee \psi$ iff $\mathcal{M}, s \models \phi$ or $\mathcal{M}, s \models \psi$.
- $\mathcal{M}, s \models \phi \to \psi$ iff $\mathcal{M}, s \models \phi$ implies $\mathcal{M}, s \models \psi$.
- $\mathcal{M}, s \models \phi \leftrightarrow \psi$ iff $\mathcal{M}, s \models \phi$ bi-implies $\mathcal{M}, s \models \psi$.
- $\mathcal{M}, s \models [\alpha]\phi$ iff for all s' such that $(s, s') \in r(\alpha)$ we have $\mathcal{M}, s' \models \phi$.
- $\mathcal{M}, s \models \langle \alpha \rangle \phi$ iff for some s' such that $(s, s') \in r(\alpha)$ we have $\mathcal{M}, s' \models \phi$.

Dynamic logic of action allows to write formulas such as $\phi \rightarrow [\alpha]\psi$, meaning that if ϕ is true, then executing action α leads to ψ being true. Is is thus possible to describe the result of an action. However this formalism can not deal with an explicit timeline, and it is not possible, for example, to assert that an action occurred at a specific time point, or that a proposition is true during a given time interval.

Event Logic. In [3], Allen developed a temporal logic, based on predicates logic, to reason about actions. This logical formalism involves properties, events, and time intervals. Allen defines a set of thirteen mutually exclusive primitive relation between intervals (see Fig. 2), originally developed in [2]. This set is $\mathcal{R}_{Allen} = \{=, <, > , m, o, d, s, f, mi, oi, di, si, fi\}$ where $=$, $<$, $>$, m, o, d, s, f respectively stands for "equals", "before", "after", "meets", "overlap", "during", "start", "finish", and each xi is the inverse of x. According to these relations, the predicates $STARTS(I, J)$, $FINISHES(I, J)$, $BEFORE(I, J)$, $OVERLAP(I, J)$, $MEETS(I, J)$ as well as $EQUAL(I, J)$ are defined, for times intervals I and J. Two other predicates are defined. The first is $HOLDS(p, I)$, where p is a property and I a time interval, meaning that property p is true during the interval I. The second predicate is $OCCURS(e, I)$, where e is an event and I a time interval, meaning that the event e occurs during the interval I, in other words e begins at the beginning of I and ends at the end of I. Whereas a property p holding during an interval I also holds for all sub-intervals of I, an event e can not be split, and its occurrence coincide exactly with the interval I. Allen also defines some other predicates about processes, causality and actions, which we will not detail here.

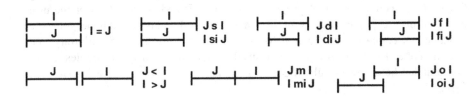

Fig. 2. Allen's primitive relations between intervals

Following this idea of reasoning about event occurrences, Siskind developed a logic known as event logic [8]. A language $\mathcal{L}_{EL}$ of event-logic expressions is defined as follow. A finite set O of constant symbols and a finite set E of primitive event-type symbols are given. An atomic event-logic expression is defined as a primitive event-type symbol of arity n applied to a sequence of n constants. Finally, an event-logic expression is either an atomic event-logic expression or a compound expression: $\neg\phi$, $\phi \vee \psi$, $\phi \wedge_R \psi$, $\Diamond_R\phi$, with $R \subseteq \mathcal{R}_{Allen}$, and ϕ and ψ event-logic expressions. An event-occurrence formula has the form $\phi @ I$ where $\phi \in \mathcal{L}_{EL}$ and I is a time interval. An interpretation $\mathcal{M}$ is a function that associate each primitive event-type symbol of arity n to a subset of $\mathcal{I} \times O^n$, where $\mathcal{I}$ is the set of all time intervals. The truth value of the formula $\phi @ I$ relatively an interpretation $\mathcal{M}$ is define by:

- $\mathcal{M} \models e(o_1, ..., o_n)@I$ iff $(I, o_1, ..., o_n) \in \mathcal{M}(e)$, for $e \in E$.
- $\mathcal{M} \models (\neg\phi)@I$ iff not $\mathcal{M} \models \phi@I$.
- $\mathcal{M} \models (\phi \vee \psi)@I$ iff $\mathcal{M} \models \phi@I$ or $\mathcal{M} \models \psi@I$.
- $\mathcal{M} \models (\phi \wedge_R \psi)@I$ iff there exists time intervals J and K such that I is the smallest super-interval of both J and K, JrK for some $r \in R$, $\mathcal{M} \models \phi@J$ and $\mathcal{M} \models \psi@K$.
- $\mathcal{M} \models (\diamond_R\phi)@I$ iff there exist some time interval J such that JrI for some $r \in R$, and $\mathcal{M} \models \phi@J$.

It is possible to define a primitive event-type, denoted $\overline{\phi}$, from a predicate ϕ. The event occurrence $\overline{\phi}@I$ is true if the predicate ϕ is true at each point of the interval I. This allows to unify the concepts of events and properties defined by Allen in [3]. As an example let's assume that we are given a set of persons, a set of rooms, and a predicate symbol $IsIn$. The predicate $IsIn(p, r)$, for a person p and a room r, is true at time t if p is present in r at time t. We can define the compound event-type expression $Move(p, r_1, r_2)$, for a person p and rooms r_1 and r_2 as follow: $Move(p, r_1, r_2) = \diamond_{\{m\}}\overline{IsIn}(p, r_1) \wedge_{\{=\}} \diamond_{\{mi\}}\overline{IsIn}(p, r_1) \wedge_{\{=\}} \overline{\neg IsIn}(p, r_1) \wedge_{\{=\}} \overline{\neg IsIn}(p, r_2)$. This states that a person p is moving from room r_1 to room r_2 during interval I iff p is in r_1 just before I, in r_2 just after I and that p in not in r_1 nor in r_2 during I.

3.2 AGM Model

The AGM model was developed by Alchourrón, Gärdenfors and Makinson as a framework for belief revision [1]. Its main goal is to define good properties of a revision operation on a belief set. A good introduction to the AGM model is given by Fermé [5]. Here we detail the main features of the AGM Model.

A belief set, or theory, K is a subset of a logical language $\mathcal{L}$ that is closed under logical consequence. Denoting Cn the consequence operation, we thus have $K = Cn(K)$. Given a belief set K a statement x, x is either believed if $x \in K$, disbelieved if $\neg x \in K$, or unsettled otherwise. The purpose of belief revision is to add or retract statements from a belief set. The AGM model define the possible revision operations on a belief set and give some postulates these operations should satisfy. Given a belief set K and a statement x, three operations are possible:

- expansion, denoted $K + x$, which changes the state of x from unsettled to believed
- contraction, denoted $K - x$, which changes the state of x from believed to unsettled
- revision, denoted $K * x$, which changes the state of x from disbelieved to believed

Expansion can be easily defined as $K + x = Cn(K \cup \{x\})$, effectively adding x to K without removing or adding information unnecessarily. Moreover, as in this case $\neg x \notin K$, if $Cn(x)$ is consistent the result is also consistent. When $\neg x \in K$, adding x to K is a revision operation. It is necessary to first remove $\neg x$ from K before adding x. The revision operation can be defined using the contraction operation through Levi identity: $K * x = Cn((K - \neg x) \cup \{x\})$. If the contraction is consistent and successful, then the revision operation is also consistent and successful.

The key of the problem is thus the contraction operation. The AGM model defines 6 main postulates a contraction operation should satisfy:

- closure: $K - x = Cn(K - x)$.
- inclusion: $K - x \subseteq K$.
- vacuity: if $x \notin K$ then $K - x = K$.
- success: if $x \notin Cn(\emptyset)$ then $x \notin K - x$.
- preservation: if $Cn(x) = Cn(y)$ then $K - x = K - y$.
- recovery: $K \subseteq Cn((K - x) \cup \{x\})$.

As a tool to define contraction, we denote $K \perp x$ the set of all maximal subset of K that does not imply x. A first naive approach to define contraction, called maxichoice contraction, is to chose $K - x$ to be one element of $K \perp x$. The maxichoice contraction has some disconcerting properties. In particular, when defining revision through the Levi identity, $K * x$ is always complete, which means that no statement is unsettled. Thus, the belief set generated by maxichoice contraction and revision might be considered "too big". A second approach, called meet contraction, is to define $K - x$ as the intersection of all elements of $K \perp x$. In this case, on the contrary, the result might be considered "too small". Indeed we have $K - x = K \cap Cn(x)$ and $K * x = Cn(x)$. In between, contraction can be defined as a partial meet contraction, which consist in selecting the most important elements of $K \perp x$. Let γ be a selection function such that $\gamma(K \perp x)$ is a non-empty subset of $K \perp x$. Partial meet contraction is defined as $K - x = \bigcap \gamma(K \perp x)$ and partial meet revision is defined through the Levi identity. Maxichoice contraction and meet contraction are extreme cases of partial meet contraction, where γ selects respectively one element or all elements of $K \perp x$. It can be shown that a contraction operation satisfies the 6 postulates if and only if it is a partial meet contraction. There is thus no general way to define contraction (and revision). Contraction requires to make some choice about the interesting beliefs to be preserved.

The AGM is a general framework for belief revision, that gives properties a revision operation should satisfy. However it does not detail practical implementation of these operation. In particular the contraction operation is not trivial to define.

3.3 Truth Maintenance Systems

Truth maintenance systems (TMS) were introduced by Doyle in [4]. As for most belief revision systems, Doyle's TMS tackles the problem of revising a belief set when a new information brings a contradiction. The two main principles of the TMS is to use a non-monotonic logic, where some facts are believed unless proved false, and to keep track of reasons why a fact is believed.

The TMS works in duality with a problem solver, which provides statements and justifications for these statements. The goal of the TMS is to decide which statement should be believed or not depending on their justifications. Within the TMS, statements are represented by node that are said to be "in" if the statement is believed or "out" otherwise. One node is marked as a contradiction and should not be "in". A justification for a node consists in two parts: a in-list and an out-list. A justification makes a node "in" iff all nodes in the in-list are "in" and all nodes in the out-list are "out". The out-list constitutes the non-monotonic part of the TMS. For example, in natural language, a justification for "Titi can fly" can be: "If Titi is a bird, Titi can fly, unless it is a penguin". In the TMS formalism, the node "Titi can fly" has a justification with the in-list "Titi is a bird" and the out-list "Titi is a penguin". There are particular of node in the TMS,called assumptions, which are nodes justified by an out-list containing their negation. An update of the TMS is triggered when a new justification is added. When the contradiction node becomes "in" after an update, a backtracking procedure is called to make the contradiction "out" again. This is done by finding the assumptions that justify (possibly indirectly) the contradiction and making one of these assumption "out" by adding a justification.

The TMS approach explains a contradiction by the fact that some assumptions were made that are not true. The contradiction is solved by disbelieving these assumptions. In our case, a contradiction can arise if a fact that was previously true becomes false because the environment is evolving. This difference makes the TMS not suitable for our problem.

4 Our Contribution

4.1 Algorithm Overview

Our algorithm assumes that we are provided information from sensors, that holds during a time interval. The time line is divided into time intervals, each time interval corresponding to a set of observations that holds during the entire interval. It is also possible to have intervals during which no information is given. In addition to these observations about the environment we are given a set of events that can make the environment evolve. We assume that these events modify our knowledge in a relatively simple way, such that, given a belief set holding before the event, we know what new belief set holds after an event occurs. The goal is to infer facts about the current environment from the consecutive observations and the possible event sequences explaining these observations.

The principle of the algorithm is to explore all possibilities of event sequences compatible with the past and current observations. Possibilities are explored by examining the consequences of adding an event to a sequence that has already been considered. The added event should be compatible with the current observations and what had already been inferred from the previous sequence hypothesis. Each time the observations change, new possibilities can be explored. Once all possibilities have been explored, we can infer that a fact about the environment is true if it is true considering every event sequence hypothesis, or possible if it is possible for at least one sequence hypothesis.

4.2 Logical Formalism

For the purpose of our problem, we found it practical to reason about continuous time and punctual events (events occurring at a precise time point). Indeed, for simplicity we assume that properties, such as the room position of a person in the house, are discrete and always well defined. As a consequence, changes on properties, such as the move of a person from one room to an adjacent room, are punctual events. Event logic provides useful operators to reason about event occurrences over time. However, for more flexibility, we chose to define a logic based on predicate logic as it was done in [3].

The main idea is to take a classical logic, later called the base logic, and augment it with time and events to construct a dynamic logic. We simply assume that the base logic contains the conjunction and the disjunction. Formulas from the base logic will be later called properties. A finite set E of punctual event symbols is given. A interpretation for our punctual event logic consists in two main elements:

- A transition model: each event symbol is associated with a transition function, which itself associates each base logic interpretation to another base logic interpretation. In other words the transition model defines how each event modifies a base logic interpretation.
- A sequence of event occurrence: An initial base logic interpretation and a sequence of events symbols associated with time points is given. Taking into account the transition model, a sequence of base interpretation associated with consecutive time intervals can be inferred, defining which properties are true at each time point.

We define two main predicates to write event logic formulas:

- $Occurs(e, t)$, with e an event symbol and t a time point, meaning that the event e occurs at time t, according to the event sequence model.
- $Holds(\phi, I)$, with ϕ a property and I a time interval, meaning that the property ϕ is true during the interval I according to the possible base logic models during this time interval.

We also define some other useful derived predicates:

- $Idle(I)$, meaning that no event occurs during the time interval I.
- $OccursSeq(s, I)$, meaning that the sequence of event $s = (e_1, ..., e_n)$ (and no other event) occurs during the time interval I
- $Holds_R(\phi, I)$, meaning that there exist a time interval J and an Allen relation $r \in R$, such that JrI and $Holds(\phi, J)$
- $Occurs_R(e, I)$ meaning that there exist a time interval I and an Allen relation $r \in R$, such that $Ir\{t\}$ and $Occurs(e, t)$
- $OccursSeq_R(s, I)$ meaning that there exist a time interval J and an Allen relation $r \in R$, such that JrI and $OccursSeq(s, J)$

This formalism gives us a framework to design our algorithm.

4.3 Transition Graph Structure

Let assume that we made a series of observations $O_0, ..., O_n$ during consecutive intervals $I_0, ..., I_n$. Observations $O_0, ..., O_n$ are sets of properties. We can thus write for each k: $Holds(O_k, I_k)$. The intervals I_k are called observation intervals. Note that the observation intervals do not necessarily coincide with the intervals during which the base logic model does not change. The observations can change without an event occurring and an event can occur without inducing a change in the observations. We assume that the transition model is known. However the event occurrence succession is unknown. Our goal is to infer properties given the observations and the transition model.

Let focus on one particular time point t in an interval I_k. The main idea of our algorithm is to make hypotheses about the event sequences that occurred from the starting time point t_0 until t. For this purpose, we associate each event sequence s to its transition function T_s, which is the composition of the transition functions associated to each of its events. Given a transition function T, we denote $Seq(T)$ the set of event sequences s such that $T_s = T$. Given a time point t, an observation interval I_k and a transition function T, we consider, as an event sequence hypothesis, the formula, denoted $N_T^k(t)$, stating that t is in I_k and that the event sequence between t_0 and t belong to $Seq(T)$:

$$N_T^k(t) = t \in I_k \wedge \exists s \in Seq(T), OccursSeq(s, [t_0; t]) \tag{1}$$

The formula $N_T^k(t)$, will be later called a belief node, as we will build a graph structure on these hypotheses. Let first notice that, for k given, the disjunction of the $N_T^k(t)$ for all transition function T is simply the statement that t belongs to I_k. For a given k, the observation interval I_k can be thus associated with the set of belief nodes $N_T^k(t)$ with T ranging over all possible transition function.

Let us now build a graph structure on belief nodes. For this purpose, we build an equivalent formula for $N_T^k(t)$ using predecessor belief nodes. Given a transition function T we consider $Pred(T)$ the set of couple (T', e), with T' a transition function and e an event symbol, such that $T = T_e \circ T'$. The hypothesis $N_T^k(t)$ is true if and only if one of the following hypothesis is true:

- for one $(T', e) \in Pred(T)$, there exists $t' < t$ such that $N_{T'}^k(t')$ and e is the only event occurring between t' and t.
- $k > 1$ and for one $(T', e) \in Pred(T)$, there exists $t' < t$ such that $N_{T'}^{k-1}(t')$, e occur at the time point between I_{k-1} and I_k and e is the only event occurring between t' and t.
- $k > 1$ and there exists $t' < t$ such that $N_T^{k-1}(t')$, and no event occurs during t' and t.
- if $k = 0$ and T is the identity, we also need to consider the hypothesis that no event occurs between t_0 and t.

Thus, each belief node can be written as a disjunction of hypotheses involving other belief nodes, which are predecessor belief nodes through different events. A predecessor belong to the same observation interval when the last event occured in the this interval, or to the previous observation interval when the last event occured at the time point between the two intervals (in this case the transition can correspond to no event).

The belief nodes can thus be organized into a graph, which we call transition graph, where vertices are belief nodes and edges correspond to events (see Fig. 3). The edges have two different types: internal edges, linking nodes corresponding to the same observation interval, and external edges, linking nodes from two consecutive observation intervals. We thus label the edges with transition symbols constructed from the event symbols and taking into account the internal or external nature of the edge. We denote this set of transition symbol $E_{tr} = E_{in} \cup E_{ex}$ with $E_{in} = \{(e, in), e \in E\}$ the set of internal transition symbols and $\{(e, ex), e \in E \cup \{idle\}\}$ the set of external transition symbols. The successor of a node N_T^k through an edge labeled by $e \in E_{tr}$ can be easily computed as $succ(N_T^k, e) = N_{T_e \circ T}^k$ if $e \in E_{in}$ and $succ(N_T^k, e) = N_{T_e \circ T}^{k+1}$ if $e \in E_{ex}$.

A walk in the transition graph starting from the initial node N_{Id}^0 gives a sequence of events for which we know the position relatively to the observation intervals. The definition of the hypothesis $N_T^k(t)$ can be refined by stating that their exist some walk w from N_{Id}^0 to $N_T^k(t)$ such that the events occurring between t_0 and t correspond to the event sequence described by w with the correct position in the observation intervals.

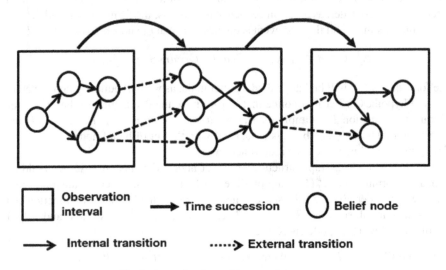

Fig. 3. Example of transition graph structure

4.4 Nodes' Belief Sets

A belief set is a set of formulas on a logical language, closed upon logical consequence. For convenience we will use belief set within logical formulas. In such cases, the belief set can be seen as the conjunction of all its elements. Similarly we sometimes define the value of a belief set through a logical formula, implicitly meaning that the belief set is the set of consequences from this formula. A belief set can also be seen as a set of interpretations, corresponding to the interpretations upon which all its formulas are true. From this point of view the conjunction (resp. disjunction) of two belief sets is the intersection (resp. union) of the corresponding sets of interpretations. In our logical formalism, a transition function can be applied to a base logic belief set, using the correspondence with set of interpretations. Notice that any transition function preserves the conjunction and the disjunction, and is monotonic relatively to the implication.

To each belief node N_T^k we associate a base logic belief set B_T^k containing all properties that can be inferred at a time point t upon the $N_T^k(t)$ hypothesis and given the past observations. In other words, we want to find B_T^k such that, for $t \in I_k$:

$$N_T^k(t) \wedge \bigwedge_{k'=0}^{k} Holds(O_{k'}, I_{k'}) \rightarrow Holds_{\{m\}}(B_T^k, \{t\}) \tag{2}$$

Let w be a walk from the initial node N_{Id}^0 to a node N_T^k. We associate w to a belief set $B(w)$ such that if the sequence of events described by w occurred between t_0 and the current time point t, and the taking into account the past observations $O_0, ..., O_k$, then we have $Holds_{\{f\}}(B(w), \{t\})$. This belief set can be defined the following way:

$$B(w) = \begin{cases} O_0 & \text{if } p \text{ is empty} \\ T_e(B(w')) \wedge O_k & \text{with } w = (w', e) \text{ and } k = n_{ex}(w) \end{cases} \tag{3}$$

where $n_{ex}(w)$ is the number of external event transitions in w. Using $Hold_{\{m\}}(B, t) \wedge Occurs(e, t) \rightarrow Holds_{\{mi\}}(T_e(B), t)$ as well as $Hold_{\{s\}}(B, I) \wedge OccursSeq(s, I) \rightarrow Holds_{\{f\}}(T_s(B), I)$, it can be shown that $B(w)$ defined this way satisfies the desired property.

As the hypothesis $N_T^k(t)$ states that their exist some walk w from N_{Id}^0 to $N_T^k(t)$ such that the corresponding sequence occurred, the belief set B_T^k can be defined as follow to satisfy Eq. 2:

$$B_T^k = \bigvee_{w \in walk(N_{Id}^0, N_T^k)} B(w) \tag{4}$$

where $walk(N_{Id}^0, N_T^k)$ is the set of walk from the initial node to N_T^k in the transition graph.

The goal of the algorithm it to compute the belief set B_T^k recursively.

4.5   Building the Graph

The goal of the algorithm is to build the transition graph and compute the nodes' belief sets recursively to match Eq. 4 so that Eq. 2 is satisfied for all belief nodes. As an input, the algorithm is provided, one after the other, the observations associated to each observation interval. Each time the observation associated to the next interval is received, the algorithm update the graph to compute the nodes associated to this interval.

The following notations are used to describe the algorithm:

- An observation interval I is identified to its set of associated nodes, so we can write $N \in I$ if the node N is associated to I.
- For an observation interval I, $next(I)$ denotes the following consecutive interval: $next(I_k) = I_{k+1}$.
- For a node N, $Obs(N)$ is the set of observation associated to the interval it belongs to.
- For a node N, $B(N)$ is the belief set associated to N.

All nodes' belief sets are initialized to be inconsistent. When the observations associated to the first observation interval is given, the $UpdateInitialInterval$ function is called (see algorithm 1). Then, each time the observations associated to the next observation interval is received, the $UpdateNextInterval$ function is called (see algorithm 2). These two function ensure that the $I_{current}$ variable refer to the last observation interval for which information has been received, and that the belief sets of nodes associated to this interval (and all previous intervals) are correctly computed. These two function both call the recursive function $UpdateNode$ (see algorithm 3), which performs a deep first exploration of the graph, updating the node's belief set when necessary.

Each call of the recursive function $UpdateNode$ corresponds to a walk in the graph. We define the set W of explored walks as the maximal set of walks such that for each node N, the associated belief set is the disjunction of all $B(w)$ with $w \in walk(N_{Id}^0, N) \cap W$. For short, we note $W_N = walk(N_{Id}^0, N) \cap W$. The algorithm is correct if at the end of all recursive calls, W contains all walks from the initial node to the current observation interval. During the algorithm execution, the following property on W is maintained: if W contains a walk w which is not in the call stack, W also contains all walks starting with w. In particular, when the algorithm terminates, the call stack is empty and, as W contains all walks in the previous interval (or the empty walk), W also contains all walks in the current interval. To maintain this property, the $UpdateNode$ function ensures that if $W_{N_{pred}}$ contains a walk w when it is called, then at the end of the execution, W contains all walks beginning with (w, e). In the recursive case, the node's belief set is updated so that W_N contains (w, e). As the function is then called recursively for all event transitions e', W should contains all walks starting with (w, e, e') for all e', and thus all walks starting with (w, e). In the base case, the belief set update has no effect, which means (w, e) is already in W_N while not in the call stack, and thus all walks beginning with (w, e) are already in W.

A key result for the termination of the algorithm is that cycles in a walk w do not impact the computation of $B(w)$. Indeed if $w = w'w_c$ with w_c a cycle, it can be shown, using the monotonicity of transition functions, that $B(w) \rightarrow B(w')$. When the $UpdateNode$ function is called for a walk $w = w'w_c$ with w_c a cycle, the corresponding node N has already been updated so that w' is in W_N. Assuming that w_c is the only cycle in w, the condition on the structure of W ensure for all walks w'' in $W_{N_{pred}}$, (w'', e) is already in W_N, except for w. As $B(w) \rightarrow B(w')$, w is also already in W_N. The update has thus no effect on the belief set and the function returns. As a consequence walks with cycles are never effectively explored, which ensure that the algorithm terminates, as long as the number of consistent nodes is finite.

Algorithm 1. $UpdateInitialInterval()$

$I_{current} := I_0$
$B(N_{Id}^0) := O_0$
for $e \in E_{in}$ **do**
    $UpdateNode(succ(N_{Id}^0), N_{Id}^0, e)$
end for

Algorithm 2. $UpdateNextInterval()$

---

  for $N \in I_{current}$ **do**
    for $e \in E_{ext}$ **do**
      $UpdateNode(succ(N, e), N, e)$
    end for
  end for
  $I_{current} := next(I_{current})$

Algorithm 3. $UpdateNode(N, N_{pred}, e)$

  $B_{old} := B(N)$
  $B(N) := B(N) \vee (T_e(B(N_{pred})) \wedge Obs(N))$
  if $B(N) \neq B_{old}$ **then**
    for $e \in E_{in}$ **do**
      $UpdateNode(succ(N, e), N, e)$
    end for
  end if

4.6 Querying the Graph

Once the transition graph is constructed, we want to know, given a time point t, which properties are true at this time point. By construction, during an observation interval, the disjunction of all its belief nodes holds. Thus, a property is true at a time point within the observation interval if it is true in all belief nodes. Additionally, a property is possible (i.e. not false) if it is possible in at least one belief node. One can also get interested in what happen at the beginning (resp. at the end) of the observation interval, by looking only at the belief nodes that have consistent predecessors (resp. successors) in the previous (resp. next) interval. For example, a property is true at the beginning of the observation interval if it is true in all nodes that have a consistent predecessor in the previous interval. Knowing which properties are true at the beginning, during or at the end of each observation interval, we can infer if a formula of the form $Holds_R(\phi, I)$ is true, false or unknown according to current knowledge. Moreover possible event sequences from t_0 to a time point t in I_k correspond to walks in the graph from the initial node N_{Id}^0 to a node associated to I_k, going through only consistent nodes.

5 Application to the Location Problem

We will now apply this algorithm to the home location problem. Here we assume that the house topology is known, and that a set devices provides two type of location information over time: information about the number of people present in one room, and information about the location of a specific person. We also assume that only known people are present in the house. We thus have a set of person P, a set of rooms R and an adjacency relation $Adj \subseteq R \times R$. The property language is build with one predicate: $IsIn(p, r)$ with $p \in P$ and $r \in R$. An event is a person moving from one room to an adjacent room. The set of event symbols is defined as: $E = \{Move(p, r_1, r_2), p \in P, (r_1, r_2) \in Adj\}$. A transition function corresponds to a subset of person moving each from one room to another room. For convenience, as they lead to similar belief sets, we chose to group in the same belief node all transition functions for which people arrive in the same position, not taking into account their initial position. We consider a belief set as a disjunction of house states, where a house state is the conjunction of predicates of the form $IsIn(p, r)$, for all $p \in P$. A house state thus describes the position of all people in the house, and can be seen as an interpretation for the base logic. Here for convenience, we use a different language for observations. An observation can be whether the predicate $Count(r, N)$, with $r \in R$ and $N \subseteq \mathbb{N}$, meaning that the number of persons in room r is in N, or the predicate $Located(p, R')$, with $p \in P$ and $R' \subseteq R$, meaning that the person p is in one of the room in R'. Adding an observation to a belief set can be simply done by removing the incompatible house states from the disjunction.

We applied this algorithm to the use case described in Sect. 2. We have $P = \{A, B\}$ for Alice and Bob, and $R = \{o, e, k, l, b\}$ for outdoor, entrance, kitchen, living-room and bedroom. The sensors deliver information about Bob's location, and the number of person in the entrance, the living-room and the kitchen. We denote $out = \{o\}$,

Table 1. Results of the algorithm applied to Alice and Bob use case

Node	Belief
Interval 1: $Located(B, out), Count(e, zero), Count(l, zero)$	
$\{\}$	$(IsIn(A, o) \wedge IsIn(B, o))$
	$\vee(IsIn(A, b) \wedge IsIn(B, o))$
	$\vee(IsIn(A, k) \wedge IsIn(B, o))$
Interval 2: $Located(B, out), Count(e, some), Count(l, zero)$	
Move(A,*,e)	$IsIn(A, e) \wedge IsIn(B, o)$
Interval 3: $Located(B, out), Count(e, zero), Count(l, some)$	
Move(A,*,l)	$IsIn(A, l) \wedge IsIn(B, o)$
Interval 4: $Located(B, home), Count(e, some), Count(l, some)$	
Move(A,*,l), Move(B,*,e)	$IsIn(A, l) \wedge IsIn(B, e)$
Interval 5: $Located(B, home), Count(e, zero), Count(l, some)$	
Move(A,*,b), Move(B,*,l)	$IsIn(A, b) \wedge IsIn(B, l)$
Move(A,*,l), Move(B,*,b)	$IsIn(A, l) \wedge IsIn(B, b)$
Move(A,*,l), Move(B,*,l)	$IsIn(A, l) \wedge IsIn(B, l)$
Move(A,*,l), Move(B,*,k)	$IsIn(A, l) \wedge IsIn(B, k)$
Interval 6: $Located(B, home), Count(e, zero), Count(l, zero)$	
Move(A,*,b), Move(B,*,k)	$IsIn(A, b) \wedge IsIn(B, k)$
Move(A,*,b), Move(B,*,b)	$IsIn(A, b) \wedge IsIn(B, b)$
Interval 7: $Located(B, home), Count(e, zero), Count(l, zero),$ $Count(k, some)$	
Move(A,*,b), Move(B,*,k)	$IsIn(A, b) \wedge IsIn(B, k)$

$home = \{e, k, l, b\}$, $zero = \{0\}$ and $some = \mathbb{N}^*$. The scenario is composed of seven steps, corresponding to observation intervals. The transition graph resulting from the algorithm is described in Table 1. Notice that in the last interval, the only possibility is that Alice is in the bedroom and Bob in the kitchen, which is more precise that what can be inferred using only the last observations. The implemented algorithm thus successfully worked on the defined test case.

6 Conclusion and Perspectives

At the application level, our work has shown that it is possible to infer accurate location information with a minimum of sparse low level measurements. For instance, as proved by our illustrative example, our approach makes it possible to find out which rooms several known occupants of the home can be located in, even if only few of them can be identified through their mobile phone or RFiD card and only very low level sensors and detector are used, only some rooms of the house are instrumented. The formalism and logical framework that we have defined multiple levels of genericity. In the Internet of Thing (IoT) domain, we can apply a similar approach to identify the status of an equipment (device, system, machine) through sparse observations of the equipment and of its environment.

On a more general level, we believe that our approach, including the modeling technique and algorithms can be applied to range of application domains. Characteristics of the target domains include the fact that information in these domains are organized as interrelated chunks of data and that it is known how modifying one chunk can affect chunks that are related to the chunk being modified.

On future work, this approach could also be extended to include probabilistic reasoning. This would allow to tackle the problem of imperfect sensors that can occasionally provide erroneous information, or to take into account the fact events and situations may occur with different probabilities.

References

1. Alchourron, C.E., Gardenfors, P., Makinson, D.: On the logic of theory change: partial meet contraction and revision functions. J. Symb. Logic **50**(2), 510–530 (1985)
2. Allen, J.F.: Maintaining knowledge about temporal intervals. Commun. ACM **26**(11), 832–843 (1983). https://doi.org/10.1145/182.358434
3. Allen, J.F.: Towards a general theory of action and time. Artif. Intell. **23**(2), 123–154 (1984). https://doi.org/10.1016/0004-3702(84)90008-0
4. Doyle, J.: A truth maintenance system. Artif. Intell. **12**(3), 231–272 (1979). https://doi.org/10.1016/0004-3702(79)90008-0
5. Fermé, E., Hansson, S.O.: The AGM Model, pp. 9–24. Springer International Publishing, Cham (2018). https://doi.org/10.1007/978-3-319-60535-7_3
6. Hoare, C.A.R.: An axiomatic basis for computer programming. Commun. ACM **12**(10), 576–580 (1969). https://doi.org/10.1145/363235.363259

7. Meyer, J.J.C.: Dynamic logic for reasoning about actions and agents. In: Minker, J. (ed.) Logic-Based Artificial Intelligence. The Springer International Series in Engineering and Computer Science, vol. 597, pp. 281–311. Springer, Boston, MA (2000). https://doi.org/10.1007/978-1-4615-1567-8_13
8. Siskind, J.: Grounding the lexical semantics of verbs in visual perception using force dynamics and event logic. J. Artif. Intell. Res. (JAIR) **15**, 31–90 (2001). https://doi.org/10.1613/jair.790

A Natural Language Generation Technique for Automated Psychotherapy

Graham Mann$^{(\boxtimes)}$ ⓘ, Beena Kishore ⓘ, and Pyara Dhillon ⓘ

Murdoch University, 90 South Street Murdoch, Perth, WA 6150, Australia
{g.mann,b.kishore,p.dhillon}@murdoch.edu.au

Abstract. The need for software applications that can assist with mental disorders has never been greater. Individuals suffering from mental illnesses often avoid consultation with a psychotherapist, because they do not realize the need, or because they cannot or will not face the social and economic consequences, which can be severe. Between ideal treatment by a human therapist and self-help websites lies the possibility of a helpful interaction with a language-using computer. A model of empathic response planning for sentence generation in a forthcoming automated psychotherapist is described here. The model combines emotional state tracking, contextual information from the patient's history and continuously updated therapeutic goals to form suitable conceptual graphs that may then be realized as suitable textual sentences.

Keywords: Natural language generation · Conceptual graphs · Model-based reasoning

1 Introduction

Many parts of the world now face a serious mental health care treatment gap, especially in low to middle income countries, and non-urban areas in high income countries [1]. The reasons are complex, but much of the shortage is caused by a lack of available skilled psychiatric professionals, and a failure of engagement by patients for economic or social stigma reasons [2]. A review of evidence shows that there are good reasons to think computerized therapy may be one effective approach to overcoming these difficulties [3]. While we do not imagine that these would be equivalent to consultation with skilled human psychiatrists, even existing mental health care apps can play a role and would often be better than nothing. In the case of "talking" therapies – those relying primarily on psychiatric interviews - software can today carry out natural conversations with a patient, simulating the role of the therapist. This paper deals with the formation and expression of appropriate responses to be used by an automated therapist during a consultation. It is a conceptual graph (CG) based language theory realized as a computer model of language generation called Affect-Based Language Generation (ABLG).

Current trends in conversational systems tend to favour machine learning (ML) approaches, typically employing neural networks (NN), but we believe that these are not ideal in this application, for the following reasons. First, the knowledge and executable

M. Cochez et al. (Eds.): GKR 2020, LNAI 12640, pp. 33–41, 2021.
https://doi.org/10.1007/978-3-030-72308-8_3

skills of a machine learning system are typically opaque, lack auditability and so lack trust [4]. This is a serious drawback in medical applications. Knowledge and skills in conceptual graph (CG) based systems are as a rule much more human-readable and subject to logical reasoning that can readily be comprehended and verified. Second, NN-based or statistical ML approaches (with the possible exception of Bayesian learners) cannot easily incorporate high level, *a priori* knowledge into their processing [5]. This disadvantages learners in domains where such high-level knowledge is available or must be policy. But by virtue of their standardized knowledge representation, CG systems can freely mix prior knowledge incoming data relatively easily. Third, ML language systems are typically very data-hungry, and while large corpuses of language knowledge are now available, using these is computationally expensive. By contrast, model-based CG systems can, with some labour, be made to work with a relatively small amount of domain-specific language knowledge and with little or no learning.

In the rest of this paper, Sect. 2 proposes a system model that draws on tracked emotional states, patient's utterances and background information about the patient with pragmatic cues and goals from a control executive to generate a suitable response in conceptual form. Section 3 briefly describes our experimental implementation, consisting of heuristics to fetch instances of the above informative content, and calling on conceptual functions to filter these and bring them together to form CGs that can be realised as linear texts. The whole process is controlled by an executive expert system implementing psychotherapeutic rules. Finally, Sect. 4 concludes with some current challenges of this approach and its prospects for testing and further development.

2 Sources Informing the Generation of Responses

Sentence generation involves the planning of conceptual content first, and then linguistically encoding it into a grammatical string of words [6]. Our idea of generating sentences is based on a therapeutic process informed by representations of the patient's current emotional state, representations of their pre-clinical interview history, and representations of their on-going utterances.

2.1 Tracking of Patient's Expressed Emotions

It is difficult to imagine a successful psychotherapist who is not concerned with the emotional state of the patient. Even behaviourist therapies that emphasise overt actions in response to stimuli over mental state today include emotions as a recognised behavioural response, if not an important internal state determining them [e.g., 7]. The evidence is clear that the patient's emotional state which is important for treatment needs to be closely monitored [8]. This state must be dealt with properly to maintain patients in a comfortable place, while at the same time empathizing, noting the significance of the emotion and helping the patient to find meaning from it. Much emotional information can be obtained by monitoring a speaker's tone of voice, facial expression or other body language. Today's mobile devices, with their microphones and cameras could hope to read these forms of expression, but since at this stage our work is about testing a theory of natural language generation, not a practical app, we use only text.

According to the survey conducted by Calvo and D'Mello [9] on models of affect, early approaches to detect emotional words in text include lexical analysis of the text to recognize words that are immanent of the affective states [10] or specific semantic analyses of the text based on an affect model [11]. The current work adapts Smith & Ellsworth's six-dimensional model [12] to make a system that can better grasp the subtleties of patient affect. Their chosen modal values on the principle component states for 15 distinguished emotional states are shown in Table 1.

Table 1. Mean locations of labelled emotional points in the range [− 1.5, +1.5] as compiled in Smith & Ellsworth's study.

Emotion	P	R	C	A	E	O
Happiness	−1.46	0.09	−0.46	0.15	−0.33	−0.21
Sadness	0.87	−0.36	0	−0.21	−0.14	1.15
Anger	0.85	−0.94	−0.29	0.12	0.53	−0.96
Boredom	0.34	−0.19	−0.35	−1.27	−1.19	0.12
Challenge	−0.37	0.44	−0.01	0.52	1.19	−0.2
Hope	−0.5	0.15	0.46	0.31	−0.18	0.35
Fear	0.44	−0.17	0.73	0.03	0.63	0.59
Interest	−1.05	−0.13	−0.07	0.7	−0.07	0.41
Contempt	0.89	−0.5	−0.12	0.08	−0.07	−0.63
Disgust	0.38	−0.5	−0.39	−0.96	0.06	−0.19
Frustration	0.88	−0.37	−0.08	0.6	0.48	0.22
Surprise	−1.35	−0.97	0.73	0.4	−0.66	0.15
Pride	−1.25	0.81	−0.32	0.02	−0.31	−0.46
Shame	0.73	1.31	0.21	−0.11	0.07	−0.07
Guilt	0.6	1.31	−0.15	−0.36	0	−0.29

A patient's textual utterance is compared to accumulated word-bags that offer clues to the expressed emotions, plus a filter to exclude references to the emotions of others. These classify the expressed emotion into one of the Smith & Ellsworth's 15 ideal values, the vectors of which locate the expression as a single point in a six-dimensional affective space. This allows mappings of complex emotional states into a consistent hypervolume so that, for example, the "distances" between two states can be computed. It also allows emotive subspaces to be defined. One way that emotional tracking can be used is for the appropriate application of sympathy. We define a "safe region" in the affective space. The therapist may continue the therapy as long as the patient's tracked emotional state stays within the safe region. A single point was chosen as the "most distressed" emotional state (we used {1.10 1.3 1.15 1.0–1.15 2.0}). The simplest model of a safe region is outside a hypersphere of fixed radius centred on this point. The process is then reduced to finding the Euclidian distance between the current emotional state and the above-defined distressed centre.

$$\Delta\Omega = \sqrt{(\mathcal{P}i - \mathcal{P}j)^2 + (Ei - Ej)^2 + (Ci - Cj)^2 + (Ai - Aj)^2 + (Ri - Rj)^2 + (Oi - Oj)^2}$$

If the calculated distance is greater than an arbitrarily defined tolerance threshold (radius), the patient's current emotional state is considered safe. The calculated $\Delta\Omega$ of an emotional state $\{1.15\ 0.09\ 1.3\ 0.15\ -0.33\ -0.21\}$ from the above-defined distress point would be 1.70. For an arbitrary tolerance radius of 2.5 units from the distress point, the patient's tracked emotive state would not be in the safe region. A more sophisticated approach would be to map examples of real patient distress into a convex volume of the emotional space and then measure the current tracked emotional state to the nearest point on that volume.

2.2 Conceptual Analysis of Patient's Utterances

Study of a reference corpus of 118 talking therapy interviews [13], reveals that these patient utterances can be long and rambling, often incoherent and quite difficult for a person, much less a machine, to comprehend. While we have a conceptual parser, SAVVY, capable of converting real, non-grammatical paragraphs into meaning-preserving CGs [14], it was not developed for use in this domain. For the present work we do not intend to improve it to the point of creating meaningful conceptual representations for most of the utterances observed in our corpus. Conceptual parsers depend on an ontology in the form of a hierarchy of concepts, a set of relations and a set of actors. Manually creating representations of all the terms used in those interviews for SAVVY would be a difficult and time-consuming task. (This most serious of drawbacks for conceptual knowledge-based systems is now being addressed in automated ontology-building machines [e.g. 15]). Our focus in this study is the *generation* of language. Yet this kind of psychotherapy is essentially conversational, so we must allow the conceptual representations of patient utterances to be an input even to test response formation. Therefore, SAVVY will be adapted to accept selected patient utterances of interest. In some cases, to keep the project manageable, we hand-write plausible input CGs to avoid diverting too much time and energy away from our generation pipeline.

2.3 Using Context to Inform the Planning Process

In regular clinical practice, the first step for a new patient is an admitting (or triage) interview, that can capture important biographical details, a presenting complaint, background histories, and perhaps an initial diagnosis. Because we wish our model of language generation to account for existing, contextual information, we will not actively model this initial interview, but rather only subsequent interviews that have access to this previously gathered background. A set of background topics that should be sought during an admitting interview is described by Morrison [16]. Our current model draws 12 topics from this source and adds three extra topics specific to our clinical model.

2.4   Executive Control

An executive system based on a theory about how therapy should be done is needed for overall control. At each conversational turn, the executive should recommend the best "pragmatic move" and therapeutic goal for the response. This allows for the selection and instantiation of appropriate high-level conceptual templates that form the therapist's utterances to support, guide, query, inform or sympathize with the patient as appropriate during the treatment process. Our executive is based on the brief therapy of Hoyt [17] and the solution-based therapy of Shoham et al. [18]. As recommended by Hoyt, the focus is on negotiating treatment practices, not diagnostic classification. However, in this experiment a working diagnosis might become available as a result of the therapy or be input as background knowledge.

For a natural interviewing style, the executive must allow its goal-seeking behaviour to be interrupted by certain imperatives imposed by conversational conventions and good clinical practice. If the patient asks a question, this deserves some kind of answer. If the patient wishes to express some attitude or feeling about some point, that should usually be entertained immediately. If the patient's estimated emotional state falls into distress, it is important that the treatment model is suspended until the patient can be comforted and settled. Similarly, if rapport with the patient is lost (the quality of the patient's responses deteriorates), special steps must be taken to recover this before anything else can be done. We call these *forced* responses, to distinguish them from less obligatory pragmatic moves, which in our model are driven by key goals in the therapy.

In most cases, a conceptual structure representing a suitable therapist's response can be formed by unifying pragmatically selected schemata with content-bearing information from the other sources. This process is to be handled by heuristic rules that must be sufficiently general to keep the number needed as low as possible. In a few cases, a single standardized expressive form can be accessed without the need for unification.

2.5   Response Generation Architecture

The proposed architecture of the ABLG system relies on three principle processes (Fig. 1): Preparing input for Therapeutic Expert, the Therapeutic Expert System, and the Surface Realization System. Based on the input sources, heuristic tests set the values of key variables controlling the behaviour of the Therapeutic Expert, such as patient type, clarity of the patient's chief complaint, the patient's readiness to change, their current emotional state, and their rapport with the therapist. At each conversational turn, the expert system recommends the best pragmatic move to the Surface Realisation System. This in turn chooses a feature structure template based on the pragmatic move recommended by the expert system. The template slot filler will fill in the template with relevant content, drawn from CG representation of the patient's recent utterances, or looked up from the background database. Lastly, YAG (Yet Another Generator) [19] realization library will convert the feature structure into a grammatically correct sentence for output. In some instances the Therapeutic Expert System will recommend a canned response, which can be directly output without using the Surface Realisation System.

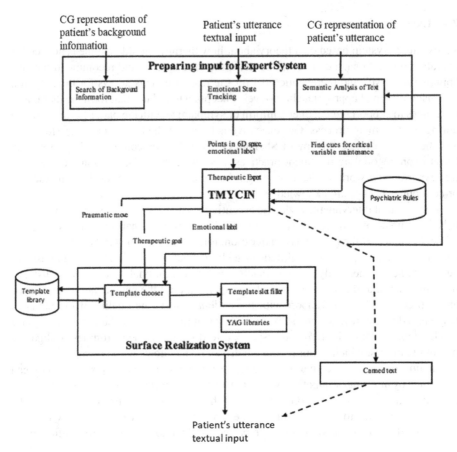

Fig. 1. Architecture of Affect Based Language Generation (ABLG) system

3   Implementation Details

To track emotions, we are experimenting with computationally "cheap" heuristics (meaning that, relative to machine learning approaches, logical rules on CGs do not consume very many CPU cycles). that can distinguish the patient's current emotional states directly from the text, though this has the disadvantage that it does not model cognitive aspects of emotion. To bring patient's conversational utterances into the picture, a text-to-CG parser is required. But even if it was feasible to construct complete representations for every utterance performed by a patient, this would not be desirable, because from analysis of the corpus, surprisingly few such representations would actually have useful implications for treatment, at least within our simplified model. Our conceptual parser, SAVVY, can do this because it assembles composite CGs out of prepared conceptual components that are already pre-selected for the domain of use to which they will be put.

A simple database currently provides background knowledge for our experiments. Each entry in the knowledgebase is a history list of zero or more CGs, indexed by both a patient identifier and one of the 15 background topics (Sect. 2.3) such as suicide_attempts, willingness_to_change and chief_complaint. Entries may be added, deleted or modified during processing, so the database can be used as a working memory to update and maintain therapeutic reasoning over sessions. Initially these entries are provided manually to represent information from the pre-existing admitting interview.

Psychiatric expertise is represented by a clinical Expert System Therapist, based on TMYCIN [20]. Consultation of the system is performed at each conversational turn, informed by the current state of variables from the inputs. Backward-chaining inference maintains internal state variables and recommends the best "pragmatic move" and "therapeutic goal". These parameters allow for the selection and instantiation of appropriate high-level templates that, when elaborated, are linearized into output texts. Further implementation details can be found in [21].

4 Conclusion

This generation component is still in development, so no systematic evaluation has yet been conducted. Some components have been coded and unit tested. Getting the heuristics of the system to interact smoothly with each other is a challenge; that is to be expected in this modelling approach. We are concerned about the number of templates that may be required, particularly at the surface expression level. If they become too difficult or too many to create, the method might become infeasible. The heuristic tests are not difficult to write, but are, of course, imperfect. Also, we have not fully tested the emotion tracking on many real patient texts so far.

Our planned evaluation has two parts. First, a systematic "glass-box" analysis will discover the strengths and limitations of the generation component, particularly with respect the generality of the techniques. Second, the "suitability", "naturalness" and "empathy" of the response generation for human use will be tested, using a series of ersatz patient interviews (to avoid the ethical complications of testing on real patients). Human judges (students in training to be psychotherapists) will be provided with background information and example patient utterances as well as the actual responses generated by the system. The judges will then rate these transcripts on those variables using their own knowledge of therapy. Finally, we reiterate that if hand-built conceptual representations can be practically built up using existing methods, the effort will be worthwhile if the systems are then more transparent and auditable than NN or statistical ML system and thus, more trustworthy.

References

1. Jack, H.E., et al.: Mutual capacity building to reduce the behavioral health treatment gap globally. Adm. Policy Mental Health (2019). https://doi.org/10.1007/s10488-019-00999-y
2. Meltzer, H.E. et. al.: The reluctance to seek treatment for neurotic disorders. Intl. Rev. Psychiat. **15**(1-2), 123–128 (2003)
3. Fairburn, C.G., Patel, V.H.: The impact of digital technology on psychological treatments and their dissemination. Behav. Res. Ther. **88**, 19–25 (2017)
4. Marcus, G.: Deep learning: a critical appraisal. arXiv preprint arXiv:1801.00631 (2018)

5. Pearl, J.: Theoretical impediments to machine learning with seven sparks from the causal revolution. arXiv preprint arXiv:1801.04016 (2018)
6. Reiter, E., Dale, R.: Building applied natural language generation systems. Nat. Lang. Eng. **3**(1), 57–87 (1997)
7. Ellis, A.: Rational-Emotive Therapy. Big Sur Recordings, pp. 32–44, CA, USA (1973)
8. Greenberg, L.S., Paivio, S.C.: Working with Emotions in Psychotherapy, vol. 13. Guilford Press, New York (2003)
9. Calvo, R.A., D'Mello, S.: Affect detection: an interdisciplinary review of models, methods, and their applications. IEEE Trans. Affect. Comput. **1**, 18–37 (2010)
10. Hancock, J.T., Landrigan, C., Silver, C.: Expressing emotion in text-based communication. In: Proceedings of the SIGCHI Conference on Human Factors in Computing Systems, pp. 929–932. Association for Computing Machinery (2007)
11. Gill, A.J., French, R.M., Gergle, D., Oberlander, J.: Identifying emotional characteristics from short blog texts. In: 30th Annual Conference of the Cognitive Science Society, pp. 2237–2242. Cognitive Science Society, Washington, DC (2008)
12. Smith, C.A., Ellsworth, P.C.: Attitudes and social cognition. J. Pers. Soc. Psychol. **48**(4), 813–838 (1985)
13. McNally, A. et. al.: Counseling and Psychotherapy Transcripts, Volume II. Alexander Street Press, Alexandria (2014)
14. Mann, G.A.: Control of a navigating rational agent by natural language. Unpublished Ph.D. thesis, University of New South Wales, Sydney, Australia (1996). https://manualzz.com/doc/42762943/control-of-a-navigating-rational-agent-by-natural-language. Accessed 15 Jan 2020
15. Leuzzi, F., Ferilli, S., Rotella, F.: ConNeKTion: a tool for handling conceptual graphs automatically extracted from text. In: Catarci, T., Ferro, N., Poggi, A. (eds.) IRCDL 2013. CCIS, vol. 385, pp. 93–104. Springer, Heidelberg (2014). https://doi.org/10.1007/978-3-642-54347-0_11
16. Morrison, J.: The First Interview: A Guide for Clinicians. Guilford Press, New York (1993)
17. Hoyt, M.F.: The temporal structure of therapy. In: O'Donohue, W.E. et al. (ed.) Clinical Strategies for Becoming a Master Psychotherapist, pp. 113–127. Elsevier (2006)
18. Shoham, V., Rohrbaugh, M., Patterson, J.: Problem-and solution-focused couple therapies: the MRI and Milwaukee models. In: Jacobson, N.S., Gurman, A.S. (eds.) Clinical Handbook of Couple Therapy, pp. 142–163. Guilford Press, New York (1995)
19. Channarukul, S., McRoy, S.W., Ali, S.S.: Enriching partially-specified representations for text realization using an attribute grammar. In: Proceedings of the 1st International Conference on NLG, vol. 14, pp. 163–170. Association for Computational Linguistics. Mitzpe Ramon, Israel (2000)
20. Novak, G.: TMYCIN expert system tool. Technical report AI87-52, Computer Science Department, University of Texas at Austin (1987). http://www.cs.utexas.edu/ftp/AI-Lab/tech-reports/UT-AI-TR-87-52.pdf. Accessed 5 Feb 2018
21. Mann, G., Kishore, B., Dhillon, P.: Conceptual reasoning for generating automated psychotherapeutic responses. In: Alam, M., Braun, T., Yun, B. (eds.) ICCS 2020. LNCS (LNAI), vol. 12277, pp. 186–194. Springer, Cham (2020). https://doi.org/10.1007/978-3-030-57855-8_14

Creative Composition Problem:
A Knowledge Graph Logical-Based AI Construction and Optimization Solution
Applied in Cecilia: An Architecture of a Digital Companion Artificial Intelligence (AI) Agent System Composer of Dialogue Scripts for Well-Being and Mental Health

Mauricio Javier Osorio Galindo[1]([envelope]) and Luis Angel Montiel Moreno[2][ORCID]

[1] Universidad de las Américas Puebla, Ex Hacienda Sta. Catarina Mártir S/N,
San Andrés Cholula, Puebla 72810, Mexico
mauricioj.osorio@udlap.mx
[2] 71 pte 1505b Puebla, Puebla 72450, Mexico
https://dblp.org/pid/o/MauricioOsorio.html

Abstract. Contribution of this work is to Define the Creative Composition Problem (CCP) for Human Well-being Optimization by Construction of Knowledge Graph using Knowledge Representation and logic-based Artificial Intelligence reasoning-planning where the computation of the Optimal Solution is achieved by Dynamic Programming or Logic Programming. The Creative Composition Problem is embedded within Cecilia: an architecture of a digital companion artificial intelligence agent system composer of dialogue scripts for Well-being and Mental Health. Where Cecilia Framework is instantiated in Well-being and Mental Health domain for optimal well-being development of first year university students. We define the 'The Problem of Creating a Dialogue Composition (PCDC)' and we propose a feasible and optimal solution of it. CCP is instantiated in this applied domain to solve PCDC optimizing the Mental Health and Well-being of the student. CCP as PCDC is applied to optimize maximizing the mental health of the student but also maximizing the smoothness, coherence, enjoyment and engagement each time the dialogue session is composed. Cecilia helps students to manage stress/anxiety to attempt the prevention of depression. Students can interact through the digital companion making questions and answers. While the system "learns" from the user it allows the user to learn from herself. Once the student discovers elements that were unnoticed by her, she will find a better way to improve when discovering her points of improvement.

Keywords: Knowledge graph · Knowledge representation · Creative composition · Reasoning planning system · Dialogue composition · Logic programming · Well-being/Mental health optimization · Digital companions

1 Introduction

The research works of the World Health Organization (WHO) [90] concludes that stress is the world mental health disease of the 21st century and may be the trigger for

© The Author(s) 2021
M. Cochez et al. (Eds.): GKR 2020, LNAI 12640, pp. 42–71, 2021.
https://doi.org/10.1007/978-3-030-72308-8_4

depression and even suicide if it is not treated correctly. WHO estimates that, in the world, suicide is the second cause of death in the group of 15 to 29 years of age and that more than 800,000 people die due to suicide every year.

Also stress illnesses generate high economic losses since sick people and those who care for them reduce their productivity both at home and at work. According to data from the WHO, 450 million people in the world, suffer from at least one mental disorder.

Well-being (meaning the absence of anxiety, depression and stress) and physical health have been studied by many Scientists. Elizabeth H. Blackburn, Carol W. Greider and Jack W. Szostak were awarded with the Nobel Prize in Physiology - Medicine 2009. They show that Telomerase activity is a predictor of long-term cellular viability, which decreases with chronic psychological distress [35]. E. H. Blackburn et al. proved that mindfulness may exert effects on telomerase activity through variables involved in the stress appraisal process [14]. According to the work of Okoshi Tadashi et al. [59] Technologies of Inclusive Well-being is a field of study that assumes positive technology has the capacity of increasing emotional, psychological, and social well-being and that investigates how information and communication technologies(ICT) empower and enhance the quality of personal experience in these areas. Economists and governments are starting to focus on well-being and "Gross National Happiness" as a new metric for measuring the statuses of the nations.

We have proposed *Cecilia* an architecture of a digital companion artificial intelligence agent system composer of dialogue scripts for Well-being and Mental Health. The core part of our proposal in the design of Cecilia as inclusive technology, is the use of Artificial Intelligence (AI) logical declarative languages used as a reasoning-planning systems that allow to implement the system responsible to define and specify the behaviour of Cecilia with the user. Cecilia should run on a smartphone and students can interact through questions and answers, while Cecilia "learns" from the user it also allows the user to learn from herself. Once the student discovers elements that were unnoticed by her, she can find a better way to improve her own well-being when discovering her points of improvement. Cecilia has been conceived as virtual digital companion assisting the student while She can improve her own skills and She freely wants to get help from the system, once the student acquires full sovereignty of herself by mastering the skills proposed by Cecilia there is no need to continue interacting with Cecilia. Therefore Cecilia is not conceived as a system generating dependency with the student, but on the contrary the aim is to help the student to achieve a mature and healthy interdependence with Herself, Relatives, Friends, Society and Nature by helping the student to acquire full sovereignty of herself by compassionate skills [16].

Cecilia is thought to be an intelligent agent system that supports all individuals with emphasis on university students and young people.

Over the years, science has shown that the brain and the mind work synergistically, that is why the brain can be reorganized, re-educated and regenerated by forming new nerve connections or paths when learning to control the mind through therapies. There are different successful techniques to support a student in overcoming their psychological difficulties such as referred in [61–63]: *Mindfulness* [9,38,78] and *Cognitive Therapy* [4,24,41] where both can be combined [46,83].

Mindfulness [9,38,78] It is a way of becoming aware of our reality, giving us the opportunity to work consciously with our stress, pain, illness, loss or in general the problems of our life. Over the past 20 years studies of mindfulness meditation are promising [15,78], and offer insight into specific cognitive processes on how it may serve as an antidote to cognitive stress states and benefit physical and psychological processes. Mindfulness minded to compassion and altruistic behaviour has been considered an important research scientific field of study [16]. For instance it has been founded the Center for Compassion and Altruism Research and Education (CCARE) [85] by Stanford University School of Medicine since 2008.

Cognitive Behaviour Therapy (CBT) [4,24,41] was initially developed by J. Beck [4] as a treatment for distorted thinking and brief depression by evaluation of negative thoughts influencing the behaviours. CBT is a psychotherapy that proposes modification of the thought to produce effective health improvement as has been shown in over 2,000 research studies [24]. Including tools such as techniques referred in [61,63] for *finding the Element* [76], reaching *Flow states* [55], *Silence in Therapy* [42] and *Poetry Therapy* [52] provide value added to our proposal particularly for college students. Mindfulness and Flow States are independent different behaviors however they can be alternated [34].

Cecilia also has the capacity to answer questions of university matters and try to create a link with the student because it considers her pleasures and hobbies. Enriching talks ("mild Therapies") proposed to be used by Cecilia are mainly based on mindfulness + cognitive therapy and advice in the professional career preferences, which are focused particularly on preventing and managing mild symptoms of stress, anxiety and depression to reduce the risk of failure in the university life due problems in learning, also to optimize mental health, well-being and behaviour of the students when they face the university challenges as it is justified in the work of Ribeiro Icaro et al. [75]. Thus, during sessions with Cecilia, it is intended that the students understand, accept and "become a friend of" their minds and emotions obtaining a better performance both in school and in their personal life. As described in the work of Luksha Pavel et al. [45] these existential skills include an ability to set and achieve goals (willpower), self-awareness/self-reflection ability (mindfulness), an ability to learn/unlearn/relearn (self-development) relevant skills (e.g. skill-formation ability), and more. Based on research of Richard Davison referred in [16] well-being is a skill to be learned. Well being has four constituents where each have received serious scientific attention: 1. Resilience, 2. Outlook, 3. Attention and 4. Generosity. Each of these four is rooted in neural circuits, and each of these neural circuits exhibits plasticity. So if any person exercise these circuits, they will be strengthen.

The core type of dialogue for every dialogue session of Cecilia is *Maieutics* described by Scraper Randy et al. in [84]. However each single agent task microdialogue as secondary type of dialogue can be one of the following according the categories stated by Douglas Walton enumerated and specified in [88]: Persuasion. Inquiry, Discovery, Information-Seeking, Casual chat, Negotiation, Deliberation and Eristic.

The Cecilia architecture has been designed to include a Theory of Mind [80] extended with emotions [60,81] of the User Agent (the student) as a Logic Programming (LP) Theory in the User Model. It is by LP Knowledge Representation that is possible to reason and plan a Dialogue Composition (DC) to help the user human development considering her beliefs, intentions, desires and emotions.

The main purpose of Cecilia is to develop Compassionate skills of the user. One property to express true creativity is to guarantee the common good of humanity, in our case we are proposing Cecilia architecture and the solution of the CCP ordering the technology for the benefit of human being, the opposite would not be creativity. In [48–50] are enumerated several results where science has shown how kindness and pro-social behaviors have a biological imperative. the creation of neural stem cells governing short term memory and the expression of genes regulating the stress response are positively affected by motherly affect, positive cognitive state influences positive immune response and vice versa, etc. As Cindy Mason [48–50] has pointed out the repeated interactions with the artifacts we create rub off on us. They are shaping and affecting us continually. Social and emotional relations influence our brain, our genes, our stress reaction and immune system and even wound healing. These findings are significant not just for AI design but to user interfaces, healthcare, education, and design intention in other fields, therefore creating and designing artifacts that support positive emotion such as kindness and compassion are essential to the goal of human-level AI. There is a strong relation between Compassion and Motherly love [48,50]. The psychophysiophilosophy related to motherly love has been a topic of research in scientific field and there are recent discoveries in neurosciences [48,50] that give hints on ways to increase motherly love in each of us, where they can be applied to Haptic Medicine into student daily lives through self-help. Cindy Mason has been a pioneer in defining Intelligence in terms of Compassion applied to the design of Artificial Intelligence artifacts. We have designed Cecilia in this line where AI is founded in a definition of Intelligence based in Compassion.

A *Knowledge Graph (KG)* [22,56] mainly describes real world entities and their interrelations, organized in a graph, defines possible classes and relations of entities in a schema, allows for potentially interrelating arbitrary entities with each other and covers various topical domains. KG are networks of entities, their semantic types, properties, and relationships between entities. KG are networks of all kind entities which are relevant to a specific domain or to an organization. They are not limited to abstract concepts and relations but can also contain instances of things like documents and datasets. Can be associated to Knowledge Representation in Logic such as RDF, Ontologies or Argumentation.

Contribution of this work is to define *the Creative Composition Problem (CCP)* for Human Well-being Optimization by Construction of Knowledge Graph using Knowledge Representation and logic-based Artificial Intelligence reasoning-planning where the computation of the Optimal Solution is achieved by Dynamic Programming or Logic Programming. The Creative Composition Problem is embedded within Cecilia: an architecture of a digital companion artificial intelligence agent system composer of dialogue scripts for Well-being and Mental Health. Where Cecilia Framework is instantiated in the Well-being and Mental Health domain for optimal well-being development of first year university students. CCP is instantiated in this applied domain for the composition of dialogues optimizing the Mental Health and Well-being of the student. We define the *The Problem of Creating a Dialogue Composition (PCDC)* and we propose a feasible and optimal solution of it. CCP as PCDC is applied to optimize maximizing the mental health of the student, but also maximizing the smoothness, coherence, enjoyment and engagement each time a dialogue session is composed. Feasibility of our Cecilia design follows a Proof of Concept strategy [40]. The objectives of Cecilia are presented in [61–63].

Our paper is structured as follows: In Sect. 2 we discuss chat-bots applied for mental health well-being. In Sect. 3 it is presented how the Creative Composition Problem (CPP) is embedded within Cecilia: an architecture of a digital companion artificial intelligence agent system composer of dialogue scripts for Well-being and Mental Health. CCP is instantiated in this applied domain for The Problem of Creating a Dialogue Composition (PCDC) optimizing the Mental Health and Well-being of the student. In Sect. 4 it is presented the definition, model and computation of the 'Creative Composition Problem (CCP)' using Graph Theory and Algorithms. In Sect. 5 it is described the Master-Agent Artificial Intelligent Composer (MAIC) as a Creative Reasoning-Planning Component formed by two modules. The first module of *Diagnosis by reasoning* based in a complex theory in a LP KB that will compose an instance of the CCP (which defines and construct the Graph input of the CCP as PCDC problem). And the second module which *Prescribes* an optimal solution for the CCP as PCDC instance to optimize well-being of the student. In Sect. 6 is presented the evaluation of Cecilia and in Sect. 7 a it is exposed a discussion of Technologies suitable to solve CCP and design of Cecilia Architecture. Finally in Sect. 8 we present our conclusions.

2   Related Work

2.1   Applied Chat-Bots for Mental Health Well-Being

Benefits of chat-bots in Health Care Well-being domain are described in [71]. In details it is delineated how chat-bots in health care may have the potential to provide patients with access to immediate medical information, recommend diagnoses at the first sign of illness, or connect patients with suitable health care providers (HCPs) across their community. Theoretically, in some instances, chat-bots may be better suited to help patient needs than a human physician because they have no biological gender, age, or race and elicit no bias toward patient demographics. Chat-bots do not get tired, fatigued, or sick, and they do not need to sleep; they are cost-effective to operate and can run 24 h a day, which is especially useful for patients who may have medical concerns outside of their doctor's operating hours. Chat-bots can also communicate in multiple different languages to better suit the needs of individual patients.

Early research in [71] has demonstrated the benefits of using health care chat-bots in many aspects, with accuracy comparable to that of human physicians. Patients may also feel that chat-bots are safer interaction partners than human physicians and are willing to disclose more medical information and report more symptoms to chat-bots. Psychological Internet interventions have frequently been evaluated and are viewed as a medium independent of time and place. They might be able to help reduce treatment barriers and expand the availability of care. Numerous studies [6] have shown that these interventions, often using cognitive-behavioral techniques, are comparable in their effectiveness to classical face-to-face psychotherapy. Psychological problems such as anxiety and depression are already being effectively addressed in this way.

As referred in [5] the work of Samuel Bell et al. introduces Woebot, a template-based chat-bot delivering basic CBT, has demonstrated limited but positive clinical outcomes in students suffering from symptoms of depression.

The work of Eileen Bendig et al. referred in [6] presents promising areas for the use of chat-bots in the psychotherapeutic context could be support for the prevention, treatment, and follow-up/relapse prevention of psychological problems and mental disorders. Also they could be used preventively in the future, for example for suicide prevention. According to the work of Samuel Bell et al. [5] in order to provide scalable treatment, several promising studies have demonstrated clinical efficacy of internet-based Cognitive Based Therapy, whereby the need for a face-to-face presence is negated.

In [89] it is reported a survey of technologies for mental Well-being. In the work of Diano Federico et al. referred in [18] it is presented an state of the art in mindfulness-based mobile applications and the design of a mindfulness mobile application to help emotional self-regulation in people suffering stressful situations. We invite the reader to check the work of Baskar Jayalakshmi et al. referred in [2] where it is reported a comparison of Applied Agents implemented for improving mental health and well-being.

In the work of Jingar Monika et al. referred in [37] it is explored how an intelligent digital companion(agent) can support persons with stress-related exhaustion to manage daily activities. Also it is explored how different individuals approach the task of designing their own tangible interfaces for communicating emotions with a digital companion.

In the work of Inkster Becky referred in [33] it is presented an empathy-driven, conversational artificial intelligence agent (Wysa) for digital mental well-being that is using mindfulness as mild therapy in combination with transfer to psychologist whenever the user ask for it. According to Samuel Bell et al. several studies have investigated the clinical efficacy of remote-, internet- and chat-bot-based therapy, but there are other factors, such as enjoyment and smoothness, that are important in a good therapy session.

In the work of Cindy Mason [43] it is exposed an Intelligent Agent Software for Medicine, it describes how software agents that incorporate learning, personalization, proactivity, context-sensitivity and collaboration will lead to a new generation of medical applications that will streamline user interfaces and enable more sophisticated communication and problem-solving.

In the work of Cidy Mason [51] it is presented how Human-Level AI Requires Compassionate Intelligence, much more than just common sense about the world, it will require compassionate intelligence to guide interaction and build applications of the future. The cognition of such an agent includes Meta-cognition: thinking about thinking, thinking about feeling, and thinking about others' thoughts and feelings. Cindy Mason summarize the core meta-architectures and meta-processes of EM-2, a meta-cognitive agent that uses affective inference and an irrational TMS.

In [28] it is showed an emotions ontology for collaborative modelling and learning of emotional responses.

In [48] it is presented the Multi-Disciplinary Case for Human Sciences in Technology Design, where it is exposed that connecting the dots between discoveries in neuroscience(neuroplasticity), psychoneuroimmunology(the brain-immune loop) and user experience (gadget rub-off) indicate the nature of our time spent with gadgets is a vector in human health - mentally, socially and physically. The positive design of our interactions with devices therefore can have a positive impact on economy, civilization and society. Likewise, the absence of design that encourages positive interaction may encourage undesirable behaviors. The consequences of the architecture of the 21stcentury conversation between man and machine may last generations. AI and the Internet of Things are primary vectors for positive and negative impacts of technology. The work of [48] describes a growing body of co-discoveries occurring across a variety of disciplines that support the argument for human sciences in technology design.

In the work of Cindy Mason [49] it is presented an Engineering Kindness architecture where it is proposed the Building of A Machine With Compassionate Intelligence.

2.2 Applied Knowledge Graph for Mental Health Well-Being

In [22] it is described definition and works on Knowledge Graph. In [56] it is described the use of Knowledge Graph in Health Well-begin application for Supporting decision making in organ transplanting using argumentation theory. In [91] it is reported a Survey of Knowledge Graph applied in Clinical Decision Support Reasoning Systems. In [79] shows a Knowledge Graph application and construction for Health Domain using Learning Techniques from electronic medical records. Finally in [31] presents different approaches on how to encode graph structure intolow-dimensional embeddings, using techniques based on deep learning and non-linear dimensionality reduction.

In [87] it is described an extension of the Knapsack problem with weighted edges in the graph, it is computed in two phases as a combination of a knapsack problem with a shortest path.

In our proposal CCP as CDP is applied to optimize maximizing the well-being and mental health of the student but also optimizing the smoothness, coherence, enjoyment and engagement each time the dialogue session is composed. As far as we know our Creative Composition Problem as an optimization problem has not been described in the literature. It differs from the work of Voloch [87] since we are maximizing with respect to vertices and weight on the edges. While Voloch is combining Knapsack with Shortest Path, our problem seems a combination between Knapsack and Travelling Sales Problem, we don't compute the optimal solution in two phases but in a single algorithm using dynamic programming.

3 Cecilia: An Architecture of a Digital Companion Artificial Intelligence Agent System Composer of Dialogue Scripts for Well-Being and Mental Health

In this section is presented the architecture of our system Cecilia which is detailed in [70].

This section has the aim to help the reader to be introduced in the context of our general 'Creative Composition Problem (CCP)', where the CCP is instantiated into a specific application domain (mental health and well-being optimization). The CCP will be discussed in the next section since the contribution of our present work is concerning the definition, model and computation of the CCP using Graph Theory, Algorithms and Logic programming solvers. The CCP is instantiated in our Cecilia architecture in order to solve the 'The Problem of Creating a Dialogue Composition (PCDC)'.

A contribution of this present work is our proposal for the definition for *The Problem of Creating a Dialogue Composition (PCDC)* and we propose a feasible and optimal solution of it in the next section.

Definition 1 *The Problem of Creating a Dialogue Composition (PCDC). Given a set of resources of AI-tasks, the profit that each AI-task contributes to development mental health and well being of student, the length that each AI-tasks lasts interacting with the student, the profit that a sequence of two distinct related AI-tasks contributes to the coherence, enjoyment and smoothness of a session, the number of AI-tasks interactions expected for a single dialogue session and the time length expected that the dialogue session may last. The problem is* **To Compose a Dialogue Session** *as a sequence of AI-Tasks such that optimizes the mental health and well being of the student with an optimal coherent, enjoyable and smoothable session.*

An optimal solution for PCDC instance is the **'Abstract Sequence Dialogue Session (ASDS)'** to be proposed by Cecilia, where for each AI-Task represented as an abstract token name. Each token is associated to Semantic Knowledge, and each token will be mapped to a script specified in a Basic Resources Script Language (BSRL). Each BSRL script is described in a machine language that an imperative language will interpret managing the dialogue interaction as a chat-bot with the User Agent (in our case the Student).

3.1   Cecilia: A Master-Slave AI Agents Digital Companion System Design

Cecilia defines a master-salve conceptual design following a centralized approach. Namely, we create hundreds of slaves (at least one thousand) such that each of them can perform a very concrete task. All the tasks correspond to interactions with the students. Each interaction are specified as atomic micro-dialogues. An example could be simple or complex task such as to teach the student how to try a meditation exercise. Each task performed by a slave-agent is programmed in the *Basic Script/Resources Language (BSRL)*. Associated to each slave we have its Semantic Knowledge. All the Semantic Knowledge of each slave plus a general theory of interaction among them is written in Logic Programming (LP) Language.

So, the LP theory corresponds to the *Master-Agent Artificial Intelligent Composer (MAIC)* that *reasons/plans* a sequence of few tasks (for a 10–15 min estimated session) that are performed by our slaves that are presented (coordinated) by a distinguished slave (a program interpreter of BSRL in Python) to the student. An analogy that we can make is the following. The LP agent is like a *master composer* of a symphony for a particular audience. The pianist is a particular slave that performs a specific task (playing the piano). The director corresponds to our distinguished *slave* that actually coordinate the rest of *slaves*. After the execution of the symphony, according to the feedback (applause, reviews, etc.), the composer hopefully learns how to create a better symphony.

The main concrete tasks of our intelligent agent described in [61–63, 70].

3.2 The Cecilia Logical-Based AI Agent Digital Companion System

Cecilia is a *Reasoning Planning System* that consist in a cycle of 4 sequential (Fig. 1) processes-modules described below.

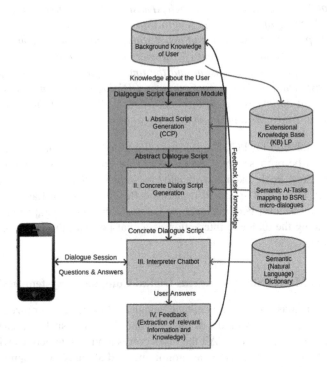

Fig. 1. Architecture of Cecilia logical-based AI agent digital companion system.

I. Abstract Script Dialogue Session (ASDS) is generated by MAIC in this process (Fig. 2). ASDS is a composition of slave agents tasks sequence to be performed by Cecilia as a single dialogue session with the student. MAIC basically consists of two modules of KB-reasoning represented and specified via ASP, the lowest one consists of a logical theory that generates -**Diagnoses** a set of recommendations (resources/assets) that would correspond *to construct a graph* a CCP as PCDC instance. The highest module consist of an ASP program that proposes the ASDS plan solving an specific problem based in the constructed graph providing a **Prescription** in dialogue to the student in order to optimize her mental health and well-being. The formal specification of this second stage in terms of an optimization problem *The Problem of Creating a Dialogue Composition (PCDC)* that is an instance of **The Creative Composition Problem**.

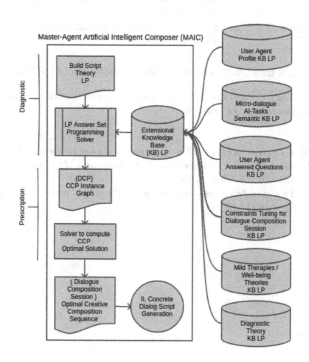

Fig. 2. I. Abstract script generation

An optimal solution for DCP instance is the intended ASDS to be proposed by Cecilia.

Figure 3 is example of an abstract dialogue session built by MAIC.

II. Concrete Dialogue Script Generation. Each AI-Task in the composed dialogue sequence (the CCP optimal solution) is translated into a single BSRL script by concatenation.

Figure 4 is an example of a concrete AI-Task dialogue script 'questioning/answering student w.r.t. Finding Element' for it's abstract token name 'c2' specified as a BRSL program.

```
<q1, c2, h2, a4, e7>
where
q1 corresponds to a 'greeting' BRSL program.
c2 corresponds to a 'questioning/aswering student wrt
                    Finding Element' BRSL program.
h2 corresponds to a 'short hobbies general dialogue'
                    BRSL program.
a4 corresponds to a 'short academic general dialogue'
                    BRSL program.
e7 corresponds to a 'short teaching a mindfulness excersise'
                    BRSL program.
```

Fig. 3. Example of an abstract dialogue session built by MAIC.

% A BSRL Code consists of two parts: instructions and text
↪ associated to labels.

```
c2
{
1   1    % Cecilia writes the sentence labeled with 1.
5   10   % The student answer yes or not and if 'yes' jump to
    ↪ label 10 in the code.
1   10   % The student answer no and Cecilia asks the sentece
    ↪ with label 10.
3   8
1   13
3   9
1   11
6  99
8   1  12
1   3
6  99
9   1  14
6  99
10  1  4
2   0
4   1
15  5
99  9  0
0   0
```

```
1  Do you think you are "in your element"?
3  Thank you.
4  What is your element? (your career, some sport, etc)
5  find_her_element (@1).
10 Do you feel passion for an activity that you love?
11 Then that activity could be your element.
12 Then you may not have found your item yet.
13 Do you want to carry out this activity with all your
   ↪ strength?
14 You may be close to being in your age.
}
```

Fig. 4. Example of a AI-Task 'questioning/answering student w.r.t. Finding Element' BRSL program.

III. Dialogue Interpreter Chat-bot corresponds to the director of the orchestra that executes the composed dialogue session (Single BSRL program) as interactions of AI-Tasks with the student.

We present a simple example of a conversation in Fig. 5.

```
Hi.
How are you?
>>> good
How good :)
Is one of your courses easy?
>>> no
How is college going?
>>> bad
No good.
We'll see.
Can you identify what goes through
your mind?(some thought for example:
I do not understand the teacher, etc)
>>> yes, I don't understand the teacher
Tell me about the matter please (a
short sentence).
>>> everything goes wrong
Tell me more about the subject please
(details).
>>> the homeworks of the teacher are very difficult
Do you consider this a problem?
>>> yes
And this problem causes you
some emotional discomfort (stress,
anxiety, depression, etc.)?
>>> stress
I get it.
Let me propose you the following meditation exercise
if you don't mind
>>> ok
[VDC explais the exercise to the student]
```

Fig. 5. Fragment of a conversation between Cecilia and a student.

IV. Feedback Module is an extraction process of relevant information and knowledge. This module filters a user conversation record to obtain the **Student Profile State (SPS)** updating the extensional Knowledge Base.

4   The Creative Composition Problem (CCP)

This section presents the definition, model and computation of *The Creative Composition Problem (CCP)* using graph theory, algorithms and logic programming solvers. It is formalized the CCP Knowledge Graph (KG) used by MAIC within Cecilia to make prescription, after this KG has been constructed by reasoning-diagnostic of MAIC. CCP corresponds to *The Problem of Creating a Dialogue Composition (PCDC)* in our instantiated mental health and well-being domain for Cecilia framework. The prescription, using the constructed Knowledge Graph by diagnostic, builds a composition sequence of AI-task interactions in form of micro-dialogues joined into a single Dialogue Composition Session, a single composed dialogue script, to optimize mental health and well-being of the student (user agent), and to optimize at the same time the links between interactions to provide a smooth, enjoyable and coherent dialogue session.

4.1   Formal Definition

CCP Graph Instance
Let $G_{L,K}$ be a complete directed graph defined as tuple $G_{L,K} = (V, E, P_V, P_E, W_V)$, where V is a set of vertexes;
E is a relation between the set of vertexes $E = V \times V$;
P_V is function $P_V : V \to \mathbb{N}$ that represents the profit that each vertex contributes in the sequence that forms the optimal composition to be created;
P_E is a function $P_E : E \to \mathbb{N} \cup \{0\}$ that represents the profit that a sequence of two distinct vertexes related in E contributes in the sequence that forms the optimal composition to be created;
W_V is a function $W_V \to \mathbb{N}$ that represents the associated size to each vertex in V that will be considered to restrict the length of the optimal composition sequence to be created.
K is the maximal length in terms of size of vertexes that an optimal composition sequence could sizes.
L is the number of vertexes that must compound the optimal composition sequence.

Feasible Solution
Is a L-tuple $X = [x_1, \ldots, x_L]$, where $\{x_1, \ldots, x_L\} \in 2^V$, $|\{x_1, \ldots, x_L\}| = L$ and $\sum_{i=1}^{L} W_V(x_i) \leq K$.

Optimal Solution
Is a feasible solution $X = [x_1, \ldots, x_L]$ such that maximizes $Z = \sum_{i=1}^{L} P_V(x_i) + \sum_{i=1}^{L-1} P_E((x_i, x_{i+1}))$.

Remark: In our instantiated domain problem for mental health and well-being there are always sufficient tasks with weight 1, hence there is always a feasible solution.

The CCP is an 'Optimal Solution' of a given 'CCP Graph Instance'. The 'Optimal Solution' is also named *Optimal Creative Composition Sequence*. A 'Feasible Solution' is also named a *Creative Composition Sequence*.

4.2 Dynamic Programming Definition of CPP

Given a CCP instance instance $G(S, K) = < V, E, Pv, Pe >$ we compute the optimal solution using a Dynamic Programming strategy. For a subset S of vertices V, an initial vertex s and a vertex j s.t. $j \neq s$, let $C(S, j, k, l)$ be the maximal profit between all feasible solutions of CCP (composition sequences of vertices in S, starting in vertex s and ending in vertex j, with l number of vertices and which cumulative sum of vertices sizes is lower equal than k).

When $|S| > 1$ we define $C(S, s, k, l) = -\infty$ where $0 \leq k \leq K, k \in \mathbb{N} \cup \{0\}, 0 < l \leq |V|, l \in \mathbb{N}$, since the composition sequence can not start and end at s.

Now, let's express $C(S, j, k, l)$ in terms of smaller sub-problems. We need to start at s and end at j; if $i \in S - \{j\}$ is the second last vertex to j in the composition sequence, then the overall profit is the profit from s to i, namely, $C(S - \{j\}, i, k - W_V(j), l - 1)$ plus the profit of the vertex j, and the profit of the (i, j) edge. We must pick the best i such that: $max\{C(S - \{j\}, i, k - W_V(j), l - 1) + P_V(j) + P_E((i, j)) : i \in S, i \neq j\}$ where $S \subseteq V, j \in S, j \neq s, 1 < l \leq |V|, l \in \mathbb{N}, W_V(j) \leq k, 0 \leq k \leq K, k \in \mathbb{N} \cup \{0\}$.

$C(V - \{s\}, j, K, L)$ is optimal solution of CCP from vertex s to vertex j, intermediate vertices are in $V - \{j\}$.

So the Recursive Definition to compute the CCP optimal solution is:

Base case
$C(\{s\}, s, k, 1) = P_V(s)$ if $W_V(s) \leq k, 0 \leq k \leq K$
$C(\{s\}, s, k, 1) = -\infty$ if $W_V(s) > k, 0 \leq k \leq K$

Recursive case
$C(S, j, k, L) = max\{C(S - \{j\}, i, k - W_V(j), L - 1) + P_V(j) + P_E((i, j)) : i \in S, i \neq j\}$ where $S \subseteq V, j \in S, j \neq s, L > 1, W_V(j) \leq k, 0 \leq k \leq K$

In our Cecilia instantiated framework, for mental health and well-being domain, it must be computed $max\ C(V - \{s\}, j, 15, 5)$ for all $j \in V - \{s\}$, where our distinguished vertex s is a 'greetings' AI-task micro-dialogue, 15 the estimated time that a dialogue session may last, and 5 the number of different interaction tasks for the student. These constants were recommended as fixed numbers according to a specialized psychological therapist, in order to compose a comfortable dialogue session for the student.

4.3 Dynamic Programming Algorithm

Using dynamic programming, based on the recursive definition to compute the CCP optimal solution, in Algorithm 1 is computed the optimal solution for a given CCP instance. It is used dynamic programming strategy to avoid duplicates in recursive call, using a memory table $C(S, j, k)$, where S is $S \subseteq V$, $j \in V$, and $0 \leq k \leq K$. In this case, for a given CCP instance, the optimal solution will be the $max\ C(S, j, K)$ for all $S \subseteq V, |S| = L, j \in V - \{s\}$

Algorithm 1. Creative Composition Problem (CCP) by dynamic programming

---

1: **function** CCP($L, K, V, E, P_V, P_E, W_V, s, C$)
2:    $Opt = -\infty$
3:    **for** $k = 0$ to K **do**
4:     **if** $(W_V(s) \leq k)$ **then**
5:       $C(\{s\}, s, k) = P_V(s)$
6:     **else**
7:       $C(\{s\}, s, k) = -\infty$
8:    **for** $c = 2$ to L **do**
9:     **for all** S s.t. $S \subseteq V, |S| = c, s \in S$ **do**
10:      $C(S, s, k) = -\infty$ s.t. $0 \leq k \leq K, k \in \mathbb{N} \cup \{0\}$
11:      **for all** $j \in S, j \neq s$ **do**
12:       **for** $k = 0$ to K **do**
13:        **if** $(W_V(j) \leq k)$ **then**
14:         $C(S, j, k) = max\{C(S - \{j\}, i, k - W_V(j)) + P_V(j) + P_E((i, j)) : i \in S, i \neq j\}$
15:         $Opt = max(Opt, C(S, j, k))$
16:        **else**
17:         $C(S, j, k) = -\infty$
18:    **return** Opt

Observe that lines 8–9, in Algorithm 1, can be easily programmed as a single iteration if the subset of fixed cardinality are already precomputed. In Algorithm 2 it is presented the pseudo code to recover all the feasible solutions that are optimal solution for a given CCP instance. Using traditional backtracking strategy, as usual in dynamic programming techniques, when it is used a memory table.

4.4 Computational Complexity of Dynamic Programming Algorithm to Compute the Optimal CCP Solution

Given a CCP instance, we would like to know the estimated computational complexity time to compute an optimal solution. When the computation definition of a problem is NP-Hard class, then complexity computation time could be intractable in terms of real run-time machine computation [20].

Sometimes, a NP-Hard problem can be parametrized in order to achieve polynomial time computation, so is the case when in an algorithm definition with a greater than factorial-exponential order complexity, commonly present in combinatorial NP-Hard

Algorithm 2. Recovers all the Optimal Composition Sequences

```
 1: function GETSOLUTIONS(Opt, L, K, V, E, P_V, P_E, W_V, s, C)
 2:   tuples = empty queue
 3:   for all S s.t S ⊆ V, |S| = L, s ∈ S do
 4:     for all j ∈ V do
 5:       for k = 0 to K do
 6:         if dcp(S, j, k) == Opt then
 7:           tuple = empty queue
 8:           getTuples(C, S, j, k, s, tuple, tuples)
 9:           break
10:   return tuples
11: procedure GETTUPLES(C, S, j, k, s, tuple, tuples)
12:   tuple.push(j)
13:   if j== s then
14:     t = tuple.getCopy().reverse()
15:     tuples.push(t)
16:   else
17:     for all i ∈ S − {j} do
18:       if C(S − {j}, i, k − W_V(j)) + P_V(j) + P_E((i, j)) == C(S, j, k) then
19:         getTuples(C, S − {j}, i, k − W_V(j), C, s, tuple, tuples)
20:   tuple.pop()
```

problems, it can be computable in polynomial time, when one of the argument of the given input instance of a problem definition is fixed as a constant number [20].

It can be easily seen that the definition to compute a CCP optimal solution, for a given CCP instance, is a combination between the well know combinatorial problems *The Travelling Sales Problem* and *The Knapsack Problem* see [13]. This since the CCP optimal composition sequence requires to compute a 'Hamiltonian path' of a fixed length, where the cost between edges is maximized, but also we would like to select those vertices subject to a capacity knapsack constraint (As in the knapsack problem definition), where also the profits of vertexes is maximized. Since the computation of an optimal solution for a given CCP instance is a combinatorial problem, then this give us an exponential time to compute the solution.

Note that between Algorithm 1 and Algorithm 2 a more complex number of computation is required to solve Algorithm 1 instead of Algorithm 2.

So let's focus in Algorithm 1 to estimate computation time complexity.

The iterative statements on lines 8–12 are greater in computation time than the iteration on line 3. The computation time on lines 8–12 can be expressed as the number of permutation $P(|V|, L)$ in the 'for' statement on lines 8–9, the computation time in the 'for' statement on line 11 can be expressed as $|V| - 1$, and computation time of the 'for' statement on line 13 can be expressed as K. Therefore the estimated computational complexity time to compute an optimal CCP solution is $O(V, L, K) = P(|V|, L) \cdot |V| \cdot K$.

However, since we have fixed limit constants as boundaries for the arguments L and K, then we have a polynomial time computation.

Specifically after receiving guidance from a psychologist and other mindfulness experts, many short dialogue sessions are suggested, not a long one, and for this it can be seen that setting the parameter $L = 5$ (five task per dialogue session) and $K = 15$ (15 min that the a whole dialogue session may last) seems to be a recommended measure. This does not exclude recommending to the student some relatively long exercise (20–30 minutes) that he can do on his own.

Since the suggested L is fixed to a value of 5, a naive strategy would require $P(|V|, 5)$ permutations, that would mean a 5 grade polynomial, which is still expensive for a large $|L|$.

For our mental health and well-being instantiated domain in Cecilia, MAIC constructs a Knowledge Graph with $|V| \leq 20$. This is possible due the logical theories in *Diagnostic Module*, and also due the structure of the nature of knowledge present in our enriching talks (mild-therapies) domain, when they are formally represented using mathematical logic by LP. Each one of the mild therapies theories presents a partial order structure as a relation between stages to progress in the acquisition of skills, for instance Mindfulness requires an ordered sequence of stages.

Then for the worst case we would have $P(20,5) = 15504$, and for a worst case where $L = 5$ and $K = 15$ we have $O(V, 5, 15) = 15504 \cdot 5 \cdot 15$, that is around $1,000,000$, which is still tractable in computation time.

A trade-off w.r.t $|V|$ could be in average cases a fixed value of 15, that can also be considered feasible in computational terms (run time). Moreover diagnostic and prescription are not computed in real time of the session, but between sessions.

It is always possible to relax the problem and use, for example, greedy techniques to obtain feasible solutions close to the optimal for a much larger instance. For example, it can be used a similar strategy such as the one used in a rational Knapsack problem computation, where the ratios between profits of objects and the cost of objects are sorted, in ascendant way, to propose a feasible solution for large inputs, getting close to the optimal solution with an approximate complexity lower than $O(V, K) = |V| log(|V|)$, lower than 400 for $|V| = 20$, and it could be considered to prescribe a KG with more than $100,000$ vertexes (AI-Tasks).

4.5 Running Example

In Appendix A there is an example of a CCP Graph Instance. In Appendix B it is shown how dcp is computed using the presented dynamic programming Algorithm 1 and Algorithm 2. Note that the computation is made as a table where sets are increasing by cardinality, then the recursive function C to obtain a DCP optimal solution is computed in terms of the memory table of simpler cases calculated before.

5 Creative Reasoning-Planning: The Master-Agent Artificial Intelligent Composer (MAIC) of Dialogue Scripts for Well-Being and Mental Health

Conceptually the MAIC in Cecilia reasons using Answer Set Programming (ASP) [27,82] and consists of two modules described in Sect. 3. The first module

Diagnoses - Reasons based in a complex theory in a LP KB that will compose an instance of the CCP KG, the diagnostic defines and construct the Knowledge Graph input of the CCP as PCDC problem, presented in the previous Sect. 4. Further details are discussed in this section. The second module *Prescribes* an optimal solution for CCP as PCDC KG instance to optimize mental health and well-being of the student but also the dialogue session interactions.

5.1 The MAIC Diagnostic: Enriching Talks (Mild Therapies) Theories Specified in ASP

It has been defined for this project 7 logic programming theories under Answer Sets Programming semantics to model the student profile, and to create a dialogue composition proposal for each session with the student.

1. **Hobbies Theory.** It suggests exercises and conversation recommendations encompassing the student likes.
2. **Emotional Well-being Theory.** It states description in logic of the OCC model of emotion [60, 80, 81, 86] that has an objective to achieve and maximize happiness of the student [70].
3. **Diagnosis of Emotional Type Theory.**It diagnoses the emotional status of the student inferred from the student conversation with Cecilia. It keeps track of the emotional status of the student through past conversation sessions to make a better diagnose.
4. **Well-being Theory.** It suggests mild therapies AI-tasks interactions to compose a enriching talk dialogue session, while considering the feedback of student profile.
5. **Academic Theory.** It suggest AI-tasks interactions with the aim to upgrade the scholar status of the student, considering academic and emotional student profile.
6. **Empathy Theory.** It suggests AI-tasks interactions with the aim of strengthening the empathy with Cecilia, but also mainly help the student to achieve a healthy emotional status.
7. **Causal Chat Theory.** It suggest AI-tasks interactions of casual chat dialogue, within the student dialogue session, with the main purpose of retrieving from the student relevant information that is out from the scope in the retrieval of traditional specific domain theories.
8. **Prescription Theory.** Obtains an optimal solution given a CCP as PCDC KG instance.

5.2 The MAIC Prescription and Recommendation: Solving the Creative Composition Problem (CCP)

The CCP as PCDC optimization problem as presented in Sect. 4 can be solved by Algorithm. But also It can naturally be encoded in logic programming, for instance it can be easely encoded in CIAO [32], DLV [29] as well as CLASP [26] solvers.

Since CCP 4 is actually a logically stratified logic program and hence we can informally say that is logically very simple program. The three codes (CIAO, DLV, CLASP) are almost the same with minor changes in coding details. The CCP can be encoded with recursive approach as presented in Sect. 4 using APOL. APOL [64] is a partial order programming [67,69] very similar to mathematical programming, where a function is minimized (or maximized) and has a set of restrictions, the difference is that the domain of values is a partial order, where partial order clauses can be expressed as normal clauses. APOL is an extension of ASP that allows to express optimization problems in a very suitable way, integrating disjunctive clauses and partial-order clauses. It performs a dynamic programming algorithm and interacts with DLV [23]. On the other hand there is also an implementation of partial order programming following a standard top-down approach [36].

Defining Profits. Recall that we have profits in the definition of CCP as PCDC instance. One kind of them are associated to each AI-task asset, recall that each AI-task asset is a micro dialogue. The other kind of them are profits associated to every pair of micro-dialogues with the intended meaning of measuring the coherence, enjoyment and smoothness of a session.

The first type of profits assignment to micro-dialogues is defined by means of a logical theory in ASP that would take into account previous answers of the user. For example, suppose the student has anxiety and that for a suggested mindfulness exercise A the user has said to Cecilia that it has been of benefit for him. Then the MAIC by ASP theory would assign a value $v1$. However, let us also assume that he has previously performed a mindfulness exercise B, and the student has been sceptic regarding the usefulness of that exercise. Then MAIC by ASP theory assign a value of $v2$ less than $v1$ to micro dialogue B. For instance $v2$ could be 1, and $v1$ could be 8, these values are adjusted through more interactions between Cecilia and the student, but also with a semi-automatic process using Machine learning specially Inductive Logic Programming (this point is still outside the scope of this paper, and for the moment we have fixed rules stated with the endorsement of an expert psychologist). The second type of profits (not yet considered in this work) we assume that it would be a learning process possibly using Machine Learning specially Inductive Logic Programming. It will consist in a combination of a priori rules stated by psychologist combined with Machine Learning rules and the answer of the student. The rules would be derived from a pilot starting group of students interacting with Cecilia, that generalizes in a universal way the concluded rules for profit assignment of the micro-dialogues.

Transition from reasoning about theories representing domain knowledge that generates by reasoning the Knowledge Graph CCP (DCP) instance is made by the following rules structure described in LP under Answer Set Programming Semantics:

To assign profit to an AI-task:
$vertices(v(x_i), P(x_i)) : - condition_m^+, \ not \ condition_n^-.$
To assign profit between two AI-tasks:
$edges(e(x_i, x_j), P_E(x_i, x_j)) : - condition_m^+, \ not \ condition_n^-.$ where $condition_m^+$ and $not \ condition_n^-.$ are predicates inferred and described from ASP Knowledge Base representing the instantiated domain knowledge.

6   Pre-evaluation of Cecilia

Cecilia was pre-evaluated by bachelor students. The pre-evaluation asked to the students about they appreciation of Cecilia conversations.

What It was made to test the software consisted in the follwing steps:

1. Semi-automatic conversations were generated using Cecilia as an automated user agent (simulating the student) to have dialogue with Cecilia.
2. It was included some Mathematics topic conversations additionally to the ones proposed in Enriching Talks Theories.
3. Some of the automated conversations were selected randomly.
4. It was asked the students what they thought of the conversation, in order to receive retrieval if the conversations are interesting or not.

The students didn't chat, this is an indirect pre-evaluation.

The pre-evaluation considered a test with the following target aspects for obtain retrieval from the students: 1) creativity, 2) easy to read/learn, 3) interesting, 4) supportive, 5) good, 6) easy, 7) motivating, 8) clear and 9) friendly. Using a discrete scale between 1 and 7, where 1 means the worst behaviour, and 7 means the best behavior. The results were in average a value of 6 for each considered aspect. Seven examples, one for each student, were pre-evaluated.

The Table 1 exposes the pre-evaluation results obtained from the students.

Table 1. Pre-evaluation retrieval obtained from the students

Q #	Question	1	2	3	4	5	6	7
1)	Creativity	6	7	7	7	7	6	7
2)	Easy to read/learn	7	4	7	6	7	7	5
3)	Interesting	7	5	7	4	7	7	7
4)	Supportive	5	4	7	5	7	7	6
5)	Good	6	6	7	5	7	7	7
6)	Easy	7	5	7	4	6	7	6
7)	Motivating	6	4	6	5	7	7	7
8)	Clear	5	7	7	7	7	7	6
9)	Friendly	5	5	7	6	7	7	7

Three comments of the students about the conversations are the following:

"I really like what I read, basically because I learn a lot of thing besides the logical exercises, I like history, and I like a little of literature with the analogy of the ying-yang and the poem, subjects that I am really in love, it's too interesting to appreciate these subjects to be combined. It makes the learning process to be much funny, that's motivated me to change my attitude talking about maths, I know maths, I just need to practice, It's like anything else, you have to practice to be a master, there's not other way. We are the only ones who are responsibles of develop our knowledge, we already have it! :)"

"It was an interesting conversation, and it helped me to better understand logical connectives. The conversation was very friendly and I liked how the concepts are simplified. Also, it was very easy to read."

"Very interesting I love it!"

Figure 6 shows an example of the Cecilia GUI application. The used language in the application is Spanish, however it will be translated to an English language version. Cecilia is designed to be independent of the knowledge scripts domain, for example, the use of Enriching Talks. Also Cecilia is independent of the used human language to dialogue with the Agent User (in our case the student).

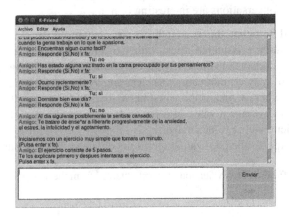

Fig. 6. Example of Cecilia's GUI

7   Technologies Suitable to Solve CCP and to Implement the Design of Cecilia Architecture

Another major issue of this paper was to justify the use of ASP besides the one present in the last subsection.

We also propose ASP for the following list of reasons.

– Flexibility to represent all major issues of the Belief Model of the student in different forms. For instance in a previous work [63] we use a standard Generate/Test technique to represent our problem. Here we use an optimization problem. Both forms were easily encoded in ASP. Default rules were very helpful in both cases. In this second approach the Well-founded semantics was sufficient to express our problem. However adding integrity constraints were useful to ensure correctness of our approach. When the system became inconsistent, due mainly because it finished all the resources that it has, we have a fixed default plan to propose.

- Availability of well known and mature solvers to be used such as CLASP and DLV. Furthermore, new interesting solvers such as s(CASP) [1,47] have potential interest in our problem. It is worth to mention that Prolog-type solvers of such as XSB and CIAO [1,32] can also be considered.
- ASP can naturally interact with *Inductive Logic Programming (ILP)*[12]. Recall that ILP [39,54] is a machine learning paradigm based on logic that allows learning from cases in order to generate rules needed to reason about future similar cases. It should be clear that learning is fundamental in Cecilia with the purpose to understand better the student. For instance, it could learn that the student become sad on Sundays.
- There are ASP approaches [3,73] that can used to help in understanding *Natural Language (NLP)*. Clearly NLP is major issue for Cecilia. Being able to understand written text by the students also allows the system to know her better, and hence have more enriching conversations.
- Updates and believe revision are also fundamental concepts required in our application. There are many well known proposed solutions based on ASP such as [17,65,92].
- There is promising work related with *ethical* chatbots [21] that could allow Cecilia to become more respectful to improve its ethical interaction with the student.
- ASP *parallelism* [19,74].
- *Planning* [23,44] for example the use of Coala in CLASP [25].
- Rapid Prototyping: Note that our generate and test code for DCP [63], and the solver to obtain the Optimal Solution of DCP KG described in this work is simply and directly written in ASP, that is one of the reasons why we are using ASP. Furthermore, for example, the use in sentiment analysis computed by solving the set covering [77] and minimal cut [72] problems. It is possible to use set covering to classify patterns where tests of properties can separate between emotions and the number of tests be minimized mapping to a set covering problem. Note that this kind of combinatorial problems are easily encoded in ASP.
- Handle Preferences and Optimization [7,8,53].

Following Gupta's advice, complex applications, as proposed in this work, will become possible if all these extensions where combined into a single system [30].

8   Conclusions

Contribution of this work[1] is to Define the Creative Composition Problem (CCP) for Human Well-being Optimization by Construction of Knowledge Graph using Knowledge Representation and logic-based Artificial Intelligence reasoning-planning where the computation of the Optimal Solution is achieved by Dynamic Programming or

---

[1] We thank the support of Psychologist Andres Munguia Barcenas.

Logic Programming. The Creative Composition Problem is embedded within Cecilia[2]: an architecture of a digital companion artificial intelligence agent system composer of dialogue scripts for Well-being and Mental Health. Where Cecilia Framework is instantiated in Well-being and Mental Health domain for optimal Well-being development of first year university students. We define the 'The Problem of Creating a Dialogue Composition (PCDC)' and we propose a feasible and optimal solution of it. CCP is instantiated in this applied domain to solve PCDC optimizing the Mental Health and Well-being of the student. CCP as PCDC is applied to optimize maximizing the mental health of the student but also maximizing the smoothness, coherence, enjoyment and engagement each time the dialogue session is composed. For Future Work Optimization of Mental Health and Well-being can be enhanced by sentiment analysis. It is possible to use set covering to classify patterns where tests of properties can separate between emotions and the number of tests to be minimized by mapping them to a set covering problem. For this it is possible to use of set covering [77] and minimal cut [72] algorithms. Note that this kind of combinatorial problems are easily encoded in ASP. Also MAIC can be enhanced with Logic Programming integrating Preferences and Optimization [7,8,53]. Following Gupta's advice complex applications as proposed in this work will become possible if all these extensions where combined into a single system [30]. In a recent paper, we investigated how to generate class notes for the development of psycho-affective learning based on a similar methodology as the one presented in this paper, namely the "Creative Composition Problem", see [10]. For future work we consider to explore the idea of representing Knowledge using alternative non-monotonic paradigms (besides from ASP) such as those found in [11,57,58,66,68,69]. As Cindy Mason stated in [49], the mechanisms for reasoning with regards to another's feelings only makes sense if there is wisdom to go along with it. This is a very important point. For a machine to engage in our world with a compassionate stance, we are faced with the task of articulating the common sense of compassion. Not all engineers and scientists are born with the gift for empathy, sympathy or compassion. We require collaboration with educators, psychologists, mothers, priests, our pets and even the kindness of strangers, to achieve the level of interaction that would enable the compassionate stance in a computational machine. The idea of programming our interfaces and embodied agents with a compassionate stance has great potential for positive influence in our cultures. This is why in our future work we will be integrating assessment of other disciplines to improve the development of compassion in our research work [48,50].

---

[2] The Cecilia application is available in https://github.com/luis-angel-montiel-moreno/efriend with the name of E-friend.

A   Appendix 1

% The following is an example of a CCP Graph Instance.% The following is an
example of a CCP Graph Instance.
% The input format consist of the numeric constants: number of vertixes, L, K.
% Following by two vectors W and P_V and one matrix P_E.

```
num_vertixes = 9.
L = 4.
K = 15.
```

#	1	2	3	4	5	6	7	8	9
W:	1	1	1	1	1	6	11	15	7
P_V:	5	2	7	12	7	1	12	12	6

P_E :

#	1	2	3	4	5	6	7	8	9
1	16	13	19	15	3	17	19	6	9
2	0	1	1	13	15	19	12	2	17
3	5	14	7	6	0	9	0	0	16
4	3	5	5	8	13	18	19	8	14
5	8	19	0	17	19	13	18	5	8
6	9	9	3	6	6	9	13	12	9
7	15	4	1	11	7	6	17	7	0
8	7	7	0	1	7	0	13	5	11
9	6	3	8	7	13	18	10	11	4

B   Appendix 2

```
dcp function is denoted as c
s={1,9}
c(s,8,8) = 20, c(s,8,9) = 20, c(s,8,10) = 20, c(s,8,11) = 20, c(s,8,12) = 20, c(s,8,13) = 20, c(s,8,14) = 20,
    c(s,8,15) = 20,
s={1,7}
c(s,6,12) = 36, c(s,6,13) = 36, c(s,6,14) = 36, c(s,6,15) = 36,
...
s={1,6,9}
c(s,5,14) = 39, c(s,5,15) = 39, c(s,8,14) = 38, c(s,8,15) = 38,
s={1,5,9}
c(s,4,9) = 40, c(s,4,10) = 40, c(s,4,11) = 40, c(s,4,12) = 40, c(s,4,13) = 40, c(s,4,14) = 40, c(s,4,15) = 40,
    c(s,8,9) = 29, c(s,8,10) = 29, c(s,8,11) = 29, c(s,8,12) = 29, c(s,8,13) = 29, c(s,8,14) = 29, c(s,8,15) =
    29,
...
s={1,5,6,9}
c(s,4,15) = 58, c(s,5,15) = 54, c(s,8,15) = 50,
s={1,4,6,9}
c(s,3,15) = 57, c(s,5,15) = 71, c(s,8,15) = 66,
...
s={1,2,3,4}
c(s,1,4) = 60, c(s,1,5) = 60, c(s,1,6) = 60, c(s,1,7) = 60, c(s,1,8) = 60, c(s,1,9) = 60, c(s,1,10) = 60,
    c(s,1,11) = 60, c(s,1,12) = 60, c(s,1,13) = 60, c(s,1,14) = 60, c(s,1,15) = 60, c(s,2,4) = 57, c(s,2,5) =
    57, c(s,2,6) = 57, c(s,2,7) = 57, c(s,2,8) = 57, c(s,2,9) = 57, c(s,2,10) = 57, c(s,2,11) = 57, c(s,2,12) =
    57, c(s,2,13) = 57, c(s,2,14) = 57, c(s,2,15) = 57, c(s,3,4) = 72, c(s,3,5) = 72, c(s,3,6) = 72, c(s,3,7) =
    72, c(s,3,8) = 72, c(s,3,9) = 72, c(s,3,10) = 72, c(s,3,11) = 72, c(s,3,12) = 72, c(s,3,13) = 72, c(s,3,14)
    = 72, c(s,3,15) = 72,
****
optimal solution of dcp
82
optimal dcp sequence (1,4,5,7)
```

References

1. Arias, J., Carro, M., Chen, Z., Gupta, G.: Constraint answer set programming without grounding and its applications. In: Datalog 2.0 2019–3rd International Workshop on the Resurgence of Datalog in Academia and Industry co-located with the 15th International Conference on Logic Programming and Nonmonotonic Reasoning (LPNMR 2019) at the Philadelphia Logic Week 2019, Philadelphia, PA (USA), 4–5 June 2019, pp. 22–26 (2019). http://ceur-ws.org/Vol-2368/paper2.pdf

2. Baskar, J., Janols, R., Guerrero, E., Nieves, J.C., Lindgren, H.: A multipurpose goal model for personalised digital coaching. In: Montagna, S., Abreu, P.H., Giroux, S., Schumacher, M.I. (eds.) A2HC/AHEALTH -2017. LNCS (LNAI), vol. 10685, pp. 94–116. Springer, Cham (2017). https://doi.org/10.1007/978-3-319-70887-4_6

3. Basu, K., Shakerin, F., Gupta, G.: Aqua: asp-based visual question answering. In: Practical Aspects of Declarative Languages - 22nd International Symposium, PADL 2020, New Orleans, LA, USA, 20–21 January 2020, Proceedings, pp. 57–72 (2020). https://doi.org/10.1007/978-3-030-39197-3_4

4. Beck, J.S., Beck, A.T.: Cognitive Therapy: Basics and Beyond. Guilford Press, New York (1995)

5. Bell, S., Wood, C., Sarkar, A.: Perceptions of chatbots in therapy. In: Extended Abstracts of the 2019 CHI Conference on Human Factors in Computing Systems, p. LBW1712 (2019)

6. Bendig, E., Erb, B., Schulze-Thuesing, L., Baumeister, H.: The next generation: chatbots in clinical psychology and psychotherapy to foster mental health-a scoping review. In: Verhaltenstherapie, pp. 1–13 (2019)

7. Bliem, B., Kaufmann, B., Schaub, T., Woltran, S.: ASP for anytime dynamic programming on tree decompositions (extended abstract). In: Friedrich, G., Helmert, M., Wotawa, F. (eds.) Proceedings of the 39th German Conference on Artificial Intelligence (KI 2016). LNCS, vol. 9904, pp. 257–263 (2016). https://doi.org/10.1007/978-3-319-46073-4

8. Brewka, G., Delgrande, J.P., Romero, J., Schaub, T.: asprin: customizing answer set preferences without a headache. In: Proceedings of the Twenty-Ninth AAAI Conference on Artificial Intelligence, 25–30 January 2015, Austin, Texas, USA, pp. 1467–1474 (2015). http://www.aaai.org/ocs/index.php/AAAI/AAAI15/paper/view/9535

9. Brown, K.W., Ryan, R.M., Creswell, J.D.: Mindfulness: theoretical foundations and evidence for its salutary effects. Psychol. Inq. **18**(4), 211–237 (2007)

10. Cervantes-Bello, G., De-Los-Santos-Goméz, A., Osorio, M., Andres, M.B.: Artificial intelligence methodology as a tool for the development of psycho-affective learning. In: proceedings of Thirteenth Latin American Workshop on New Methods of Reasoning (LANMR) 2020 in CEUR Workshop Proceedings (CEUR-WS.org). Logic/Languages, Algorithms and New Methods of Reasoning (2009)

11. Confalonieri, R., Nieves, J.C., Osorio, M., Vázquez-Salceda, J.: Possibilistic semantics for logic programs with ordered disjunction. In: Link, S., Prade, H. (eds.) FoIKS 2010. LNCS, vol. 5956, pp. 133–152. Springer, Heidelberg (2010). https://doi.org/10.1007/978-3-642-11829-6_11

12. Corapi, D., Russo, A., Lupu, E.: Inductive logic programming in answer set programming. In: Inductive Logic Programming - 21st International Conference, ILP 2011, Windsor Great Park, UK, 31 July–3 August 3 2011, Revised Selected Papers, pp. 91–97 (2011). https://doi.org/10.1007/978-3-642-31951-8_12

13. Dasgupta, S., Papadimitriou, C.H., Vazirani, U.V.: Algorithms. McGraw-Hill Higher Education New York (2008)

14. Daubenmier, J., Lin, J., Blackburn, E., Hecht, F.M., Kristeller, J., Maninger, N., Kuwata, M., Bacchetti, P., Havel, P.J., Epel, E.: Changes in stress, eating, and metabolic factors are related to changes in telomerase activity in a randomized mindfulness intervention pilot study. Psychoneuroendocrinology **37**(7), 917–928 (2012)

15. Davidson, R.J., et al.: Alterations in brain and immune function produced by mindfulness meditation. Psychosom. Med. **65**(4), 564–570 (2003). https://www.ncbi.nlm.nih.gov/pubmed/12883106

16. Davidson Richard: the four keys to well being. Greater Good Magazine (2016). https://greatergood.berkeley.edu/article/item/the_four_keys_to_well_being

17. Delgrande, J., Peppas, P., Woltran, S.: Agm-style belief revision of logic programs under answer set semantics. In: Logic Programming and Nonmonotonic Reasoning, 12th International Conference, LPNMR 2013, Corunna, Spain, 15–19 September 2013. Proceedings, pp. 264–276 (2013)
18. Diano, F., Ferrata, F., Calabretta, R.: The development of a mindfulness-based mobile application to learn emotional self-regulation. In: PSYCHOBIT (2019)
19. Dovier, A., Formisano, A., Pontelli, E.: Parallel answer set programming. In: Handbook of Parallel Constraint Reasoning, pp. 237–282 (2018). https://doi.org/10.1007/978-3-319-63516-3_7
20. Downey, R.G., Fellows, M.R.: Fundamentals of Parameterized Complexity. TCS. Springer, London (2013). https://doi.org/10.1007/978-1-4471-5559-1
21. Dyoub, A., Costantini, S., Lisi, F.A.: Towards ethical machines via logic programming. arXiv preprint arXiv:1909.08255 (2019)
22. Ehrlinger, L., Wöß, W.: Towards a definition of knowledge graphs. In: SEMANTiCS (Posters, Demos, SuCCESS), p. 48 (2016)
23. Eiter, T., Faber, W., Leone, N., Pfeifer, G., Polleres, A.: The dlv^k planning system: progress report. In: Logics in Artificial Intelligence, European Conference, JELIA 2002, Cosenza, Italy, 23–26 September, Proceedings, pp. 541–544 (2002). https://doi.org/10.1007/3-540-45757-7_51
24. Friedman, E.S., Koenig, A.M., Thase, M.E.: Cognitive and Behavioral Therapies. In: Fatemi, S.H., Clayton, P.J. (eds.) The Medical Basis of Psychiatry, pp. 781–798. Springer, New York (2016). https://doi.org/10.1007/978-1-4939-2528-5_35
25. Gebser, M., Grote, T., Schaub, T.: Coala: a compiler from action languages to ASP. In: Janhunen, T., Niemelä, I. (eds.) JELIA 2010. LNCS (LNAI), vol. 6341, pp. 360–364. Springer, Heidelberg (2010). https://doi.org/10.1007/978-3-642-15675-5_32
26. Gebser, M., Kaufmann, B., Kaminski, R., Ostrowski, M., Schaub, T., Schneider, M.: Potassco: the potsdam answer set solving collection. AI Commun. **24**(2), 107–124 (2011)
27. Gelfond, M., Kahl, Y.: Knowledge Representation, Reasoning, and The Design of Intelligent Agents: The Answer-Set Programming Approach. Cambridge University Press, New York (2014)
28. Gil, R., Virgili-Gomá, J., García, R., Mason, C.: Emotions ontology for collaborative modelling and learning of emotional responses. Comput. Hum. Behav. **51**, 610–617 (2015)
29. Grasso, G., Leone, N., Manna, M., Ricca, F.: ASP at work: spin-off and applications of the DLV system. In: Balduccini, M., Son, T.C. (eds.) Logic Programming, Knowledge Representation, and Nonmonotonic Reasoning. LNCS (LNAI), vol. 6565, pp. 432–451. Springer, Heidelberg (2011). https://doi.org/10.1007/978-3-642-20832-4_27
30. Gupta, G.: Next generation logic programming systems: reaching for the holy grail of computer science (2017)
31. Hamilton, W.L., Ying, R., Leskovec, J.: Representation learning on graphs: methods and applications. arXiv preprint arXiv:1709.05584 (2017)
32. Hermenegildo, M.V., et al.: An overview of ciao and its design philosophy. TPLP **12**(1–2), 219–252 (2012). https://doi.org/10.1017/S1471068411000457
33. Inkster, B., Sarda, S., Subramanian, V.: An empathy-driven, conversational artificial intelligence agent (wysa) for digital mental well-being: real-world data evaluation mixed-methods study. JMIR mHealth and uHealth **6**(11), e12106 (2018)
34. Jackson, S.: Flow and Mindfulness in Performance. Current Perspectives in Social and Behavioral Sciences, pp. 78–100. Cambridge University Press, New York (2016)
35. Jacobs, T.L., et al.: Intensive meditation training, immune cell telomerase activity, and psychological mediators. Psychoneuroendocrinology **36**(5), 664–681 (2011)
36. Jayaraman, B., Moon, K.: Subset logic programs and their implementation. J. Log. Program. **42**(2), 71–110 (2000). https://doi.org/10.1016/S0743-1066(99)00005-9

37. Jingar, M., Lindgren, H.: Tangible communication of emotions with a digital companion for managing stress: an exploratory co-design study. In: Proceedings of the 7th International Conference on Human-Agent Interaction, pp. 28–36 (2019)
38. Kabat-Zinn, J.: Wherever You Go, There You Are: Mindfulness Meditation in Everyday Life. Hachette Books, Paris (2009)
39. Katzouris, N., Artikis, A., Paliouras, G.: Incremental learning of event definitions with inductive logic programming. Mach. Learn. **100**(2–3), 555–585 (2015). https://doi.org/10.1007/s10994-015-5512-1
40. Kendig, C.E.: What is proof of concept research and how does it generate epistemic and ethical categories for future scientific practice? Sci. Eng. Ethics **22**(3), 735–753 (2016)
41. Knapp, P., Beck, A.T.: Cognitive therapy: foundations, conceptual models, applications and research fundamentos, modelos conceituais, aplicações e pesquisa da terapia cognitiva. Rev Bras Psiquiatr. **2008**(30 Suppl II), S54–64 (2008). http://citeseerx.ist.psu.edu/viewdoc/download?doi=10.1.1.611.1005&rep=rep1&type=pdf
42. Levitt, H.M.: Sounds of silence in psychotherapy: the categorization of clients' pauses. Psychother. Res. **11**(3), 295–309 (2001)
43. Lieberman, H., Mason, C.: Intelligent agent software for medicine. In: Studies in Health Technology and Informatics, pp. 99–110 (2002)
44. Lifschitz, V.: Answer set programming and plan generation. Artif. Intell. **138**(1–2), 39–54 (2002). https://doi.org/10.1016/S0004-3702(02)00186-8
45. Luksha, P., Cubista, J., Laszlo, A., Popovich, M., Ninenko, I.: Educational ecosystems for societal transformation (2017)
46. MacKenzie, M.B., Abbott, K.A., Kocovski, N.L.: Mindfulness-based cognitive therapy in patients with depression: current perspectives. Neuropsychiat. Dis. Treat. **14**, 1599 (2018)
47. Marple, K., Salazar, E., Gupta, G.: Computing stable models of normal logic programs without grounding. CoRR abs/1709.00501 (2017). http://arxiv.org/abs/1709.00501
48. Mason, C.: The multi-disciplinary case for human sciences in technology design. In: AAAI Fall Symposia (2014)
49. Mason, C.: Engineering kindness: building a machine with compassionate intelligence. Int. J. Synth. Emot. (IJSE) **6**(1), 1–23 (2015)
50. Mason, C., Mason, E.: Haptic medicine. Stud. Health Technol. Inf. **149**, 368–385 (2009)
51. Mason, C.L.: Human-level AI requires compassionate intelligence. In: AAAI Workshop on Meta-Cognition (2008)
52. Mazza, N.: Poetry Therapy: Theory and Practice. Routledge, London (2016)
53. Morak, M., Pichler, R., Rümmele, S., Woltran, S.: A dynamic-programming based ASP-solver. In: Janhunen, T., Niemelä, I. (eds.) JELIA 2010. LNCS (LNAI), vol. 6341, pp. 369–372. Springer, Heidelberg (2010). https://doi.org/10.1007/978-3-642-15675-5_34
54. Muggleton, S.H., Tamaddoni-Nezhad, A., Lisi, F.A. (eds.): ILP 2011. LNCS (LNAI), vol. 7207. Springer, Heidelberg (2012). https://doi.org/10.1007/978-3-642-31951-8
55. Nakamura, J., Csikszentmihalyi, M.: The Concept of Flow. Flow and the Foundations of Positive Psychology, pp. 239–263. Springer, Dordrecht (2014). https://doi.org/10.1007/978-94-017-9088-8_16
56. Nieves, J.C., Cortés, U., Osorio, M., Centia, S., Mártir, C.: Supporting decision making in organ transplanting using argumentation theory. In: LA-NMR (2006)
57. Nieves, J.C., Cortés, U., Osorio, M., Olmos, I., Gonzalez, J.A.: Defining new argumentation-based semantics by minimal models. In: Seventh Mexican International Conference on Computer Science, ENC 2006, 18–22 September 2006, San Luis Potosi, Mexico. pp. 210–220. IEEE Computer Society (2006). https://doi.org/10.1109/ENC.2006.10
58. Nieves, J.C., Osorio, M., Zepeda, C.: A schema for generating relevant logic programming semantics and its applications in argumentation theory. Fundam. Informaticae **106**(2–4), 295–319 (2011). https://doi.org/10.3233/FI-2011-388

59. Okoshi, T., Nakazawa, J., Ko, J.G., Kawsar, F., Pirttikangas, S.: Wellcomp 2019: second international workshop on computing for well-being. In: Adjunct Proceedings of the 2019 ACM International Joint Conference on Pervasive and Ubiquitous Computing and Proceedings of the 2019 ACM International Symposium on Wearable Computers, pp. 1146–1149 (2019)

60. Ortony, A., Clore, G.L., Collins, A.: The Cognitive Structure of Emotions. Cambridge University Press, New York (1990)

61. Osorio, M., Zepeda, C., Carballido, J.L.: Myubot: towards an artificial intelligence agent system chat-bot for well-being and mental health. (2020)

62. Osorio, M., Zepeda, C., Carballido, J.L.: Towards a virtual companion system to give support during confinement. In: CONTIE (2020)

63. Osorio, M., Zepeda, C., Castillo, H., Cervantes, P., Carballido, J.L.: My university e-partner. In: CONTIE, pp. 150–1503 (2019)

64. Osorio, M., Corona, E.: The a-pol system. In: Answer Set Programming, Advances in Theory and Implementation, Proceedings of the 2nd International ASP 2003 Workshop, Messina, Italy, 26–28 September 2003 (2003). http://ceur-ws.org/Vol-78/asp03-final-osorio-apol.pdf

65. Osorio, M., Cuevas, V.: Updates in answer set programming: an approach based on basic structural properties. CoRR abs/cs/0609167 (2006)

66. Osorio, M., Jayaraman, B.: Aggregation and negation-as-failure. New Gener. Comput. **17**(3), 255–284 (1999). https://doi.org/10.1007/BF03037222

67. Osorio, M., Jayaraman, B., Plaisted, D.A.: Theory of partial-order programming. Sci. Comput. Program. **34**(3), 207–238 (1999)

68. Osorio, M., Nieves, J.C.: PStable semantics for possibilistic logic programs. In: Gelbukh, A., Kuri Morales, Á.F. (eds.) MICAI 2007. LNCS (LNAI), vol. 4827, pp. 294–304. Springer, Heidelberg (2007). https://doi.org/10.1007/978-3-540-76631-5_28

69. Osorio, M., Nieves, J.C., Jayaraman, B.: Aggregation in functional query languages. J. Funct. Logic Program. **2004** (2004). http://danae.uni-muenster.de/lehre/kuchen/JFLP/articles/2004/A2004-02/A2004-02.html

70. Osorio, M.J., Montiel-Moreno, L.A., Rojas-Velázquez, D., Nieves, J.C.: E-friend: a logical-based ai agent system chat-bot for emotional well-being and mental health. In: To be published in Communications in Computer and Information Science CCIS. Accepted in 1st International Workshop on Deceptive AI at ECAI2020, 30 August 2020. Santiago de Compostela, Spain (2020)

71. Palanica, A., Flaschner, P., Thommandram, A., Li, M., Fossat, Y.: Physicians' perceptions of chatbots in health care: Cross-sectional web-based survey. J. Med. Internet Res. **21**(4), e12887 (2019)

72. Pang, B., Lee, L.: A sentimental education: sentiment analysis using subjectivity summarization based on minimum cuts. In: Proceedings of the 42nd Annual Meeting on Association for Computational Linguistics, p. 271. Association for Computational Linguistics (2004)

73. Pendharkar, D., Gupta, G.: An ASP based approach to answering questions for natural language text. In: Practical Aspects of Declarative Languages - 21th International Symposium, PADL 2019, Lisbon, Portugal, 14–15 January 2019, Proceedings, pp. 46–63 (2019). https://doi.org/10.1007/978-3-030-05998-9_4

74. Perri, S., Ricca, F., Sirianni, M.: Parallel instantiation of ASP programs: techniques and experiments. TPLP **13**(2), 253–278 (2013). https://doi.org/10.1017/S1471068411000652

75. Ribeiro, I.J., Pereira, R., Freire, I.V., de Oliveira, B.G., Casotti, C.A., Boery, E.N.: Stress and quality of life among university students: a systematic literature review. Health Prof. Educ. **4**(2), 70–77 (2018)

76. Robinson, K., Aronica, L.: Finding Your Element: How to Discover Your Talents and Passions and Transform Your Life. Penguin Books, London (2014)

77. Rodríguez, R.S., Roldán, C.Y.C., Eisele, J.G., del Pilar Gómez Gil, M., Galindo, M.J.O.: Algorithms for the typing of related DNA sequences. In: 15th International Conference on Electronics, Communications, and Computers (CONIELECOMP 2005), 28 February 2005–2 March 2005, Puebla, Mexico, pp. 268–271 (2005). https://doi.org/10.1109/CONIEL.2005.17

78. Rosenkranz, M.A., Dunne, J.D., Davidson, R.J.: The next generation of mindfulness-based intervention research: what have we learned and where are we headed? Curr. Opin. Psychol. **28**, 179 (2019)

79. Rotmensch, M., Halpern, Y., Tlimat, A., Horng, S., Sontag, D.: Learning a health knowledge graph from electronic medical records. Sci. Rep. **7**(1), 1–11 (2017)

80. Sarkadi, Ş., Panisson, A.R., Bordini, R.H., McBurney, P., Parsons, S., Chapman, M.: Modelling deception using theory of mind in multi-agent systems. AI Commun. **32**(4), 287–302 (2019)

81. Sarlej, M.: A lesson learned: using emotions to generate stories with morals. Ph.D. thesis, Doctoral dissertation). Computer Science and Engineering, University of New 2026 (2014)

82. Schaub, T., Woltran, S.: Answer set programming unleashed!. KI-Künstliche Intelligenz **32**(2–3), 105–108 (2018)

83. Schwarze, M.J., Gerler Jr., E.R.: Using mindfulness-based cognitive therapy in individual counseling to reduce stress and increase mindfulness: an exploratory study with nursing students. Prof. Counselor **5**(1), 39 (2015)

84. Scraper, R.L.: The art and science of maieutic questioning within the socratic method. In: International Forum for Logotherapy. Viktor Frankl Inst of Logotherapy (2000)

85. Stanford Medicine: the center for compassion and altruism research and education. CCARE (2020). http://ccare.stanford.edu/

86. Steunebrink, B.R., Dastani, M., Meyer, J.J.C.: The OCC model revisited. In: Proceedings of the 4th Workshop on Emotion and Computing. Association for the Advancement of Artificial Intelligence (2009)

87. Voloch, N.: Finding the most efficient paths between two vertices in a knapsack-item weighted graph. Int. J. Adv. Comput. Res. **7**(28), 15 (2017)

88. Walton, D.: The place of dialogue theory in logic, computer science and communication studies. Synthese **123**(3), 327–346 (2000)

89. Woodward, K., et al.: Beyond mobile apps: a survey of technologies for mental well-being. IEEE Trans. Affect. Comput. (2020)

90. World Health Organization: World health organization. WHO (2020). https://www.who.int/

91. Xiang, X., Wang, Z., Jia, Y., Fang, B.: Knowledge graph-based clinical decision support system reasoning: a survey. In: 2019 IEEE Fourth International Conference on Data Science in Cyberspace (DSC), pp. 373–380. IEEE (2019)

92. Zhuang, Z., Delgrande, J.P., Nayak, A.C., Sattar, A.: A new approach for revising logic programs. CoRR abs/1603.09465 (2016)

Set Visualisations
with Euler and Hasse Diagrams

Uta Priss[✉]

Zentrum für erfolgreiches Lehren und Lernen, Ostfalia University, Wolfenbüttel, Germany
http://www.upriss.org.uk

Abstract. This paper discusses set visualisations with concept lattices in the sense of Formal Concept Analysis (FCA) in contrast to visualisations with Euler diagrams. Both types of visualisations have advantages and disadvantages. Because of the connection between both fields and the body of knowledge that exists in both fields it is of interest to investigate whether results from either field can contribute to the other.

1 Introduction

Sets and their intersections can be visualised with Venn and Euler diagrams but also using mathematical lattice theory and a certain type of diagram (*Hasse diagram*) that is commonly used with lattices. It is therefore of interest to compare Euler and Hasse diagrams both with respect to what can be observed from the diagrams but also with respect to underlying theoretical constructs. While a translation between lattices and Venn diagrams is straightforward, the connection between *well-formed* Euler diagrams and lattices is not trivial. Lattice theory has produced a large body of knowledge which could potentially be beneficial for research about well-formed Euler diagrams. The research about Venn and Euler diagrams provides, for example, applications and algorithms which could be of interest for Hasse diagrams as well.

The version of lattice theory used in this paper is called Formal Concept Analysis (FCA) and has been developed since the 1980s as an applied mathematical theory of knowledge representation (Ganter and Wille 1999). Venn and Euler diagrams are well-established as a visualisation of sets that is used, for example, in schools when students are first introduced to set theory. Hasse diagrams may be less intuitive at first sight and require some training. Priss (2017) discusses misconceptions that students initially have about Hasse diagrams of concept lattices in general. If restricted to specific tasks, Eklund et al. (2004) show, however, that novice users can be instructed to use Hasse diagrams fairly effectively.

As far as we know, the relationship between FCA and Euler diagrams has so far not been investigated in any great depth[1]. The intention of this paper is to elaborate the basic connections between both fields. This paper provides an introduction to both fields and basic translations between Venn/Euler and Hasse diagrams. It discusses the application of some lattice-theoretical properties to Euler diagrams. We suspect that

---

[1] As evidenced by a query on Google Scholar for "Formal concept analysis" and "Euler diagrams" which retrieves very little.

M. Cochez et al. (Eds.): GKR 2020, LNAI 12640, pp. 72–83, 2021.
https://doi.org/10.1007/978-3-030-72308-8_5

many researchers from either field are not aware of all of the connections. Because each field has a slightly different focus, it is conceivable that a combination might provide further interesting results. Many questions about the relationship between well-formed Euler diagrams and lattices still remain open.

Sections 2 and 3 of this paper provide introductions to Venn, Euler and Hasse diagrams and FCA. Section 4 covers Venn diagrams and their (well-known) relationship to Boolean lattices. Sections 5, 6, 7 discuss different aspects of the relationship between Euler and Hasse diagrams. Although most of the individual mathematical aspects presented in this paper are not new, we believe that the compilation and elaboration of details with respect to the examples presented in this paper is new. A possibly provocative conclusion of this paper is that although many people may find Euler diagrams "intuitive" as a representation of sets, from a structural viewpoint Hasse diagrams are potentially more suitable for visualising set theory than Venn and Euler diagrams.

2 A Brief Introduction to Euler and Venn Diagrams

Venn and Euler diagrams are a means for graphically representing sets and their intersections and unions. A more detailed introduction and further background is, for example, provided by Rodgers (2014). Venn diagrams contain all possible intersections for a powerset (i.e. set of all subsets of a set). For example, D1 and D2 in Fig. 1 show Venn diagrams for 3 and 4 sets. Venn diagrams for more than 3 sets cannot be represented by only using circles. Euler diagrams are similar to Venn diagrams but exclude zones which are known to be empty.

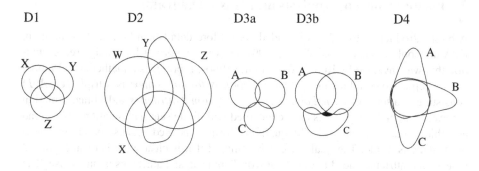

Fig. 1. Venn diagrams (D1 and D2) and non-well-formed Euler Diagrams (D3a, D3b and D4)

The following terminology applies to Venn and Euler diagrams in this paper: Venn and Euler diagrams consist of closed *curves* which have *labels*. *Minimal regions* are the smallest areas in a diagram which are surrounded by lines and not divided further. *Regions* are sets of minimal regions. *Zones* are maximal regions that are within a set of curves and outwith the remaining curves. For a set L of curve labels, the notation $E(L)$ is used in this paper for a *set of zones*. In other words, $E(L)$ is a subset of the powerset of L that corresponds to the zones of an Euler diagram.

The reason for distinguishing minimal regions and zones is that zones are the smallest set-theoretically meaningful areas in a diagram whereas minimal regions are the smallest visible areas in a diagram. In a *well-formed* Euler diagram, zones correspond to minimal regions. Further conditions for being well-formed are defined slightly differently by different authors (e.g. Flower et al. (2008)). In order to be well-formed, a diagram should not contain a zone that is *disconnected* and split into several minimal regions (as in D3b in Fig. 1 where the black region in the middle belongs to the outer region). Diagrams should not contain *n-points* for $n > 2$ that is points where more than 2 curves cross (as in D3a). Different curves should not be *concurrent* (as in D4). Each curve should have at most one label. Curves should not intersect themselves. There should not be any brushing points where several curves meet without crossing.

In universal algebra or algebraic logic, relationships are established between equational classes and algebraic structures. For example, the powerset of a set with operations $\cap$, $\cup$ and complementation corresponds to a Boolean algebra or Boolean lattice which can be defined as an equational class. Any subset of a powerset that is closed under $\cap$ and $\cup$ corresponds to a distributive lattice which can also be defined as an equational class. While a single (fairly simple) equation is needed to determine whether a lattice is distributive, no similar simple equation or property has yet been found that determines whether a set $E(L)$ can be represented as a well-formed Euler diagram. Although it seems visually clear what Euler diagrams are and what they look like, from an algebraic viewpoint well-formed Euler diagrams are neither simple nor intuitive. So far algorithms have been provided for deciding whether an Euler diagram is well-formed (for example, Flower et al. (2008)) but not an equational characterisation.

3   Formal Concept Analysis and Hasse Diagrams

A brief introduction to FCA is included here. More details can be found in the main FCA textbook by Ganter and Wille (1999). FCA is a theory of knowledge representation that was invented by Rudolf Wille in the 1980s. It provides a mathematical model for conceptual hierarchies using lattice theory. A *formal context* is a triple (O, A, I) consisting of a set O of *formal objects*, a set A of *formal attributes* and a binary relation I between them. This paper is only concerned with finite sets. The relation oIa is read as "object o has attribute a". The qualifier "formal" is used because being an object or attribute is a role. The qualifier can be omitted if it is clear what is meant. Formal objects and attributes need not be "real world" objects and attributes in any sense. The left-hand side of Fig. 2 shows an example of a formal context with types of animals as formal objects and "female", "juvenile" and "male" as formal attributes. The right-hand side shows a concept lattice (as defined below) using a visualisation for partially ordered sets called *Hasse diagram*.

Concepts are formed by starting with a set of objects, then collecting all attributes which they have in common and then adding any further objects that also have these attributes. Dually, one can also start with attributes. Formally, all common attributes of a set $O_1 \subseteq O$ of objects are denoted by $O_1' := \{a \in A \mid oIa \text{ for all } o \in O_1\}$. All common objects of a set $A_1 \subseteq A$ of attributes are denoted by $A_1' := \{o \in O \mid oIa \text{ for all } a \in A_1\}$. A *formal concept* is a pair (O_1, A_1) where $O_1 = A_1'$ and $A_1 =$

	juvenile	male	female
lamb	x		
filly	x		x
colt	x	x	
calf	x		
foal	x		

({foal,calf,lamb,filly,colt},{juvenile})

({filly},{juvenile,female})   ({colt},{juvenile,male})

({ },{juvenile,female.male})

Fig. 2. A formal context and concept lattice

O_1'. The right-hand side of Fig. 2 shows 4 formal concepts. The set O_1 of a formal concept (O_1, A_1) is called the concept's *extension*; the set A_1 is called the concept's *intension*. For example, ({filly}, {juvenile, female}) is a formal concept with extension {filly} and intension {juvenile, female}. The pair ({calf, lamb}, {juvenile}) is not a formal concept because it fulfils $O_1' = A_1$ but not $A_1' = O_1$. It follows from the definition of the $'$-operation that for any set S of objects or attributes $S' = S'''$ and $S \subseteq S''$.

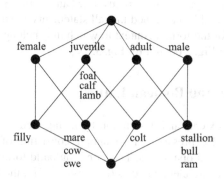

female   juvenile   adult   male

foal
calf
lamb

filly   mare   colt   stallion
         cow   bull
         ewe   ram

Fig. 3. A concept lattice with minimal labelling

A concept (O_1, A_1) is a subconcept of a concept (O_2, A_2) if $O_1 \subseteq O_2$. This is equivalent to $A_1 \supseteq A_2$ (as can be observed in Fig. 2). The set of formal concepts together with a subconcept ordering forms a mathematical lattice. In a Hasse diagram of a concept lattice, nodes denote concepts and edges connect adjacent concepts according to the subconcept ordering. In Fig. 2 the full concepts are written within the nodes. Figure 3 shows a different concept lattice, this time with *minimal labelling* because each object is written slightly below the lowest concept it belongs to and each attribute is written slightly above the highest concept it belongs to. Such objects/attributes are called *immediate* objects/attributes of a concept in this paper. In the remainder of this paper only minimal labelling is employed. An extension can then be read by collecting all objects on every downwards path from a concept and an intension by collecting all attributes on every upwards path from a concept. The top concept of a lattice has all objects in its extension. It can but does not need to have an attribute in its intension and represents some sort of global or universal concept. The bottom concept has all attributes in its intension and corresponds to some sort of *Null* concept. It can but does not need to have an object in its extension.

In a finite lattice, each set of concepts has an infimum (called *meet* and denoted by $\wedge$) and a supremum (called *join* and denoted by $\vee$). A meet is the largest shared concept below a set of concepts. Dually, a join is the smallest shared concept above a set of concepts. A concept in a lattice that has exactly one adjacent upper concept (i.e., one edge going up from the node) is called $\wedge$-irreducible and must have at least one immediate attribute. This is the case for all nodes that have immediate attributes in Figs. 2 and 3 except for the top concept in Fig. 2 (with attribute "juvenile") because a top concept is the meet of an empty set and thus $\wedge$-reducible. Dually, a concept with exactly one adjacent lower concept is called $\vee$-irreducible and must have at least one immediate object. In Fig. 3 the concept with immediate objects {foal, calf, lamb} is $\vee$-reducible. If the objects {foal, calf, lamb} were removed from the formal context the resulting lattice would still be isomorphic to the one in Fig. 3. But if "filly" or "colt" were removed from the formal context, then the lattice structure would change.

For concept lattices, logical implications amongst attributes can be read from the Hasse diagram because the attributes of a subconcept imply the attributes of a super-concept. For example, in Fig. 2 "male $\Longrightarrow$ juvenile" and in Fig. 3 "female $\wedge$ male $\Longrightarrow$ juvenile $\vee$ adult". It should be cautioned that all statements about concepts and implications are only valid for the formal context to which they belong. For example, "male $\Longrightarrow$ juvenile" is true for Fig. 2 but not for Fig. 3.

4   Venn Diagrams and Boolean Lattices

Sets naturally have an extensional description by listing elements and an intensional description using logical expressions, for example consisting of labels of other sets together with set-theoretical operations. Thus, one can build formal contexts $(U, L, \in)$ where the formal objects are elements of a (universal) set U, the formal attributes are labels (in L) corresponding to subsets of U and the incidence relation is the element-of relation ($\in$). The Hasse diagrams below are to be interpreted in that manner. For Venn (or Euler) diagrams only set labels are required, set elements are optional but can be written into zones. In some of the Venn (and Euler) diagrams below, set elements are included in order to emphasise the correspondence between Venn and Hasse diagrams.

In a concept lattice of a context $(U, L, \in)$, the lattice-theoretical $\wedge$-operation correlates with a $\cap$-operation amongst subsets of U. For example in Lattice 1 in Fig. 4, $(\{a, b\}, \{X\}) \wedge (\{a, c\}, \{Y\}) = (\{a\}, \{X, Y\})$ corresponds to $\{a, b\} \cap \{a, c\} = X \cap Y$. In such lattices, the lattice-theoretical $\vee$-operation correlates with a $\cap$-operation amongst subsets of L. For example, in Lattice 2, $\{Y, Z\} \cap \{Y, W\} = \{Y\}$. In either case, only containment holds for $\cup$-operations. For example, $(\{F, B, a\}, \{Y, Z\}) \vee (\{G, B, a\}, \{Y, W\}) = (\{F, G, B, a, l\}, \{Y\})$ but $(Y \cap Z) \cup (Y \cap W) \subset Y$.

Lattices corresponding to Venn diagrams (Fig. 4) are Boolean lattices and contain 2^n concepts (for n labels) each of which relates to a zone in a Venn diagram. Their Hasse diagrams form hypercubes. The dotted lines in Lattice 2 correspond to zones in Diagram 2 that are not neighbours in the Venn diagram even though they could

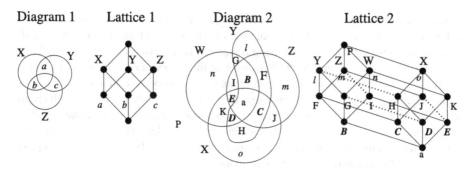

Fig. 4. Venn and Hasse diagrams of Boolean lattices

(or should) be neighbours. For example: the zone with the immediate object H is in $X \cap Y$. But while it is a neighbour of the zone with the immediate object o (in X) it is not a neighbour of the zone with the immediate object l (in Y) even though structurally the relationship between X and $X \cap Y$ is isomorphic to the relationship between Y and $X \cap Y$. Thus Lattice 2 shows relationships which are not as easily visible in Diagram 2.

Flower et al. (2008) define a *dual graph* of an Euler diagram as a labelled graph which has a vertex for each zone and an edge if the zones are neighbours. Each edge is labelled by the set labels which distinguish their vertices. For example, an edge between X and $X \cap Y$ is labelled by Y. Flower et al. show that for well-formed Euler diagrams, each edge has exactly one label. This condition is called *single-label condition* in the remainder of this paper. A *superdual graph* contains all possible edges with exactly one label. Thus the dual graph of Diagram 2 corresponds to the solid lines in the diagram for Lattice 2 (as an undirected graph) whereas the superdual graph corresponds to the solid together with the dotted lines. A superdual graph represents an abstract set of zones of an Euler diagram that is independent of how the diagram is exactly drawn. The next section shows that not every abstract set of zones of a well-formed Euler diagram forms a lattice and not every lattice corresponds to a set of zones of a well-formed Euler diagram.

5   Sets of Zones as Well-Formed Euler Diagrams and Lattices

In this section a different construction is used for the formal contexts compared to the previous section. For each Euler diagram, a formal context $(E(L), L, \ni)$ is created by taking the set $E(L)$ of the set of labels of each zone as formal objects, the set L of set labels as formal attributes and by defining the incidence relation for $z \in E(L), l \in L$ as follows: $z \ni l :\Longleftrightarrow l$ is an element of the set z of labels. Graphically this is equivalent to z (as a zone) being within curve l. Contrary to the construction of $(U, L, \in)$ in the previous section this construction uses zones represented by labels without specifying elements of the sets.

The question arises as to whether any given set of zones $E(L)$ can be represented as a well-formed Euler diagram or a Hasse diagram of a concept lattice. Obviously, the condition for being representable as a concept lattice is that the set of zones must form a lattice. This means that in the context $(E(L), L, \ni)$ the set $E(L)$ must be closed with respect to intersections. If the set of zones itself does not form a lattice, it can still be embedded into a lattice. Constructing a concept lattice for a context $(E(L), L, \ni)$ achieves such an embedding. In the remainder of this paper, any concept in the lattice of $(E(L), L, \ni)$ that is added for the embedding (i.e. does not have an immediate object in the lattice of $(E(L), L, \ni)$) is represented by an empty node in the Hasse diagram and called a *supplemental concept*. Because it does not correspond to a zone and thus does not have an immediate object, the extension of a supplemental concept equals the union of the extensions of its lower neighbouring concepts. If the bottom concept is supplemental (as in Lattice 3 in Fig. 5), its extension is empty.

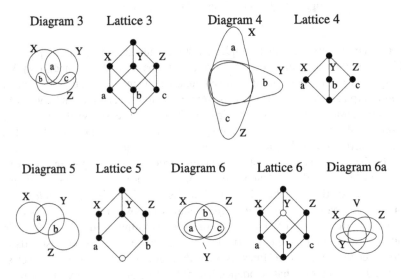

Fig. 5. Euler diagrams and concept lattices

Diagram 1 (in Fig. 4) presents a Venn diagram that is also a well-formed Euler diagram and can be represented as a lattice without supplemental concepts (cf. Lattice 1). Lattice 3 and Diagram 3 (in Fig. 5) represent a set of zones which can neither be a well-formed Euler diagram nor a lattice without supplemental concepts. The set of zones in Lattice 4 forms a lattice without supplemental concepts, but does not correspond to a well-formed Euler diagram (because it contradicts the single-label condition). Last but not least, Diagram 5 displays an example of a well-formed Euler diagram which does not correspond to a lattice without supplemental concepts. Thus the examples show that any of the four possible constellations of being a well-formed Euler diagram and a lattice without supplemental concepts exists.

Supplemental concepts can occur higher up in the lattice ordering as well. Lattice 6 contains a supplemental concept which is required in order to attach attribute Y to a node but this node does not correspond to a zone in Diagram 6. Lattice 6 would still be a lattice even if the supplemental concept was removed. But in that case instead of a curve Y, two curves would need to exist, one as a subset of X and the other one as a subset of Z. Thus a corresponding lattice without a supplemental concept would have one attribute more than Lattice 6. Its corresponding Euler diagram would not be well-formed because the single-label condition would not be fulfilled.

It should be mentioned that adding or deleting a curve can change a well-formed Euler diagram into a non-well-formed one and vice versa. Diagram 6 can be embedded into a well-formed Euler diagram by adding a curve as shown in Diagram 6a. Similarly in Diagram 2, deleting curve W or X would yield a non-well-formed diagram which, in this case however, can be transformed into a well-formed diagram. For the purposes of this paper this fact about Euler diagrams is stated as the set of well-formed Euler diagrams not being *closed with respect to recursive generation*.

6   Conditions for Well-Formed Euler Diagrams

It appears to be easier to identify conditions that determine that a set of zones cannot be a well-formed Euler diagram than those that determine that it can be a well-formed Euler diagram. Such conditions from the literature (see below) tend to not use lattice theory. Therefore this section discusses some conditions based on lattice theory.

- **C1:** if a $\wedge$-reducible concept has an immediate attribute then the corresponding Euler diagram is not well-formed. Proof: a curve corresponding to such an attribute is concurrent with the intersection of other curves which contradicts the single-label condition.
- **C2:** if a $\wedge$-reducible concept with n adjacent upper concepts in a concept lattice without supplemental concepts is not the bottom node of a Boolean sublattice with 2^n elements, then the corresponding Euler diagram is not well-formed. Proof: if a concept c has n adjacent upper neighbours then the intensions of these concepts must all differ by one attribute from the intension of c because of the single-label condition. This means that any pair of the n concepts shares all attributes except that each one has one extra attribute. If one forms all intersections of such n intensions in order to build a lattice without supplemental concepts then one obtains a Boolean sublattice.

Condition C2 is relevant for Lattice 4 and the discussion about Lattice 6 above. Because of condition C2, lattices without supplemental concepts that correspond to well-formed Euler diagrams look like they are hypercubes that are glued together. But this is still not a necessary and sufficient condition. Lattice 9 in Fig. 6 does not correspond to a well-formed Euler diagram because the zone $\{X, W\}$ which is shaded in black is disconnected.

A next attempt might be to consider whether distributivity plays a role but Fig. 6 demonstrates that it does not. Lattice 7 is not distributive but Diagram 7 is well-formed. Lattices 8–10 are distributive. Lattices 8 and 10 can be represented as well-formed Euler diagrams (as shown in Diagrams 8 and 10) but Lattice 9 cannot. In the case of a single disconnected zone as in Diagram 9, adding a further zone yields a well-formed diagram as demonstrated for Diagram 6 and 6a, Diagram 9 and 10 and Diagram 5 (modified to correspond to a lattice without supplemental concepts) and Diagram 7. Each represents

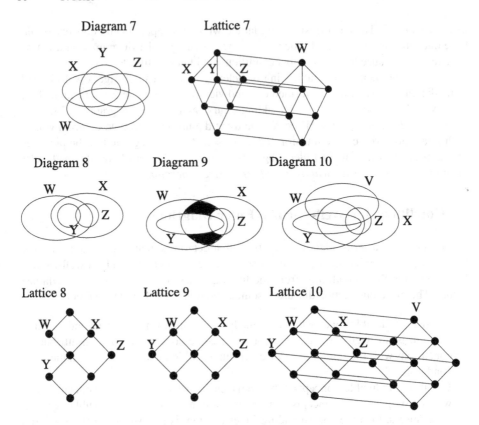

Fig. 6. Euler diagrams and distributive lattices

an example of the set of well-formed Euler diagrams not being closed with respect to recursive generation.

The fact that Lattices 4 and 9 cannot be represented as well-formed Euler diagrams can also be described in terms of irreducible concepts (i.e. concepts that are simultaneously ∧- and ∨-irreducible): in Lattice 4 a meet of three irreducible concepts contradicts the single-label condition and in Lattice 9 two irreducible concepts that have pairwise meets with the same concept and a joined meet cause a similar problem. It might also be of interest to consider well-formed Euler diagrams for lattices such as Lattice 5 where only the bottom concept is a supplemental concept.

Flower et al. (2008) provide further necessary conditions for well-formed Euler diagrams, for example a connectivity condition: a dual graph serves the connectivity condition if it is connected, all subgraphs induced by deleting any vertex containing a selected label are connected and all subgraphs induced by deleting any vertex not containing a selected label are also connected. If the bottom node was missing in Lattice 6, then its graph would be disconnected after removal of all concepts which do not contain Y. Thus attributes attached to supplemental concepts can be necessary, but not sufficient for the connectivity condition.

A further condition from Flower et al. (2008) is that the dual graph of an Euler diagram must be planar or must be reducible to a planar graph which still passes the connectivity condition. This does not imply that the corresponding Hasse diagram also must be planar because a Hasse diagram is a directed graph whereas a dual graph is undirected. For example Lattice 1 in Fig. 4 is not planar and cannot be converted into a planar Hasse diagram. But if the graph is converted into an undirected graph and the top node (or the bottom node) is placed into the middle then it can be drawn as a planar graph. The same holds for Lattice 2 without the dotted lines. Again, the negation is not valid: Lattice 9 shows an example that fulfils the single-label condition, the connectivity condition and is a planar Hasse diagram but is not drawable as a well-formed Euler diagram. Flower et al. remaining condition is a "face condition" which checks the sequence of curve labels around each "face" of a dual graph for a certain property. It is not clear whether and how that could be translated into a lattice-theoretical property.

7 Reading Implications from Euler and Hasse Diagrams

The question of which Euler diagrams can be drawn as well-formed diagrams is important because well-formed diagrams are presumably easier for users to visually parse than non-well-formed diagrams. A further question about Euler diagrams is what information can be extracted from them so that they can be employed as a tool for information visualisation. In Sect. 3 it was mentioned that implications can be read from concept lattices. The same is true for Euler diagrams. For example, one can read $X \implies Y$ and $Y \implies Z$ both from Diagram 11 as well as from Lattice 11 (in Fig. 7).

Stapleton et al. (2017) use Diagram 12 as an example of an *observational advantage* of Euler diagrams. The diagram shows that $P \cap Q = \emptyset \Rightarrow R \cap Q = \emptyset$. Stapleton et al. argue that Euler diagrams have a maximum observational advantage because any similar set-theoretical statement that is valid for the data in the diagram can be read from the diagram. We argue that Hasse diagrams have an even higher observational advantage than Euler diagrams if one considers further set-theoretical operations.

The implication $P \cap Q = \emptyset \Rightarrow R \cap Q = \emptyset$ can also be observed from Lattices 12a and 12b[2]. Lattices 12a and 12b both contain the implication $R \Rightarrow P$ and the corresponding $R \cap Q \subseteq P \cap Q$. Lattice 12a also contains $P \cap Q \Rightarrow R$ and thus $P \cap Q = R \cap Q$ which is difficult, or impossible, to see in Diagram 12 because it involves a statement about the empty set as a bottom concept which exists in Lattice 12a but is a missing zone in Diagram 12. Lattice 12b contains all intersections that are still possible if the implication $R \Rightarrow P$ is assumed. The supplemental concepts in Lattice 12b correspond to two missing zones in Diagram 12. In Lattice 12b, the implication $P \cap Q = \emptyset \Rightarrow R \cap Q = \emptyset$ is not an intensional implication but an implication that involves $R \cap Q \subseteq P \cap Q$ and the extensional information that $P \cap Q = \emptyset$.

While it is possible to observe that zones are missing in an Euler diagram, one can argue that statements that assert that two missing zones are equal (as in Lattice 12a) or involve information about extensions (as in Lattice 12b) cannot be observed from Euler diagrams. Thus one might argue that for someone who can read Hasse diagrams,

---

[2] It should be noted that implications and their generalisations are well-known in the FCA community and discussed, for example, in the textbook by Ganter and Obiedkov (2016).

Lattices 12a and 12b have a higher observational advantage than Diagram 12. Further-more, Hasse diagrams are not restricted to representing simple relationships amongst sets. Ganter and Obiedkov (2016) discuss many other applications, for example, involv-ing clauses and other more complex logical statements instead of just implications.

It should be mentioned, however, that lattices have the same problem as Venn and Euler diagrams in that they become very difficult to visually parse if they are too large. In cases such as Lattice 4 in Fig. 5 where "many intersections are missing", the lattice is less complex than a Boolean lattice. But in cases such as Lattice 3, a Boolean lattice is required. While it is theoretically possible to draw Hasse diagrams for Boolean lat-tices of any size, it becomes difficult to see anything in such a lattice for more than 4 sets. Therefore presenting diagrams to users is not necessarily the main goal of FCA applications which instead often use FCA for computational purposes.

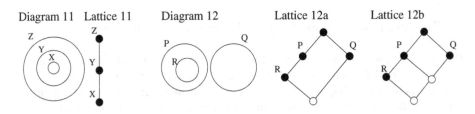

Fig. 7. Implications amongst set-theoretical statements

8   Conclusion

This paper provides a discussion of representing sets with Hasse diagrams of concept lattices compared to Euler diagrams. The basic relationship between the two types of diagrams is explained. Examples of well-formed Euler diagrams exist that do not cor-respond to lattices without supplemental concepts and lattices without supplemental concepts exist that do not correspond to well-formed Euler diagrams. Conditions for determining which Euler diagrams can be represented as concept lattices without sup-plemental concepts are discussed. While some Euler diagrams that are not well-formed can be near impossible to draw, having supplemental concepts in a lattice does not affect how a Hasse diagram is drawn or read. Supplemental concepts serve a purpose with respect to implications. Both Euler diagrams and Hasse diagrams become diffi-cult to read if they get too large. While many people find Euler diagrams much more intuitive to read than Hasse diagrams, the overall expressive power of Hasse diagrams might be higher than that of Euler diagrams. Furthermore, lattice theory can quite likely provide more insights with respect to a theory of well-formed Euler diagrams.

One potentially provocative conclusion of this paper is that well-formed Euler dia-grams may not actually be an ideal representation for sets. Set theory is often introduced to students using the visualisation of Venn and Euler diagrams. Thus students may start to think of sets as *being like* Venn and Euler diagrams. But because well-formed Euler diagrams can only represent some subsets of powersets and because it is not clear what the algebraic nature of well-formed Euler diagrams precisely is, one could argue that in some sense Hasse diagrams are more suitable for representing set theory than Euler diagrams.

References

Eklund, P., Ducrou, J., Brawn, P.: Concept lattices for information visualization: can novices read line-diagrams? In: International Conference on Formal Concept Analysis, pp. 57–73. Springer, Berlin (2004)

Flower, J., Fish, A., Howse, J.: Euler diagram generation. J. Vis. Lang. Comput. **19**(6), 675–694 (2008)

Ganter, B., Wille, R.: Formal Concept Analysis. Mathematical Foundations. Springer, Berlin (1999)

Ganter, B., Obiedkov, S.: Conceptual Exploration. Springer, Berlin (2016)

Priss, U.: Learning thresholds in formal concept analysis. In: Bertet, K., Borchmann, D., Cellier, P., Ferré, S. (eds.) ICFCA 2017. LNCS (LNAI), vol. 10308, pp. 198–210. Springer, Cham (2017). https://doi.org/10.1007/978-3-319-59271-8_13

Rodgers, P.: A survey of Euler diagrams. J. Vis. Lang. Comput. **25**(3), 134–155 (2014)

Stapleton, G., Jamnik, M., Shimojima, A.: What makes an effective representation of information: a formal account of observational advantages. J. Logic Lang. Inform. **26**(2), 143–177 (2017)

Usage Patterns Identification Using Graphs and Machine Learning

Ovidiu-Dan Sonea[✉]

Babes-Bolyai University, Cluj-Napoca, Romania
ovidiu.dan.sonea@gmail.com

Abstract. During the past years, the number of platforms that are introducing a subscription plan is steadily increasing. This phenomenon helps support the developers as well as continuing to provide quality content. Since not so many individuals are willing to spend money or some simply do not have the means, they resort to sharing an account that has a subscription plan. This behavior can, in some instances, be harmful for the developers and, even if it is not, any provider can benefit from knowing what type of clients they have. The solution depicted and explored in this article will focus on using data that is easily available and structuring it in a way that can provide insight into each account activity.

1 Introduction

Since sharing credentials is very easy and many people don't see it as a problem, this practice continues to expand. This phenomenon leads many content creators to be interested in developing a way of identifying shared accounts but often it is not enough just to know if an account is shared or not; content creators want to know how an account is shared. This means that the algorithm must also classify users into patterns that are predefined by the provider to suite their needs. In the end, based on the constrains of each pattern and other metrics calculated, mostly using graph theory, the algorithm provides a sharing probability for each account. Most providers have access to massive amounts of data which, most likely, means that they have the necessary tools to identify password sharing, they just have not found an efficient way processing at the data in order to solve this problem. Given that the algorithm, which will be detailed in the next pages, uses only information that most content providers already have access to, it can be easily implemented successfully on a large number of platforms.

Although there are several solutions that are implemented, these approaches cannot provide a definitive answer for the problem previously described. A few examples are:

1. Fraud Detection attempts to identify individual events/transactions as "fraudulent" do not work in our case, while we need to label the entire subscriber activity as "shared" or not.
2. "Anomalies" spotted within a subscriber activity are not necessarily an indication for account sharing, while sharing can happen with no visible anomalies if the account is shared from the beginning.

It is necessary to detect usage patterns. Having only the label "shared" or "not shared" is insufficient, because the content creator may want to allow certain types of sharing that

M. Cochez et al. (Eds.): GKR 2020, LNAI 12640, pp. 84–92, 2021.
https://doi.org/10.1007/978-3-030-72308-8_6

do not harm their business. An example from the streaming industry can be a teenager that went to college and is sharing an account with his/her parents.

2 The Problem

The problems that demand a solution are identifying accounts that are shared and classifying users into usage patterns. The end goal is to give providers insights on their subscribers so they can take action on the users from a certain usage pattern. The solution should also be implemented in a reliable and testable way.

3 Approach

In solving this problem we used several graph theory algorithms to structure the data in a way that ensures the validity of our assumptions and assures that the data was not corrupted in a prior step.

The proposed solution will analyse the subscriber's activity during a given time period, classify the subscriber into a known usage pattern and it will provide a password sharing probability. Moving forward, we will describe the capabilities and functions of the proposed solution on an example from the TV industry.

The raw data, that will be inserted in the algorithm, observes the activity of real users during a month. This data was collected and provided by a client from the industry and contains the following fields: user id (as defined in the clients database), the coordinates at which an event took place, device type, device id and the time at which an event occured. All the data gathered in a time interval will be processed and the end result for each user will be:

- Number of devices – the number of unique devices per subscriber per analysed time interval;
- Location clusters – that are determined by finding common locations between subscriber's devices. The devices that have been seen in a common location will be considered to belong to the same cluster. But at the same time, two devices can be in the same cluster even though they do not have common locations, but they are connected through the locations of other devices from that cluster;
- Type of location clusters – mobile or static cluster;
- The minimum distance between location clusters – the sum of distances between the closest points of different clusters;
- The minimum number of persons behind an account – determined by looking at the subscriber's activity in a chronological order and analysing successive events which are produced by different devices. Here we are determining the cases where the usage cannot be made by a single person.

Based on the detailed criteria, each subscriber will be labeled into a single usage pattern and after that, they will be given an account sharing probability. The table that follows shows how this particular client has chosen to define the patters in order to extract information they considered valuable. The algorithm allows for the patterns to be defined in

Table 1. Detailed view of Usage patterns defined criteria

Usage pattern label	Devices	Cluster configuration	Min. distance between all clusters
1. Single location usage	Less than 5	Only one location	N/A
2. Traveling User	Less than 5	1 static cluster or/and 1 mobile cluster, or 2 mobile clusters	Unspecified
3. Large Family	More than 4 but less than 21	Less than 3 and at most 1 static	Less than 100 Km
4. Multiple houses at close distance	Unspecified	2 or 3 static clusters and the total number less than 5	Less than 100 Km
5. Heavy usage across multiple locations	Unspecified	3 or more static and the total number more than 5	More than 100 km
6. Multiple distant locations	Unspecified	2 or more static but the total number less than 5	Unspecified
7. Concurrent usage from different locations	Less than 5	1 static cluster or/and 1 mobile cluster, or 2 mobile clusters	Unspecified
8. Secondary location	Less than 8	2 clusters and at most one static	Unspecified
9. Few clusters close to each other	Unspecified	Less than 4 clusters but at most one static	Less than 100 km
10. Multiple clusters close to each other	Unspecified	More than 3 but at most one static	Less than 100 km
11. Few clusters distant from each other	Unspecified	Less than 4 clusters but at most one static	More than 100 km
12. Multiple clusters on multiple distant location	Unspecified	More than 3 but at most 1 static	More than 100 km

many ways without them affecting its performance. There are, however, a few limitations when it comes to defining these usage patterns. The limitations are: the defined patterns must be mutually exclusive, meaning that a subscriber must fit into only one pattern and that the entire pool of subscribers must be fitted into the defined patterns (there can't be subscribers that don't have a pattern assigned).

4   Implementation

The algorithm is structured in way in which it achieves the intended goal by following nine steps (Table 2).

Step 1. This step mainly deals with the input processing by reading the raw data from the specified time period and filtering out inputs that might not be relevant for the algorithm.

Step 2. After the input is validated, the data must be arranged in a meaningful way for it to provide the desired results. This means grouping entries by users and sorting them in chronological order. For the algorithm to be more efficient, this step also deals with data compression. Meaning that, if there are multiple consecutive entries from the same device, they will be considered as being a single event with the starting date of the most recent and the end date of the last entry from the consecutive sequence.

Step 3. A square matrix is created with the size being the number of devices squared. This matrix represents a way to track which devices are being used by different persons. If such a case is found, the values in the matrix corresponding to the found devices will be marked with "1". Additionally, we create a buffer that contains events which span at most 48 h (we assumed that in this time period you can physically get to any two points in the United States). In this buffer, we recreate the activity of the subscriber by adding each event from the chronological event array, one by one, and check if it is physically possible. We have two ways of analysing if the activity is done by one person or more. The first one is by looking at two consecutive events and the second one is by checking three or more events (maximum is determined by the number of events in buffer) and analysing them with a machine learning algorithm (we used XGBoost Classifier with the objective of logistic regression). Choosing which consecutive events are analysed (and how) is a challenge by itself, since there can be multiple occurrences of the same device in buffer. To solve this, we created an occurrence array in which we store the last occurrence of each device. If a device that is already in the buffer is added again, then we analyse with a XGBoost algorithm the loop created by the two devices, as well as the whole buffer. For an example please look at Fig. 1.

Step 4. At this point, we can start calculating the minimum number of persons that is needed for the subscribers activity to be physically possible. Having the matrix from Step 3, we can consider it to be a graph represented as a matrix where we know that the values of one indicate that the devices corresponding to the line and the column

Table 2. List of used terms.

Term	Description
Static device	A device that has very low mobility (e.g.: GameConsole, SetTopBox, TV, etc.)
Mobile device	A device that has high mobility (e.g.: MobilePhone, Tablet, Laptop, etc.)
Cluster	A cluster is created by finding common locations between devices. The devices that have been seen in a common location will be considered to belong in the same cluster. Two devices can be in the same cluster even though they do not have common locations but can be connected through the locations of other devices
Mobile cluster	A cluster that has no static devices
Static cluster	A cluster that has at least one static device

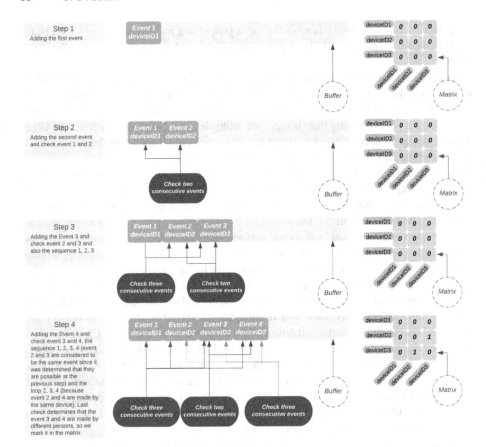

Fig. 1. Graphical representation of Step 3

are used by different persons. At the same time, in graph theory, we can say that these two vertices are adjacent. At this point, the problem can be solved by a simple Graph Coloring algorithm [1]. To ensure that an optimal solution is found, we need to apply the algorithm from each vertex since this problem is NP-complete. From an efficiency point of view, this would seem extreme and inefficient, but we deal with small graphs, and in our experiments we had no issues. On average, in the data we had, the number of devices per account was around four, and only in extreme cases the count exceeded thirty. The end result will contain all the optimal solutions of coloring the graph, since, in most cases, it is not just one. Translating from graph theory, this means we found the minimum number of persons and all the possible ways of pairing a person with one or more devices.

Step 5. In this part of the algorithm, we implemented a method that is able to quantify how connected is the activity of a user. This quantifier is represented by the number of clusters, a term which was previously explained. Since we know the locations visited by a device, we can consider each device as being a graph and the visited locations as the vertices of this graph. Now, we have multiple graphs with common vertices but we don't know which of these vertices are mutual. If two graphs have a common vertex, that means they can be considered as one big graph. In the end, each remaining graph translates to a cluster. To solve this problem in an efficient way, we devised an algorithm based on a balanced binary search tree [2]. The information, contained in the nodes that create the tree, represents the location (which serves as a search key) and the device id (which is unique for an account). We add, one by one, all the locations that were visited by a user and if that location already exists in the tree, we know which device was already seen there. By having an array where we keep track of such cases, in the end, we can determine all the clusters. The previously mentioned array has the size equal to the number of devices. Each value in the array represents the index of a cluster in which a device is positioned.

Step 6. Each device has a degree of mobility, these degrees being "mobile" or "static", based on the type of the device. Using the result from Step 5 we can determine which cluster is mobile and which one is static. A static cluster has at least one static device and a mobile cluster does not have any static devices. If a subscriber has two or more distinct static clusters, we can safely label this account as being shared. Having the processed clusters at this step, we can also calculate the minimum distance between all clusters. To do this, we have to find the closest locations between each two clusters and after that, apply the Dijkstra algorithm [5] to create a minimum spanning tree. The sum of all remaining edges represents the minimum distance between all clusters.

Step 7. By using the results from Step 4 and 5, we can find distinct persons belonging to one or more clusters that have not visited other clusters and have never been in contact with the persons belonging to those clusters. In this instance, we can safely assume that we detected account sharing but, because Step 4 does not always return a single solution, we must check that the number of cases where we identified account sharing, divided to the total number of cases, is 1, before labeling an account as shared. The result of the division will be taken into account when calculating the sharing probability.

Step 8. Using the results from the steps above, we determined some thresholds that create a pattern and fit each subscriber in the corresponding usage pattern.

Step 9. In the end, using a machine learning algorithm (XGBoost Regressor with the objective of linear regression) a sharing probability is calculated. The algorithm takes into account the number of clusters, the number of devices, minimum number of persons, the usage pattern and the number obtained from Step 7.

5 Technologies

We decided to put XGBoost [4] at the core of this algorithm since it is very efficient, flexible, and it can learn really quickly. This was highly important because we didn't had any pre-labeled data and creating multiple thousands of repetitive entries in order to train a neural network would have been really difficult and time consuming. Using this approach we only had to label about one thousand for each model. All mentioned factors make the implementation of these types of gradient boosted decision trees to be the perfect solution for this problem.

The model used at Step 3 has an XGBClassifier with a structure as displayed in Table 3(a). The end result for this model was achieving an accuracy of 91.87% for the

Table 3. XGBClassifier Structures

(a) Step 3		(b) Step 9	
Parameter name	Value	Parameter name	Value
max_depth	1	max_depth	1
min_child_weight	3	min_child_weight	1
learning_rate	0.065	learning_rate	0.05
n_estimators	500	n_estimators	700
Objective	binary:logistic	Objective	reg:linear
Gamma	0	Gamma	0
Subsample	0.9	Subsample	0.4
colsample_bytree	0.7	colsample_bytree	0.5
colsample_bylevel	1	colsample_bylevel	1
scale_pos_weight	1	scale_pos_weight	1

training data and an accuracy of 93.24% for the validation data, which means that there was no over fitting.

For the model at Step 9 we used XGBRegressor with the specifications shown in Table 3(b). The accuracy for the training data was 89.22% and for the validation data 93.11%. For both models, the evaluation metric used was area under the curve(auc) [3]. During the tests made to find an optimal model for these tasks, we obtained an accuracy close to 100% for the training data but, for the validation, the accuracy was much lower, meaning that the model just learned the results.

6 Results and Analysis

We had access to a large data set. The Figs. 2, 3 and 4 are created from a data set with more than 13 million subscribers. Each subscriber had one or more events, meaning that, at least for the situations it was tested for, the algorithm produces results that can be considered to reflect reality.

Looking at Fig. 2, we notice that most users are classified as having either less than 20%, either 100% sharing probability, meaning that the algorithm is fairly certain of it's prediction. This is very important, since it would be troublesome to predict a high probability to a user that is not sharing the account.

Observing Fig. 3, it is obvious how unbalanced the distribution of patterns is. However, looking at Fig. 4, this represents good news for the provider of this data since the patterns that have the highest number of users represent a low risk of sharing.

Overall, 10% of shared accounts may not seem as a large number. However, taking into consideration that these users share their account with at least another person, it means that, if all those who benefit from sharing would get a subscription, the number of subscribers would increase with at least 10%. From a marketing point of view, this is a considerable and very favorable percentage for providers.

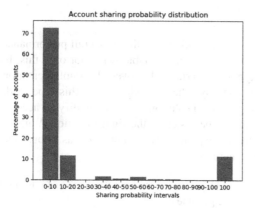

Fig. 2. Sharing probability distribution

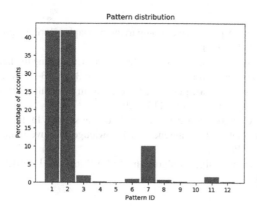

Fig. 3. Pattern distribution where the bar index represents the pattern from Table 1

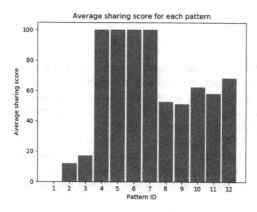

Fig. 4. Average sharing score for each pattern where the bar index represents the pattern from Table 1

7 Conclusion

Looking at the results, we are satisfied with the overall performance since we found a way to identify account sharing in a reliable way. Not only this, but we can actually determine multiple types of sharing. Moreover, the implementation of this algorithm is simple and can be done by other providers since this type of data is easily available. Even though the presented solution does not identify all accounts which are being shared, we consider this to be a step in the right direction. With further research, we are confident that more usage patterns will emerge and as a consequence the number of shared accounts might increase.

Acknowledgements. I would like to thank Dr. Christian Săcărea for his kindness, help and time invested in making this article possible.

References

1. Aslan, M., Baykan, N.: A performance comparison of graph coloring algorithms. Int. J. Intell. Syst. Appl. Eng. **4**, 1–1 (2016)
2. Austern, M., Stroustrup, B., Thorup, M., Wilkinson, J.: Untangling the balancing and searching of balanced binary search trees. Softw. Pract. Exper. **33**, 1273–1298 (2003)
3. Bradley, A.P.: The use of the area under the roc curve in the evaluation of machine learning algorithms. Patt. Recogn. **30**(7), 1145–1159 (1997)
4. Chen, T., Guestrin, C: Xgboost: a scalable tree boosting system. In: Proceedings of the 22nd ACM SIGKDD International Conference on Knowledge Discovery and Data Mining, pp. 785–794. ACM, New York (2016)
5. Javaid, A.: Understanding Dijkstra algorithm. SSRN Electron. J. (2013). https://doi.org/10.2139/ssrn.2340905

Collaborative Design and Manufacture: Information Structures for Team Formation and Coordination

Iain Duncan Stalker[1]([✉]) [iD] and Nikolai Kazantsev[2] [iD]

[1] Institute of Management, University of Bolton, Bolton, UK
IS4@bolton.ac.uk
[2] Alliance Manchester Business School, The University of Manchester, Manchester, UK
nikolai.kazantsev@manchester.ac.uk

Abstract. Our interest here lies in supporting important, but routine and time-consuming activities that underpin success in highly distributed, collaborative design and manufacturing environments; and how information structuring can facilitate this. To that end, we present a simple, yet powerful approach to team formation, partner selection, scheduling and communication that employs a different approach to the task of matching candidates to opportunities or partners to requirements (matchmaking): traditionally, this is approached using either an idea of 'nearness' or 'best fit' (metric-based paradigms); or by finding a subtree within a tree (data structure) (tree traversal). Instead, we prefer concept lattices to establish notions of 'inclusion' or 'membership': essentially, a topological paradigm. While our approach is substantive, it can be used alongside traditional approaches and in this way one could harness the strengths of multiple paradigms.

Keywords: Concept lattices · Information structures · Team formation

1 Introduction

The first couple of decades of the twenty-first century have seen many Original Equipment Manufacturers (OEMs) in high value industries, such as the automotive and aerospace sectors, significantly streamline their supply chains, developing strategic partnerships with a reduced number of Tier 1 Suppliers, devolving to them key responsibilities for procurement and management of other suppliers. OEMs were motivated primarily by a need to rationalise adminstrative burden and to promote agility in response to increasing technical complexity of products and ever shortening product lifecycles. As such, traditional hierarchies have evolved into much flatter organisational structures, where interaction is dynamic and opportunistic, membership fluid, and decision-making decentralised. Unfortunately, these flatter structures have led to more complex coordination and collaboration procedures, posing challenges for small- and medium-sized enterprises (SMEs) to enter contemporary supply chains. It would be beneficial for SMEs to find a means of increasing visibilities to promote inclusion in contemporary supply chains: one possibility is for them to form clusters of complementary expertise so that they leverage appropriate market opprtunities. Subsets of partners from a cluster

M. Cochez et al. (Eds.): GKR 2020, LNAI 12640, pp. 93–104, 2021.
https://doi.org/10.1007/978-3-030-72308-8_7

would pool resources—according to availability, capacity and requirements—to form a short term, dynamic partnership (an *agile partnership*) to respond as a single entity to a specific business opportunity.

A typical opportunity is when an OEM publishes an invitation to tender for a technical system or module, e.g., an interior. Timely response to this by an agile partnership requires rapid coordination of product development activities such as preliminary conceptual design of appropriate subsystems and (conceptual) integration of the resulting specification, among (potential) partners from the cluster. Automated support could accelerate this coordination and improve response to opportunities. Thus, our motivating research question was: *How can we enable quick assembly and informed coordination of agile partnerships in highly distributed, dynamic manufacturing environments?*

Essentially, the problem of assembling an agile partnership is one of matchmaking: identifying requirements and locating suppliers to fulfil these. Traditionally, this is approached using either an idea of 'nearness' or 'best fit' (metric-based paradigms); or by finding a subtree within a tree (data structure) (tree traversal). Here, we present an approach that uses concept lattices and rests on notions of 'inclusion' or 'membership': essentially, a topological paradigm.

Our intention here is to present the approach and outline its applications; we defer a critical comparison with alternatives and discussion of how to integrate with traditional approaches to another work. The paper is structured as follows. In Sect. 2 we briefly summarise the initial and current research contexts for the work; in Sect. 3 we introduce key elements of the formal apparatus and we briefly outline our approach; and in Sect. 4 we provide some simplified examples. We close with some concluding remarks in Sect. 5.

2 Research Context

The initial research context for the work here was in the automotive sector; in particular, working with SMES forming collaborative clusters known as *Networks of Automotive Excellence* (NoAEs) [5–7]. Membership of these NoAEs is fluid, with partners participating in a number of networks; interaction is dynamic and opportunistic, and decision-making is decentralised. Subsets of partners within an NoAE pool resources, forming short-term, dynamic alliances to respond as a single entity to opportunities in appropriate markets [5]. In these contexts, the responsibility of OEMs is shifting from purchasing and supplier management to brand positioning and design for assembly; convening such networks through Tier 1 Suppliers [6].

The current research context has enlarged to include Industry 4.0 initiatives in aerospace and related industries. DIGICOR (https://www.digicor-project.eu/) is developing a collaboration platform, tools, and services to facilitate the set up and coordination of a production network; these are informed by case specific governance tools and procedures for collaboration, knowledge protection, and security [2]. The platform aims to provide seamless connectivity to existing automation solutions, smart objects, and real-time data sources across the network; this will enable manufacturing companies and service providers to create and operate collaborative networks across the value chain. A key aims is to foster the integration of non-traditional, small, but innovative companies into the complex supply chain of large OEMs. DIGICOR governance rules aim to significantly reduce the burden of setting up collaborative networks and shorten the time to jointly respond to business opportunities.

3 Preliminaries

We briefly introduce some of the formal apparatus underpinning our approach.

3.1 Formal Concept Analysis

Formal Concept Analysis (FCA) [4] is a powerful, elegant method of analysis which identifies (conceptual) structures within data sets. The qualifier *formal* typically precedes many of the terms in the vocabulary of FCA to emphasise that these are mathematical notions, which do not necessarily reflect everyday use of the terms. We shall dispense with the qualifier here for convenience.

Definition 1 (Context and Concept). *A* context *is a triple* (G, M, I), *where G is a set of* objects, *M is a set of* attributes *and $I \subseteq G \times M$ is an* incidence relation. *We write gIm for $(g, m) \in I$. Let $A \subseteq G$ and $B \subseteq M$. Define $A^{\triangleright} = \{m \in M \mid gIm, \forall g \in A\}$, then $A^{\triangleright}$ is the set of attributes shared by all objects in the set A. Similarly define $B^{\triangleleft} = \{g \in G \mid gIm, \forall m \in B\}$, then $B^{\triangleleft}$ is the set of all objects possessing the attributes in the set B. These maps are called* derivation operators. *A* concept *of the context (G, M, I) is a pair (A, B), such that $A^{\triangleright} = B$ and $A = B^{\triangleleft}$. The* extent *of the concept (A, B) is A and the* intent *is B.*

Definition 2 (Concept Lattice). *Denote the set of all concepts of a context $\mathcal{B}(G, M, I)$, or simply $\mathcal{B}$ where the context is clear. Define a partial order, $\leq$, on $\mathcal{B}$ as follows: $(A_1, B_1) \leq (A_2, B_2) \Leftrightarrow A_1 \subseteq A_2 \Leftrightarrow B_1 \supseteq B_2$. Then $(\mathcal{B}, \leq)$ is called the* associated complete lattice of concepts, *or simply* concept lattice, *of the context (G, M, I).*

Table 1. A simple context for the planets; after [3].

	Size			Distance		Moon	
	Small	Medium	Large	Near	Far	Yes	No
Mercury	×			×			×
Venus	×			×			×
Earth	×			×		×	
Mars	×			×		×	
Jupiter			×		×	×	
Saturn			×		×	×	
Uranus		×			×	×	
Neptune		×			×	×	
Pluto	×				×	×	

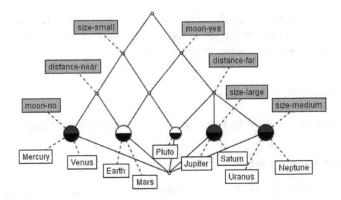

Fig. 1. A concept lattice for the planets from Table 1; after [3].

We illustrate the basics of FCA through a simple example. Table 1 illustrates a simple context for the planets (objects) of the solar system, categorising these according to a number of attributes such as size, distance from the Sun and whether a planet has a moon. Consider the set {Mercury, Venus}. The attributes of this set are {Mercury, Venus}$^{\triangleright}$ = {size-small, distance-near, moon-no}. and the pair ({Mercury, Venus}, {size-small, distance-near, moon-no}) is a concept of the simple context of Table 1, since {size-small, distance-near, moon-no}$^{\triangleleft}$ = {Mercury, Venus}. Now consider the set {Mercury, Venus, Earth, Mars}. The attributes of this set are {Mercury, Venus, Earth, Mars}$^{\triangleright}$ = {size-small, distance-near}. The pair ({Mercury, Venus, Earth, Mars}, {size-small, distance-near}) is a concept of the simple context of Table 1. Moreover, since ({Mercury, Venus}, {size-small, distance-near, moon-no}) ≤ ({Mercury, Venus, Earth, Mars}, {size-small, distance-near}) the former is a subconcept of the latter.

We can provide pictorial representation of the concepts of our context and their interrelations using a Hasse diagram [3]; see Fig. 1[1]. The concept lattice is read in the following way: objects accumulate from the bottom upwards; and attributes accumulate from the top downwards. For example, the concept at the node marked distance-near includes {size-small, distance-near} as attributes and {Me, V, E, Ma} as objects. The concept lattice for a given context provides a direct manner in which to identify whether a relationship exists between two given concepts; and further, clarifies the nature of this relationship. For example, the concept lattice for a given context allows us to identify the immediate subconcept (respectively, superconcept) of any two concepts of a given context.

---

[1] The node colourings provide useful information concerning filters and ideals [4] furnished by the tool used to produce this figure, *Concept Explorer* (http://sourceforge. net/projects/conexp). This information is additional to our current purposes, thus we do not discuss here.

3.2   Galois Connection

Once information about a domain is structured in concept lattices, we can use Galois Connections to interrelate different concept lattices, or even different concepts in the same lattice. A Galois Connection is a pair of "opposite" functions between two partially ordered sets, often powersets, which respects the orders in the sets [1].

Definition 3 (Galois Connection). *Let $(X, \sqsubseteq_X)$ and $(Y, \sqsubseteq_Y)$ be partially ordered sets. A Galois Connection between the two sets is a pair of maps $\alpha : X \to Y$ and $\gamma : Y \to X$ such that, for all $x \in X$ and $y \in Y$,*

$$\alpha(x) \sqsubseteq_Y y \Leftrightarrow x \sqsubseteq_X \gamma(y) \tag{1}$$

We denote the Galois Connection between X and Y by (X, α, Y, γ).

Definition 4 (Closure Operator). *Let $(X, \sqsubseteq_X)$ be a partially ordered set. A closure operator on X is a map $c : X \to X$, such that, for all $x, y \in X$, c is*

- Extensive, *i.e.*, $x \sqsubseteq_X c(x)$;
- Monotonic, *i.e.*, $x \sqsubseteq_X y \Leftrightarrow c(x) \sqsubseteq_X c(y)$; and
- Idempotent, *i.e.*, $c(c(x)) = c(x)$.

Accordingly, any element $x \in X$ is called closed *if and only if $x = c(x)$. We refer to the structure which results from the application of a closure operator to a poset as a closure system or simply closure.*

Amongst the many interesting properties of a Galois Connection is that the consecutive application, the *composition*, of the two "opposite" functions constitutes a closure operator; that is it "collects" upwards, preserves the order and two applications produce the same effect as one.

Lemma 1. *Let (X, α, Y, γ) be a Galois Connection between two partially ordered sets, $(X, \sqsubseteq_X)$ and $(Y, \sqsubseteq_Y)$. Then (composing from left to right) $\alpha\gamma : X \to X$ defines a closure operator on X and $\gamma\alpha : Y \to Y$ defines closure operator on Y. (See [3] for proof.)*

3.3   Galois Connections and Concept Lattices

Recall the derivation operators from Subsect. 3.1 used to establish a relation from sets of objects to sets of attributes (shared by these objects) and vice-versa. These can be thought of as; are in fact functions on the powersets of objects and attributes. The lemma below shows that these constitute a Galois Connection between the two powersets.

Lemma 2. *Let (G, M, I) be a context. Recall the derivation operators $^{\triangleright} : \wp(G) \to \wp(M)$ and $^{\triangleleft} : \wp(M) \to \wp(G)$. Then $(\wp(G), ^{\triangleright}, \wp(M), ^{\triangleleft})$ is a Galois Connection between the posets $(\wp(G), \subseteq)$ and $(\wp(M), \supseteq)$. (See [4] for proof.)*

Any powerset and its dual are complete lattices [3], so we have that $(\wp(G), \subseteq)$ and $(\wp(M), \supseteq)$ are complete lattices. Thus, we can combine the results of Lemmas 1 and 2.

Corollary 1. *Let (G,M,I) be a context. Recall the derivation operators $^{\triangleright}$: $\wp(G) \to$ $\wp(M)$ and $^{\triangleleft}$: $\wp(M) \to \wp(G)$. Then $^{\triangleright\triangleleft}$: $\wp(G) \to \wp(G)$ is a closure operator on $(\wp(G), \subseteq)$ and $^{\triangleleft\triangleright}$: $\wp(M) \to \wp(M)$ is a closure operator on $(\wp(M), \supseteq)$.*

Remark 1 (**Notation**). We write simply $\wp(G)$ for $(\wp(G), \subseteq)$, when it is clear that the partial order is the usual subset inclusion; and we write $\wp(M)^{\partial}$ for $(\wp(M), \supseteq)$. We denote the closures of these under the compositions of the derivation operators $\overline{\wp(G)}$ and $\overline{\wp(M)}^{\partial}$, respectively.

For a particular context, (G,M,I), the actions of these closure operators, $^{\triangleleft\triangleright}$ on $\wp(M)^{\partial}$ and $^{\triangleright\triangleleft}$ on $\wp(G)$, generate the concept intents and extents, respectively. Moreover, the structures of the closure systems induced on $\wp(M)^{\partial}$ and $\wp(G)$ are identical; and these structures are co-located in the concept lattice, $\mathscr{B}(G,M,I)$. Informally, we can think of the closure operators as removing redundancy:

- $^{\triangleleft\triangleright}$ removes from $\wp(M)^{\partial}$ (sub)sets of attributes that do not combine to describe an object. For example, size-large and distance-near do not apply in tandem to any of the planets in Table 1. Thus, {size-large, distance-near} $\in \wp(M)^{\partial}$, but {size-large, distance-near} $\notin \overline{\wp(M)}^{\partial}$.
- $^{\triangleright\triangleleft}$ removes from $\wp(G)$ (sub)sets of objects that have no attributes in common. For example, Mercury is a small planet, near the sun without a moon, whereas Jupiter is a large planet, far from the sun with at least one moon. Thus, these share none of the attributes in Table 1 and are conceptually distinct and should not appear together in the extent of any concept. Hence, {Mercury, Jupiter} $\in \wp(G)$, but {Mercury, Jupiter} $\notin \overline{\wp(G)}$.

3.4 Observations

FCA identifies those objects which are indistinguishable under a given incidence relation to a particular set of attributes: indistiguishable objects belong to the same element of the associated closure (and comprise the extent of the related concept). For example, Mercury and Venus are indistinguishable using the attributes of the context in Table 1; thus, they are identified as the same "element" in the closure.

Different attribute sets will give rise to different closures: in particular, subsets will give rise to substructures. In FCA, a context derived from another by considering only a subset of attributes (or objects) is called a *subcontext* [4]. For example, the lattice in Fig. 2 derives from a subcontext of Table 1 that considers only attributes for size and distance; and ignores presence or absence of a moon. Again, the lattice derives from closures on the associated power sets[2]. When we use the subset of attributes (from the subcontext), we see that Mercury and Venus are still indistinguishable from each other, but now, Venus is also indistinguishable from these; thus, they are identified as the same "element" in the new closure, which is a coarser system. Of course, all of the

---

[2] Furthermore, a Galois connection obtains between the concept lattice of the full context (full lattice) and the concept lattice of the subcontext (sub-lattice). Thus, the above sub-lattice is also a closure of the full lattice.

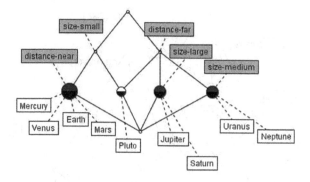

Fig. 2. Concept lattice for a reduced context of planets.

information of the sub-lattice is actually contained in the full lattice; however, identifying a subset attributes of interest and using these to project onto a sub-lattice makes the relationships and indistinguishable elements much clearer (as redundant information is removed); and indeed, more visible. This becomes more valuable as the number of objects and attributes increase. This means that for a given context, we can use subsets of attributes to explore more directly the interrelationships of objects from different perspectives; and visualise these. This is essentially what we do when we use lattices to match suppliers with requirements, coordinate meetings, etc., as illustrated in Sect. 4.

4 Application

We provide some (simplified) examples of how the approach can be applied in the aerospace industry to facilitate team formation for responses to invitations to tender (Subsect. 4.1), to coordinate meetings (Subsect. 4.2), to identify membership of project subgroups and identify key interactions of team members (Subsect. 4.3).

4.1 Invitations to Tender

An *Invitation to Tender* is a formal invitation made by an OEM to suppliers to make an offer, i.e., propose terms, for the supply of specific goods or services. Typically, an ordinary aerospace tender includes a statement of requirements that clarify expectations of suppliers, specify products and services needed and identify volumes, time frames and key dates. An OEM will only consider tenders from suitably qualified partnerships and demands will usually address:

- size of partners, reflected in capacity and turnover constraints;
- systems capabilities, reflected in standards and certifications, such as ASD 9100, ISO 16949 and NADCAP;
- proximity to the place of assembly; and nowadays
- a commitment to corporate social responsibility.

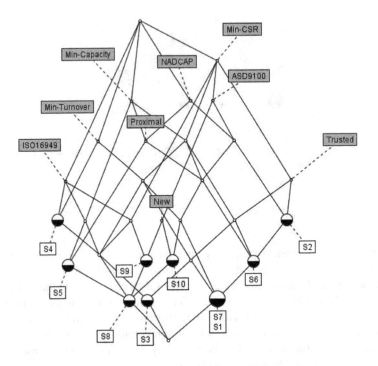

Fig. 3. A concept lattice for suppliers

An OEM may also require that a submitting partnership has a working history (thus, that partners are trusted by each other and are not new entrants to the cluster).

It is a simple matter to construct a context that allows us to characterise the suppliers (objects) in our cluster using relevant descriptors (attributes); Fig. 3 shows a simplified context for ten suppliers (S1, ..., S10) characterised using attributes relating to these descriptors (Min-Turnover, Min-Capacity, Trusted, New, ASD 9100, ISO 16949, NAD-CAP, Proximal and Min-CSR). We read the lattice as usual: the white labels collect upwards and the grey labels collect downwards. Here, a "concept" indicates which suppliers fulfil various requirements captured by subsets/combinations of the attributes. This provides information which can be invaluable for coordinating for tenders. Moreover, manipulating the lattice and projecting onto sub-lattices according to different subsets can reveal which suppliers meet certain criteria more directly.

Suppose that the OEM requires that the partnership has a sound working history and has stipulated minimum capacity, NADCAP capability, locating within a specific proximity and appropriate CSR certification. By collapsing the full lattice to an appropriate sub-lattice (for subcontext of attributes: Min-Capacity, Trusted, NADCAP, Proximal and Min-CSR), see Fig. 4, we see immediately that only suppliers S1, S6 and S7 are suitable partners for the tender (from the current set). Of course, we have made a number of simplifications here: we have not, for example, considered whether the expertise of these three would be sufficient. It is more likely that the ten suppliers would be for a particular aspect of the tender, the same aspect, and that our projection onto a sub-lattice

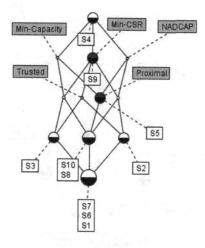

Fig. 4. A concept lattice for suppliers

would be used to identify potential candidates. We may then select one from these three
or ask the three to coordinate on that aspect of the tender: this would build redundancy
into the supply chain, if the tender were accepted, thus fostering resilience.

4.2 Coordinating Meetings

Consider the following (extremely) simplified subset of interior features of a fuselage
for an airliner: chairs, windows, vents, internal panels, lighting systems and (overhead)
lockers. Table 2 combines these with a relevant (again, extremely simplified) subset
of service providers—Paneller, HVAC Supplier, Upholsterer, Lighting Specialist, Fix-
ture Systems Provider, Seating Specialist, and Specialist Glass provider—into a context
which gives rise to the concept lattice in Fig. 5. Again, we read the lattice with white
labels collecting upwards and grey labels accumulating downwards. Here, a "concept"
indicates which suppliers associate, i.e. have an interest in or contribute expertise necessary for a particular feature or set of features. This provides information which can

Table 2. A simple context for a fuselage interior.

	Chairs	Windows	Vents	Panels	Lights	Lockers
Paneller		×	×	×	×	×
HVAC			×	×	×	
Upholst.	×					
Lighting				×	×	×
Fixtures	×		×	×	×	×
Seating	×					
Spec. glass		×	×	×		

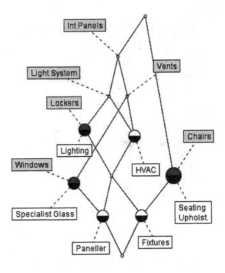

Fig. 5. A concept lattice for fuselage suppliers

be invaluable for arranging meetings. For example, we can infer from the node carrying the label "Windows" that the interests of the Specialist Glass Supplier and the Paneller coincide and that it is only these two that need to meet to finalise the relevant specifications. Thus, we know that we shall need to coordinate meetings between these two for purposes of discussing the Windows. We can also see that no single supplier needs to meet about every feature, as the lowest node in the lattice has no object (supplier) associated with it. Moreover, We can also see that no single feature requires the input of every supplier, as the highest node in the lattice has no attribute (feature) associated with it. Of course, we can draw these conclusions quite easily from the context; however, this would become increasingly difficult as a context enlarges.

4.3 Project Subgroups

As the complexity of a product or technical system increases, the more convenient it is to have formal subgroups working on different aspects of development. Projecting the full concept lattice of Fig. 5 directly onto the sub-lattices deriving from the subcontext generated for a particular feature makes directly clear those suppliers who must be part of the subgroup. For example, Fig. 6 shows directly who is needed for the Light System Project Subgroup.

Finally, selecting those features for relating to a specific supplier and projecting the full concept lattice of Fig. 5 directly onto the sub-lattice deriving from the relevant subcontext reveals essential interactions, specifically subgroups and meetings, from the perspective of that supplier. For example, Fig. 7 shows directly the interactions of the HVAC Supplier. Interestingly, every feature that requires the expertise of the HVAC Supplier requires that of both the Paneller and the Fixtures Provider; however, we *cannot* infer the converse.

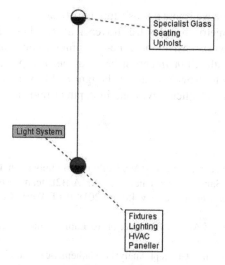

Fig. 6. A concept lattice for the light system subgroup

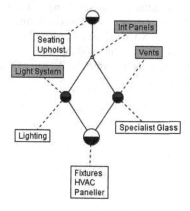

Fig. 7. Meetings and subgroups for the HVAC supplier

5   Concluding Remarks

We have reported on investigations into information structuring to facilitate the automation of important, but routine and time-consuming activities of agile partnerships operating within highly distributed, collaborative environments. These explorations are
grounded in the domains of Networks of Automotive Excellence and Industry 4.0 initiatives in aerospace. We have outlined how a synthesis of mathematical notions provides
a simple, yet powerful approach to facilitate *inter alia* partnership formation; the selection of working groups from partnerships; and the scheduling of workshops and subgroup meetings, identifying the subject matter for these. We believe that our approach
is innovative in that we re-think the problem of matching candidates to opportunities or

partners to requirements; we frame this as a topological notion of set membership rather than taking traditional metric-based or tree traversal approaches, which, while effective, can be computationally expensive and time-consuming. Our aim is not to challenge established methods; rather, our intention here has been to present the approach and outline its applications to provide food for thought and to stimulate discussion. Thus, we defer a comparison with alternatives and in-depth critique to another work.

References

1. Birkhoff, G.: Lattice Theory, 3rd edn. AMS Colloquium Publication, Providence (1967)
2. Cisneros-Cabrera, S., Sampaio, P., Mehandjiev, N.: A B2B team formation microservice for collaborative manufacturing in industry 4.0. In: 2018 IEEE World Congress on Services, pp. 37–38 (2018)
3. Davey, B.A., Priestley, H.A.: An Introduction to Lattices and Order, 2nd edn. Cambridge University Press, Cambridge (2002)
4. Ganter, B., Wille, R.: Formal Concept Analysis. Mathematical Foundations. Springer, Heidelberg (1999). https://doi.org/10.1007/978-3-642-59830-2
5. Grefen, P., Mehandjiev, N., Kouvas, G., Weichhart, G., Eshuis, R.: Dynamic business network process management in instant virtual enterprises. Comput. Ind. **60**(2), 86–103 (2010)
6. Mehandjiev, N., Grefen, P.: Dynamic Business Process Formation for Instant Virtual Enterprises. Advanced Information and Knowledge Processing Series. Springer, London (1983)
7. Stalker, I.D., Mehandjiev, N.D.: Facilitating collaboration in highly distributed design and manufacturing environments – extended abstract. In: Adaptive Computing in Design and Manufacture (ACDM 2006) (2006)

Invited Additional Contributions

Approximate Knowledge Graph Query Answering: From Ranking to Binary Classification

Ruud van Bakel[1,2], Teodor Aleksiev[1,3], Daniel Daza[1,2,4],
Dimitrios Alivanistos[1,4], and Michael Cochez[1,4(✉)]

[1] Computer Science, Vrije Universiteit Amsterdam, Amsterdam, The Netherlands
ruudvanbakel@yahoo.co.uk, {d.dazacruz,d.alivanistos,m.cochez}@vu.nl
[2] University of Amsterdam, Amsterdam, The Netherlands
[3] Leiden University, Leiden, The Netherlands
aleksiev.teodord@gmail.com
[4] Discovery Lab, Elsevier, Amsterdam, The Netherlands
https://discoverylab.ai

Abstract. Large, heterogeneous datasets are characterized by missing or even erroneous information. This is more evident when they are the product of community effort or automatic fact extraction methods from external sources, such as text. A special case of the aforementioned phenomenon can be seen in knowledge graphs, where this mostly appears in the form of missing or incorrect edges and nodes.

Structured querying on such incomplete graphs will result in incomplete sets of answers, even if the correct entities exist in the graph, since one or more edges needed to match the pattern are missing. To overcome this problem, several algorithms for approximate structured query answering have been proposed. Inspired by modern Information Retrieval metrics, these algorithms produce a ranking of all entities in the graph, and their performance is further evaluated based on how high in this ranking the correct answers appear.

In this work we take a critical look at this way of evaluation. We argue that performing a ranking-based evaluation is not sufficient to assess methods for complex query answering. To solve this, we introduce Message Passing Query Boxes (MPQB), which takes binary classification metrics back into use and shows the effect this has on the recently proposed query embedding method MPQE.

Keywords: Query answering · Geometric representation · Box embeddings · Approximation

1 Introduction

In many organizations, a vast amount of complex information is used in operations daily. This data is often stored in various databases or file systems while information can be retrieved using query languages and information retrieval

© The Author(s) 2021
M. Cochez et al. (Eds.): GKR 2020, LNAI 12640, pp. 107–124, 2021.
https://doi.org/10.1007/978-3-030-72308-8_8

techniques. During the past decade, several companies have started taking up knowledge graphs (KG) [10], as a way to represent heterogeneous data and make it useful for a large variety of applications [14]. To make said data accessible, various querying languages like SPARQL and Cypher have been developed. Such querying languages allow for accessing nodes in the graph, traversing them via specific relations, or retrieve nodes that match a specific pattern. At the core of these languages lie graph patterns. These patterns can be thought of as graph shaped structures where some nodes and edges can correspond to nodes existing in the graph, while others correspond to variables (with specific variable names). When a match for this pattern is found in the graph, the variables are bound and the appropriate values are returned as the result.

However, the performance of the previously described process is heavily dependent on the level of completeness in the graph.

To go in detail, completeness refers to whether it contains all the nodes and edges in the graph pattern, and has a binding for all variables. Having a single node or edge missing from the graph, which represents a comparatively small bit of information, results in missing answers. This phenomenon could be good, in case of an erroneous piece of information, or bad, in case of information missing from the graph.

In this paper, we focus on this issue, specifically the case of missing edges in the graph. Ideally, we would like a query system that can still give answers when the phenomenon described before applies. We would like to have *approximate query answering*.

One way to approach this, is by performing link prediction. In link prediction, one would try to predict missing links in the graph, by training a machine learning model on the known parts of it. While not trivial, it is possible to use the single link prediction mechanism to answer queries with missing links. Another way to approach this problem is by using the so-called query encoders. These encoders take a query as input and produce an embedding (a high dimensional vector representation) for it. This query embedding is later compared to learned embeddings for the entities in the graph. This machine learning system is optimised in such a way that entities close to the query embedding in vector space, are also its probable answers.

In this paper we focus on the analysis and evaluation of these systems. Typically, such systems return a series of candidate answers to the query, accompanied by a likelihood or distance from the query embedding in vector space. In the evaluation phase, this ranking is compared to, not a ground truth ranking, but rather the set of correct answers to the query. To do this, typical measures like hits@n (how many correct answers out of n) and mean reciprocal rank (MRR – what is the average reciprocal of the rank of correct answers) are used. While these measures are appropriate for information retrieval systems, they fall short when it comes to query systems. In the latter, the results are not ranked, but are rather the correct answer or not.

This is also reflected in how these measures are usually adapted by modifying them to filtered versions. In this case, measures like hits@n and MRR are computed such that true answers higher in the returned ranking are ignored when computing for example the rank for lower ranked entities.

We argue that we need to look into metrics that are not based on specific ranking of the results, but rather on a crisp set of results retrieved from these systems. A main argument for why this is necessary is that many downstream tasks using the aforementioned results need to get a finite set of answers from the knowledge graph, not just a ranked list of all possible entities. That is, we need a query engine that does not just act as a ranking system, but as a binary classifier: it must provide a set of entities that are answers to the query while all other entities are not. In this scenario, the evaluation would be the same as what has traditionally been used for classification problems, with measures such as precision and recall.

This paper is structured as follows: in Sect. 2, we provide an example for several algorithms used for approximate query answering. Then, in Sect. 3 we discuss how metrics for binary classification can provide additional insight on top of the metrics used for ranking. We end that section with a general direction on how this could be achieved in the existing systems using volumetric query embeddings. Sect. 4 details a first approach for solving this problem using axis-aligned hyper-rectangles for these queries. We describe the MPQB model, a proof-of-concept, in the section after that. Finally, we provide a conclusion and future outlook.

This work is largely based on the Bachelor thesis works of Ruud van Bakel [3] and Teodor Aleksiev [1], who both worked under the supervision of Michael Cochez at the Vrije Universiteit Amsterdam.

2 Approximate Query Answering on Knowledge Graphs

We define a knowledge graph as a tuple $\mathcal{G} = (\mathcal{V}, \mathcal{R}, \mathcal{E})$, where $\mathcal{V}$ is a set of entities, $\mathcal{R}$ a set of relation types, and $\mathcal{E}$ a set of binary predicates of the form $r(h, t)$ where $r \in \mathcal{R}$ and $h, t \in \mathcal{V}$. Each binary predicate represents an edge of type r between the entities h and t, and thus we call $\mathcal{E}$ the set of edges in the knowledge graph.

A query on a KG looks for the set of entities that meet a particular condition, specified in terms of binary predicates whose arguments can be constants (i.e. entities in $\mathcal{V}$), or variables. As an example, consider the following query (adapted from [4]): "Select all projects P, such that topic T is related to P, and both *Alice* and *Bob* work on T". In this query, the constants entities are *Alice* and *Bob*, and the variables are denoted as P and T. We can define such a query formally in terms of a conjunction of binary predicates, as follows:

$$q = P.\exists T, P : \text{related}(T, P) \wedge \text{works\_on}(\text{Alice}, T) \wedge \text{works\_on}(\text{Bob}, T). \quad (1)$$

More formally, we are interested in answering *conjunctive queries*, that have the following general form:

$$q = V_t.\exists V_1, \ldots, V_m : r_1(a_1, b_1) \wedge \ldots \wedge r_m(a_m, b_m), \quad (2)$$

In this notation, $r_i \in \mathcal{R}$, and a_i and b_i are constant entities in the KG, or variables from the set $\{V_t, V_1, \ldots, V_m\}$.

Recent works have proposed to use machine learning methods to answer such queries. These methods operate by learning a vector representation in a space $\mathbb{R}^d$ for each entity and relation type. These representations are also known as *embeddings*, and we denote them as $\mathbf{e}_v$ for $v \in \mathcal{V}$ and $\mathbf{e}_r$ for $r \in \mathcal{R}$. Similarly, these methods define a *query embedding function* ϕ (usually defined with some free parameters), that maps a query q to an embedding $\phi(q) = \mathbf{q} \in \mathbb{R}^d$.

Given a query embedding $\mathbf{q}$, a score for every entity in the graph can be obtained via cosine similarity:

$$\text{score}(\mathbf{q}, \mathbf{e}_v) = \frac{\mathbf{q}^\top \mathbf{e}_v}{\|\mathbf{q}\|\|\mathbf{e}_v\|}.$$

The entity and relation type embeddings, as well as any free parameters in the embedding function ϕ, are optimized via stochastic gradient descent on a specific loss function. Usually the loss is defined so that for a given embedding of a query, the cosine similarity is maximized with embeddings of entities that answer the query, and minimized for embeddings of entities sampled at random.

The dataset used for training consists of query-answer pairs mined from the graph. Once the procedure terminates, the function ϕ can be used to embed a query. The entities in the graph can then be ranked as potential answers, by computing the cosine similarity of all the entity embeddings and the embedding of the query.

Note that in contrast with classical approaches to query answering, such as the use of SPARQL in a graph database, this approach can return answers even if no entity in the graph matches exactly every condition in the query.

In the next sections we review the specifics of recently proposed methods, which consider particular geometries for embedding entities, relation types, and queries; as well as scoring functions.

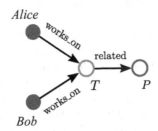

Fig. 1. The query $q = P.\exists T, P : \text{related}(T, P) \land \text{works\_on}(\text{Alice}, T) \land \text{works\_on}(\text{Bob}, T)$ can be represented as a directed acyclic graph, where the leaves are constant entities, the intermediate node T is a variable, and P is the target entity. (Adapted from a figure in [4])

2.1 GQE

Conjunctive queries can be represented as a directed acyclic graph, where the leaf nodes are constant entities, any intermediate nodes are variables, and the root node is the target variable of the query. In this graph, the edges have labels that correspond to the relation type involved in a predicate.

We illustrate this in Fig. 1 for the example query introduced previously. In Graph Query Embedding (GQE) [9], the authors note that this graph can be employed to define a computation graph that starts with the embeddings of the entities at the leaves, and follows the structure of the query graph until the target node is reached.

GQE was one of the first models that defined a query embedding function to answer queries over KGs. The function relies on two different mechanisms, each of which handles paths and intersections, respectively. This requires generating a large dataset of queries with diverse shapes that incorporate paths and intersections.

2.2 MPQE

Graph Convolutional Networks (GCNs) [5, 8, 11] are an extension of neural networks to graph-structured data, that allow defining flexible operators for a variety of machine learning tasks on graphs. Relational Graph Convolutional Networks (R-GCNs) [17] are a special case that introduces a mechanism to deal with different relation types as they occur in KGs, and have been shown to be effective for tasks like link prediction and entity classification.

In MPQE [4], the authors note that a more general query embedding function can be defined in comparison with GQE, if an R-GCN is employed to map the query graph to an embedding. The generality stems from the fact that the R-GCN uses a general message-passing mechanism to embed the query, instead of relying on specific operators for paths and intersections.

2.3 Query2Box

Both GQE and MPQE embed a query as a single vector (i.e., a point in space). Query2Box [15] deviates from this idea and uses a box shape to represent a query. The method further narrows the allowed embedding shape to axis-aligned hyperrectangles. We will discuss more in Sect. 4 why that is beneficial. This method has several benefits, especially for conjunctive queries; for these queries, the answer set can be seen as the intersection of the answers to the conjuncts. Such an operation can be imagined with an embedded volume, but not with a vector embedding.

While this method would have made it possible to create a binary classifier, the model is not specifically trained, nor evaluated for multiple answers.

2.4 Complex Query Decomposition

Complex Query Decomposition (CQD) [2], is a recently proposed method for query answering based on using simple methods for 1-hop link prediction to answer more complex queries. In CQD, the link predictors used are DistMult [21] and ComplEx [20]. Such link predictors are more data efficient than the previous methods, since they only need to be trained with the set of observed triples. In contrast, to be effective the previous methods require mining millions of queries covering a wide range of structures.

In CQD, a complex query is decomposed in terms of its binary predicates. The link predictor is used to compute scores for each of them, and the scores are then aggregated with t-norms, which have been employed in the literature as continuous relaxations of the conjunction and disjunction operators [12,13,18].

CQD provides an answer to the query by providing a ranking of entities based on the maximization of the aggregated scores. Therefore, the evaluation procedure for CQD is the same as the previous methods.

3   From Ranking Metrics to Actual Answers

As discussed above, there are merits to returning a hard answer set as opposed to returning a ranking. One way to obtain such binary classifications is to define a threshold within a ranking. As we will further describe in Sect. 4, one can create such a threshold by using shapes (e.g. axis aligned hyper-rectangles) for query embeddings.

3.1 Closed-World Assumption

Binary classification does introduce new challenges. One such challenge can be seen in the definition of a loss function that can act differently for entities within the set and entities not in the set. Since the knowledge graph may contain missing edges, the retrieved target set may be a subset of the ground truth. This in turn could result in entities being incorrectly used within the loss function (i.e. an incorrect closed-world assumption).

However, this is not necessarily problematic. We define $\mathcal{T}$ to be the ground truth target set of a query and $\mathcal{T}'$ to be the retrieved target set (i.e. when directly querying the KG). Assuming the number of entities missing from $\mathcal{T}'$ is considerably smaller than $\mathcal{V} - \mathcal{T}$, most entities that do not belong in $\mathcal{T}'$ are also not answers to the query (i.e. not in $\mathcal{T}$). This means that if we sample a relatively small subset of the inverse found target set ($\mathcal{V} - \mathcal{T}'$) it will likely not contain entities that are also in $\mathcal{T}$.

In the case where we need to be certain that our sample from $\mathcal{V} - \mathcal{T}'$ does not contain entities in $\mathcal{T}$ we could restrict our sampling process to entities which could never appear in $\mathcal{T}$. This is possible for example, by sampling entities which are incompatible with the domain and range of specific relations in a query (e.g. house entities will never appear in a has_sibling(a,b) relation). Potential downsides of such methods include a potential slow down during learning or a limit in the model's overall performance, as having very different entities in T and our sample from $V - T'$ could prevent our model from learning the differences between the two sets. On the other hand, if these two sets are very similar the model would be forced to uncover differences even when they are not very apparent. In fact, it is often good practise to use so-called "hard" negative samples, which are similar to entities in T'. A better alternative for finding entities not in T would be using more advanced techniques as proposed in [16].

3.2 From Ranking to Classification

Another focal point where binary classification differs from ranking as a metric, is in the way performance is measured (e.g. F-score against Mean Reciprocal Rank). On binary classification, a common performance measure would be the F-score, which is the harmonic mean between Precision and Recall, while in a ranking setting we encounter the Mean Reciprocal Rank.

While these metrics differ significantly, there are ways for them to relate. This insight can be evident, considering that rankings could be turned in binary classifications, using a threshold. In particular, we notice that ranking metrics typically focus on having entities in T' higher in the rank. As a result, having many high-ranking entities that are not in T' is also penalised. Effectively these measures then provide some notion of how well T' and $V - T'$ can be separated. This means that in the case of a low ranking measure, the binary classification can also under-perform. Moreover, it could either result in low precision, recall or both, depending on where the threshold is placed among the ranking.

Geometrically, there is also a correspondence between a ranking with a cutoff point and a system where all answer embeddings withing a given distance would be included as answers. One could view a classifier with high precision and low recall as having an embedding with relatively small volume, while viewing a classifier with high recall and low precision as having an embedding with relatively large volume instead. In this setting, the interpretation of a ranking measure would be whether entities in T' are closer to our geometric query embedding than entities not in T'. This measure of closeness is defined via a distance metric (e.g. the L1 norm) and can be used in the loss function [15].

4   Using Axis-Aligned Boxes for Query Embedding

As discussed in Sect. 2 an entity is a valid answer to a specific structured query if it satisfies the query. The ultimate aim is to find the set of all valid answers, as entities in the Knowledge Graph, that satisfy the given query even when a missing edge in the KG is required for the binary predicates. As discussed, we could either attempt to use a cut-off point in the ranking to obtain a binary classifier, or we could train the embedding model such that it indicates a volume in the embedded space that contains the answers. In this section we present a first possible design of such a system to show the feasibility. We alter the earlier work done on query2box [15] method in two ways. First, we do interpret the boundaries of the hyperrectangle used for the embedding as a bounding box. All entities within the box are predicted answers to the query, while answers outside are predicted to not be answers. Second, we do not use the embedding procedure proposed in query2box, but rather perform the embedding using the technique devised in MPQE.

Now, we could choose to embed entities using points, as is done in other query embedding methods. Then, entities that get embedded inside the box would be seen as answers to the query, while points outside of it would be seen as non-answers. This is illustrated in Fig. 2.

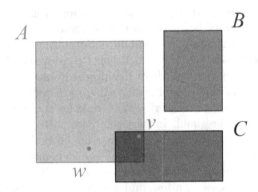

Fig. 2. A small 2D query box embedding: Here there are three queries A, B and C, and two entities v and w. In this case v is an answer to A and C, whilst w is only an answer to A. (Source [3])

But, as we will discuss in more detail in the following subsection, we can also use hyper-rectangles for these. The choice we make in the experiments in this paper is to consider an entity, embedded as a box, to be valid answer to the query if there is an intersection between the two boxes. This is also illustrated in Fig. 3, for the two-dimensional case. An alternative choice could be to consider an entity and answer in case the entity box is completely inside the query box.

To formalize this, we operate on the embedding space $\mathbb{R}^d$. What we want is to describe an axis-aligned hyper-rectangle in this space. We do this by keeping two vectors, one to indicate the center of the box and one to indicate the offset of the sides of the box. So, in the described model every entity $v \in V$ has an embedding $\mathbf{e}_v \in \mathbb{R}^{2d}$. Additionally an embedding for the query is defined that maps the full vector of the query: $\mathbf{q} \in \mathbb{R}^{2d}$.

The boxes in $\mathbb{R}^d$ corresponding to the $2d$-dimensional vectors are defined as $p = (Cen(p), Off(p)) \in \mathbb{R}^{2d}$:

$$Box_p = \{v \in \mathbb{R}^d : Cen(p) - Off(p) \preceq v \preceq Cen(p) + Off(p)\}, \qquad (3)$$

where $\preceq$ denotes element-wise inequality.

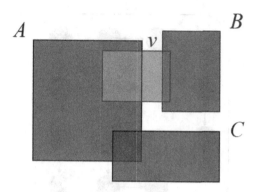

Fig. 3. A small 2D query and entity box embedding: Here there are three queries A, B and C, and one entity v. In this case v is an answer to A and B, but not to C. (Source [3])

Note that a completely analog definition could be made by keeping two extreme counterpoints of the box rather than a center and offset.

4.1 Boxes for Entities

It was already mentioned in the previous section that we represent our entity embeddings with boxes, as well. This idea comes forward from the fact that entities could play different roles in different contexts. For example, we could have a person who both works at a university, buy is also a member of a political party. Having a single point to represent that person forces a query asking for members of that political party and a query asking for people working at that university to overlap. If we instead use a box for the entity, the query embeddings do not have that additional problem. The issue is also illustrated in Figs. 4 and 5. The nodes representing Alice and Bob are close to each other in the one context, but far away in the other one. In the embedding of the entities in Fig. 5 shows that with boxes it is possible to have the entities close to each other and far away from each other at the same time. With the entities as boxes, we can have it as an answer to two disjoint queries as illustrated in Fig. 3.

5 Proof of Concept

In this section, we perform an evaluation of the system we discuss above. Note that our goal is not to provide state-of-the-art results. Firstly, this is because what we propose is just a proof of concept for an approximate embedding system which can find a set of answers for a query. But, the main reason we cannot really compare with other systems is because they are evaluated with ranking metrics as discussed in Sect. 3.

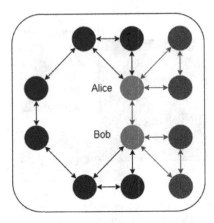

Fig. 4. Here Alice and Bob are closely related in context of a specific relations (1 relation minimum), but they are not very closely related in other context (5 hops minimum). (Source [3])

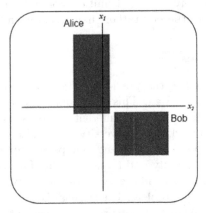

Fig. 5. Here Alice and Bob are have relatively close points (seen near the origin), but also very distant points. (Source [3])

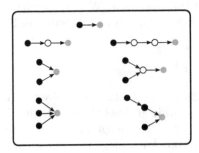

Fig. 6. Used query structures for evaluation on query answering. Black nodes correspond to anchor entities, hollow nodes are the variables in the query, and the gray nodes represent the targets (answers) of the query. (Source [4])

5.1   Experimental Setup

Figure 6 shows seven distinct query graph structures. We only consider these structures when training and testing our model for the query answering task. These structures were originally proposed in GQE [9]. Each of these structures starts with actual entities from a graph (i.e. anchor entities) and ends with a set of target entities. Some of these structures are chains without any intersections (e.g. $B.\exists A, B$: knows(Alice, A) $\wedge$ is_related_to(A, B)), whilst other only have intersections (e.g. $B.\exists B$: knows(Alice, B) $\wedge$ is_related_to(Bob, B)) or even combinations of both. Our goal is to train a model that finds the answer set of a given query, using a query embedding. This is in contrast to other related work [4,9,15] as we want to be able to find multiple answers. As mentioned before, we could create such a set by embedding the query as box, thus getting a hard boundary for separating entities in and not in the target set.

Datasets. While previous work [4,9] incorporated multiple datasets, our implementation has yet solely been tested on the AIFB dataset. This dataset is a knowledge graph of academic institution in which persons, organizations, projects, publications, and topics are the entities. Table 1 give some statistics of this dataset and also for two more datasets often used for the evaluation of approximate query answering.

Table 1. Statistics of the knowledge graphs that were used for training and evaluation.

	AIFB	MUTAG	AM
Entities	2,601	22,372	372,584
Entity types	6	4	5
Relations	39,436	81,332	1,193,402
Relation types	49	8	19

Query Generation. To train our model we have to sample for query graphs from our dataset. This is done by initially sampling anchor nodes and relations which are later used to form graphs based on specific query patterns (Fig. 6).

After acquiring the anchor nodes and the relations connecting them, we can obtain the target set. Although this may appear straightforward, there are some caveats. The biggest one is that some queries contain considerable sets of potential target entities (over 100,000 answers). Because we sample for edges first these particular graphs actually appear often.

Luckily, for most query structures this was not the case, but specifically the 2-chain and 3-chain query structures occasionally suffer from it. This is likely explained by the fact that knowledge graphs contain "hub nodes", nodes with a very high degree, to which a plethora of other nodes connect via a certain relation. Table 2 shows the average size of the target sets of sampled queries for the aforementioned datasets. One interesting thing to note is that for the AM dataset the 3-chain-inter structure actually had the largest average target set. This could indicate that this problem is indeed very graph-dependent. Since this is a problem with the AIFB dataset, we limit the query target sets to a maximum of 100 answers.

We also sample for entities not in the target set to be used as negative samples during training. For the query structures that contain an intersection we incorporate hard negative samples by finding entities that would have been in the target set if the conjunctive intersections were to be relaxed to disjunctions.

Table 2. Average number of multiple answers to different queries structures, across the used datasets. (Results were earlier reported in [1])

Structure	AIFB		MUTAG		AM	
	Train	Test	Train	Test	Train	Test
1-chain	3.4	1.2	1.9	1.1	1.2	1.0
2-chain	34.5	6.4	13.4	4.7	10.2	3.5
3-chain	**47.0**	**7.2**	**17.6**	**5.4**	13.8	3.7
2-inter	9.3	3.2	1.6	1.3	9.1	3.5
3-inter	5.1	2.8	1.0	1.0	7.4	2.9
3-inter-chain	15.5	4.2	1.9	1.7	10.3	3.5
3-chain-inter	22.8	5.6	2.6	2.3	**15.2**	**4.4**

Evaluation. In order to test whether the model is actually able to find answers to queries that involve edges which are not in the graph, careful preparation of our data splits was necessary. We started by our original graph and marked 10% of the edges to be removed (they are still there at this stage). Then, we sample the graph for the query patterns. If the sample makes use of any edge marked as removed, it will be added to either the validation set or the test set (10/90 split). If the sample contains no such marked edge, then we put it in the training set. This way, we end up with validation and test queries that make use of at least one edge that is not in the graph seen during training.

Post sampling, we end up with around 2 million targets and the corresponding query graphs to be used in the training set. For the validation set we used about 30,000 targets worth of queries and for the test set we will had approximately 300,000 targets worth of query graphs. The validation set is also used to perform early stopping in case specific conditions were not met.

Since our method uses boxes, which allow for binary classification, we report our model's performance in the form of a confusion matrix (see Fig. 7). Given the fact that our entities are also boxes, we have more freedom to choose when an entity is considered an answer.

This is because entities now inhabit more space than a single point which allows for partial overlap with query boxes. In order to allow flexibility we have decided that an entity is considered an answer to a query if its box representation overlaps with the box representation of the respective query box. Naturally, other more strict conditions could be applied such as requiring full overlap or define a fraction based threshold (e.g. requiring at least 50% overlap). We expect these conditions to change based on the potential downstream task [22].

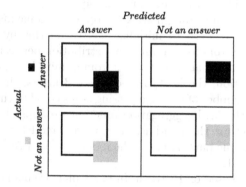

Fig. 7. Model of the confusion matrix used for evaluation of the results, the empty box is representation of a query, the black and the gray box are respectively a valid and a invalid answer to the query. (Source [1])

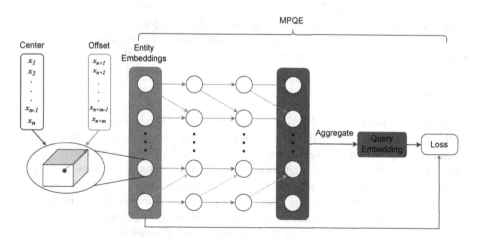

Fig. 8. The MPQB model used in this proof of concept. (Adapted from a figure in [3])

Model. Our model has the same basic functionality as the MPQE [4] model. MPQE is used as an embedding component, but the input and output are interpreted as boxes (as illustrated in Fig. 8). MPQE first performs several steps of message passing using an R-GCN architecture after which the node states are aggregated to form the query embedding. With this query embedding a loss function is evaluated which is used as a signal (using SGD) to update the embeddings and weights in the network. For the aggregation operation we have several options (*SUM, MAX, TM, MLP*) at the end of our model. We test our model with some of these different aggregation functions.

Since we train an embedding matrix (as opposed to having a latent embedding to start with) we need to initialize it. We do this by sampling the 32 dimensional center vectors from a uniform distribution between 0 and 10, whilst sampling the 32 dimensional offset vectors from a unit Gaussian with a mean 3.

For TM aggregation, the MPQE model uses 3 layers; the TM aggregation function requires a number of message passing steps equal to the query diameter, in our case 3. For the MLP aggregation function we applied a two layer fully-connected MLP. As for the non-linearities in our model, we used the ReLU function. To update the parameters of the model we used Adam optimizer with a learning rate of 0.01.

Our code base is based on PyTorch. In particular, we made use of the library PyTorch Geometric [7], which is a PyTorch extension specialised for graph-based models. While there are potential baselines to consider [4,9], they are not suitable for our work. This happens because we perform a binary classification as opposed to ranking-based methods. To our knowledge there have not been any related work that performed binary classification in the context of approximate graph querying. In the area of link prediction, we do find some work, like the early work on Neural Tensor Networks [19] and a more recent one which looks at triple classification [6]. This did not prove to be a major concern, as our main goal was not to achieve state-of-the-art results, but rather explore whether this direction of research may prove worthwhile.

5.2   Results

After having trained the MPQB model for over 200,000 iterations it appeared to still not have converged. After this amount of iterations the query boxes seemed to not overlap with any target boxes (i.e. no entities in T' were returned). Apart from training the model for longer and on multiple epochs, there are some other settings that could still be experimented with. For example, how many samples are in each epoch (less samples allow for training on more epochs), whether we use T' fully during train or use a subset, and how many entities should be in our sample from $V - T'$. The latter two settings also influence how many distinct queries we could train on within a given time span. In may be worth noting that previous works [4,9,15] train using single positive samples. While we want to focus on answering queries with multiple answers, we do not necessarily need to train on multiple answers. In theory, if a method can produce a good ranking, it should also be able to produce a good classification, given that the optimal thresholds for these rankings could be found.

Since we do not have direct result in a manner we would have liked, we will instead analyse the trained models to see if there are relevant insights to be found. For this we looked at models using different aggregation functions, trained on the AIFB dataset.

While we have no intersections between query boxes and target boxes, we could still look whether the target boxes (from T') appear relatively close to the entity boxes, when compared to the box representations of entities in $V-T'$. This effectively provides some measure as to whether the produced rankings are good. Table 3 shows these results. While these scores may not indicate state-of-the-art results, they do seem to suggest that the model did at least produce decent non-trivial rankings using the SUM and TM aggregators. This could suggest that further research is indeed in order. The fact that TM outperformed SUM is not surprising considering that it is a more involved method that also takes query diameter into account. This result is also in line with the findings in [4]. A more surprising result is that the MLP method did not seem to perform well at all. This could be a result of a faulty implementation, or an implementation that simply does not work for boxes as is. Overall, the results seem promising.

Table 3. Percentage (%) of answers embedded closer to the query box compared to a non answer, with regard to the query structure, using different aggregation function. Tested on AIFB dataset. (Results were earlier reported in [1])

Structure	AIFB		
	SUM	TM	MLP
1-chain	67.48	**69.84**	0.0
2-chain	68.78	**75.85**	0.0
3-chain	76.55	**79.86**	0.0
2-inter	62.09	**63.10**	0.0
3-inter	63.32	**63.35**	0.0
3-inter-chain	67.61	**67.91**	0.0
3-chain-inter	68.87	**72.43**	0.0

6   Conclusion and Outlook

In this work, we looked critically at the currently prevailing evaluation strategy for approximate complex structured query algorithms for knowledge graphs. Typically, these systems take a query as an input and produce a ranking of all entities in the KG as an output. The performance of these systems is than determined using metrics typically used in information retrieval.

What we propose is to augment the current evaluations by also requiring these systems to produce a binary classification of the nodes into a class of answers and one of non-answers. This is needed because many applications can simply not work with a ranking and need a fixed set of answers to work with.

As a first proof of concept, we have adapted ideas from MPQE and query2Box, and created an embedding algorithm that represents the queries and the entities as axis-aligned hyper-rectangles. We noticed that the performance of this system is pretty low, and expect that future works can heavily improve upon this first attempt.

As future research directions, we see a need to expand our experiments to include other query types (disjunctions, negations, filters, etc.), in order to show the generalizability of our approach. This will, however, require new representation for the volumes as these operations are not possible if we would stay with just boxes. For example, the negation of a box, would no longer be a box.

Moreover, we it needs to be investigated how our method can be applied on different kinds of graphs. This will give us insights as to what changes need to be made in terms of training data (via query generation) as well as the effects on model performance. Also, it seems worth experimenting with different geometric representations for the parts of the query (anchor, variables and targets). Finally, since our experiments were relatively small-scale, further research could also start by simply experimenting with different settings for our current architecture.

References

1. Aleksiev, T.: Answering approximated graph queries, embedding the queries and entities as boxes. BSc. thesis, Computer Science, Vrije Universiteit Amsterdam, Supervised by Cochez, M. (2020)
2. Arakelyan, E., Daza, D., Minervini, P., Cochez, M.: Complex query answering with neural link predictors. In: International Conference on Learning Representations (2021). https://openreview.net/forum?id=Mos9F9kDwkz
3. van Bakel, R.: Box R-GCN: Structured query answering using box embeddings for entities and queries. BSc. thesis, Computer Science, Vrije Universiteit Amsterdam, Supervised by Cochez, M. (2020)
4. Daza, D., Cochez, M.: Message passing query embedding. In: ICML Workshop - Graph Representation Learning and Beyond (2020). https://arxiv.org/abs/2002.02406
5. Defferrard, M., Bresson, X., Vandergheynst, P.: Convolutional neural networks on graphs with fast localized spectral filtering. In: Advances in Neural Information Processing Systems, pp. 3844–3852 (2016)
6. Dong, T., Wang, Z., Li, J., Bauckhage, C., Cremers, A.B.: Triple classification using regions and fine-grained entity typing. In: Proceedings of the AAAI Conference on Artificial Intelligence, vol. 33, pp. 77–85 (2019)
7. Fey, M., Lenssen, J.E.: Fast graph representation learning with PyTorch Geometric. arXiv preprint arXiv:1903.02428 (2019)
8. Gilmer, J., Schoenholz, S.S., Riley, P.F., Vinyals, O., Dahl, G.E.: Neural message passing for quantum chemistry. In: Proceedings of the 34th International Conference on Machine Learning, ICML 2017, Sydney, NSW, Australia, 6–11 August 2017, pp. 1263–1272 (2017)

9. Hamilton, W., Bajaj, P., Zitnik, M., Jurafsky, D., Leskovec, J.: Embedding logical queries on knowledge graphs. In: Bengio, S., Wallach, H., Larochelle, H., Grauman, K., Cesa-Bianchi, N., Garnett, R. (eds.) Advances in Neural Information Processing Systems, vol. 31, pp. 2026–2037. Curran Associates, Inc. (2018). https://proceedings.neurips.cc/paper/2018/file/ef50c335cca9f340bde656363ebd02-fd-Paper.pdf

10. Hogan, A., et al.: Knowledge graphs. arXiv preprint arXiv:2003.02320 (2020)

11. Kipf, T.N., Welling, M.: Semi-supervised classification with graph convolutional networks. arXiv preprint arXiv:1609.02907 (2016)

12. van Krieken, E., Acar, E., van Harmelen, F.: Analyzing differentiable fuzzy implications. In: Proceedings of the 17th International Conference on Principles of Knowledge Representation and Reasoning, pp. 893–903 (2020). https://doi.org/10.24963/kr.2020/92

13. Minervini, P., Demeester, T., Rocktäschel, T., Riedel, S.: Adversarial sets for regularising neural link predictors. In: UAI. AUAI Press (2017)

14. Noy, N., Gao, Y., Jain, A., Narayanan, A., Patterson, A., Taylor, J.: Industry-scale knowledge graphs: lessons and challenges. Commun. ACM **62**(8), 36–43 (2019)

15. Ren, H., Hu, W., Leskovec, J.: Query2box: reasoning over knowledge graphs in vector space using box embeddings (2020)

16. Safavi, T., Koutra, D., Meij, E.: Evaluating the calibration of knowledge graph embeddings for trustworthy link prediction (2020)

17. Schlichtkrull, M., Kipf, T.N., Bloem, P., van den Berg, R., Titov, I., Welling, M.: Modeling relational data with graph convolutional networks. In: Gangemi, A., et al. (eds.) ESWC 2018. LNCS, vol. 10843, pp. 593–607. Springer, Cham (2018). https://doi.org/10.1007/978-3-319-93417-4_38

18. Serafini, L., d'Avila Garcez, A.S.: Logic tensor networks: Deep learning and logical reasoning from data and knowledge. CoRR abs/1606.04422 (2016). http://arxiv.org/abs/1606.04422

19. Socher, R., Chen, D., Manning, C.D., Ng, A.: Reasoning with neural tensor networks for knowledge base completion. In: Burges, C.J.C., Bottou, L., Welling, M., Ghahramani, Z., Weinberger, K.Q. (eds.) Advances in Neural Information Processing Systems, vol. 26, pp. 926–934. Curran Associates, Inc. (2013). https://proceedings.neurips.cc/paper/2013/file/b337e84de8752b27eda3a1236310-9e80-Paper.pdf

20. Trouillon, T., Welbl, J., Riedel, S., Gaussier, É., Bouchard, G.: Complex embeddings for simple link prediction. In: ICML, JMLR Workshop and Conference Proceedings, vol. 48, pp. 2071–2080. JMLR.org (2016)

21. Yang, B., Yih, W., He, X., Gao, J., Deng, L.: Embedding entities and relations for learning and inference in knowledge bases. In: Proceedings of the 3rd International Conference on Learning Representations, ICLR 2015, Conference Track Proceedings, San Diego, CA, USA, 7–9 May 2015 (2015)

22. Pellegrino, M.A., Altabba, A., Garofalo, M., Ristoski, P., Cochez, M.: GEval: a modular and extensible evaluation framework for graph embedding techniques. In: Harth, A., et al. (eds.) ESWC 2020. LNCS, vol. 12123, pp. 565–582. Springer, Cham (2020). https://doi.org/10.1007/978-3-030-49461-2_33

Galois Connections for Patterns: An Algebra of Labelled Graphs

David A. Cohen[1], Martin C. Cooper[2(✉)], Peter G. Jeavons[3], and Stanislav Živný[3]

[1] Royal Holloway, University of London, Egham, UK
dave@cs.rhul.ac.uk
[2] IRIT, University of Toulouse, Toulouse, France
cooper@irit.fr
[3] University of Oxford, Oxford, UK
{peter.jeavons,standa.zivny}@cs.ox.ac.uk

Abstract. A pattern is a generic instance of a binary constraint satisfaction problem (CSP) in which the compatibility of certain pairs of variable-value assignments may be unspecified. The notion of forbidden pattern has led to the discovery of several novel tractable classes for the CSP. However, for this field to come of age it is time for a theoretical study of the algebra of patterns. We present a Galois connection between lattices composed of sets of forbidden patterns and sets of generic instances, and investigate its consequences. We then extend patterns to augmented patterns and exhibit a similar Galois connection. Augmented patterns are a more powerful language than flat (i.e. non-augmented) patterns, as we demonstrate by showing that, for any $k \geq 1$, instances with tree-width bounded by k cannot be specified by forbidding a finite set of flat patterns but can be specified by a finite set of augmented patterns. A single finite set of augmented patterns can also describe the class of instances such that each instance has a weak near-unanimity polymorphism of arity k (thus covering all tractable language classes). We investigate the power of forbidding augmented patterns and discuss their potential for describing new tractable classes.

Keywords: Constraint satisfaction · Tractability · Forbidden patterns · Galois connection · Lattice

The authors were supported by EPSRC grant EP/L021226/1. Martin Cooper was supported by the grants ANR-18-CE40-0011 and ANR-19-PI3A-000. Stanislav Živný was supported by a Royal Society University Research Fellowship. This project has received funding from the European Research Council (ERC) under the European Union's Horizon 2020 research and innovation programme (grant agreement No 714532). The paper reflects only the authors' views and not the views of the ERC or the European Commission. The European Union is not liable for any use that may be made of the information contained therein.

M. Cochez et al. (Eds.): GKR 2020, LNAI 12640, pp. 125–150, 2021.
https://doi.org/10.1007/978-3-030-72308-8_9

1   Introduction

The CSP (Constraint Satisfaction Problem) is a classical abstract framework for the modelling of finite-domain constrained assignment problems [8,32]. Although first inspired by applications in computer vision and artificial intelligence, it's generic nature has allowed it to become a programming paradigm in its own right used in, for example, scheduling, product configuration, planning and bio-informatics. It is well known that the CSP is NP-complete and remains so even when restricted to binary constraints since all instances have an equivalent dual instance which is binary [22,40].

An interesting avenue of theoretical research on CSPs consists in the characterisation of tractable subproblems defined by placing a restriction on the type of constraints that can occur (the constraint language) and again it is known that it is possible to limit attention to languages of binary relations [5,10]. A major advance towards the recent characterisation of tractable constraint languages [3,41] was the algebraic approach based on the study of pointwise closure operations of constraint relations, known as polymorphisms, and the identities satisfied by these polymorphisms [1,4]. Of particular interest is the Galois connection between (sets of) polymorphisms and (sets of) relations [27]. In parallel, tractable subproblems of the CSP based on restrictions on the (hyper)-graph of constraint scopes (the constraint (hyper)graph) were also characterised [26].

In order to define new classes, we need to go beyond placing restrictions on constraint languages or on the structure of the constraint (hyper)-graph. A natural way of defining sets of instances is to consider properties of the microstructure of binary CSP instances [30]. A *pattern* can be seen as a partial microstructure (i.e. a binary CSP instance in which the compatibility of some assignments may be left undefined) or, more abstractly, as a graph with vertices labelled by names of variables and edges which may be positive or negative. Defining sets of binary CSP instances by forbidding patterns has led to the discovery of novel tractable classes [9,18]. For example, in each of the following cases, forbidding a simple 3-variable pattern defines a tractable class of binary CSP instances which strictly generalises a known tractable class:

- The Broken-Triangle Property (BTP) [16] includes all instances whose constraint graph is a tree. It has also led to the discovery of interesting reduction operations [14] and has been extended in different ways to define larger tractable classes [12,35–37].
- The Joint-Winner Property (JWP) [17] includes all CSP instances defined by a single All-Different constraint [38] together with arbitrary unary constraints.
- The Extended Max-Closed (EMC) class [19] includes all binary max-closed instances [29]. The stable marriage problem [31] is just one example of a class of problems that can be expressed as binary max-closed CSPs [25].
- The T_4 pattern [15] generalises the ZOA language class [13] which is itself a generalisation of 2SAT. Three other patterns have also recently been shown to define tractable classes that generalise 2SAT [7].

In this paper we initiate the study of the underlying theory of forbidden (sets of) patterns, an essential foundation on which to build a characterisation of all tractable classes defined by forbidden (sets of) patterns. We begin by studying what we call flat patterns before studying augmented patterns with extra structure, such as partial orders on variables or domain values. Adding such structure is not only essential to define certain hybrid classes such as BTP [16] and EMC [19], but, as we will show in Sect. 6, also allows us to define (families of) polymorphisms [28] and bounded tree-width [20] within the same framework.

For both flat and augmented patterns, we exhibit a Galois connection between sets of patterns and sets of instances. In each case, we investigate the tractability consequences of the Galois connection, including the possibility of defining new tractable classes by combination of known tractable classes via the lattice operations. We notably show that tractable classes form a sublattice.

2   Definitions and Notation

We assume that there is a countable collection of variables $\mathcal{X}$ and a countable domain $\mathcal{D}$ of values. A variable-value pair (x, a), representing the assignment of value $a \in \mathcal{D}$ to variable $x \in \mathcal{X}$, is known as a *point*. A *flat pattern* (or simply a *pattern*) $P = \langle A_P, \rho_P \rangle$ is a subset A_P of $\mathcal{X} \times \mathcal{D}$ equipped with a (partial) function ρ_P from the pairs of points $(x, a), (y, b)$ of P such that $x \neq y$ to {negative, positive}. Thus P consists of a set of variable-value assignments (x, a) together with a set of negative and positive edges representing the compatibility of pairs of assignments. In figures we represent negative edges by dashed lines, positive edges by solid lines and points corresponding to assignments to the same variable are grouped into ovals. Three patterns $P1$, $P2$, $P3$ are shown in Fig. 1.

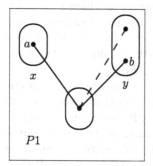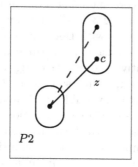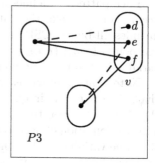

Fig. 1. Examples of the occurrence of a pattern in another pattern: $P1 \rightarrow P2$, $P2 \rightarrow P1$, $P1 \rightarrow P3$, $P2 \rightarrow P3$.

We give a recursive definition of connectedness. Two points $(x, a), (y, b)$ in a pattern P are *connected* if $x = y$ or $\rho_P((x, a), (y, b)) \in \{\text{negative, positive}\}$ or if $(x, a), (y, b)$ are both connected to some point (z, c) of P. Clearly, each pattern has a decomposition into connected components according to this definition of connectedness.

A *completely specified binary CSP instance* (or simply an *instance*) is a pattern $I = \langle A_I, \rho_I \rangle$ in which the function ρ_I is total, i.e. the compatibility of each pair of variable-value assignments (to distinct variables) is specified. Given an instance I on n variables, a *solution* to I is a clique of positive edges of size n, which corresponds to a pairwise-compatible assignment of values to variables. The question associated with an instance is the existence of a solution. An instance I is *arc consistent* if for all points (x, a) of I and all variables $y \neq x$ of I, (x, a) has a support at y, i.e. $\exists b \in \mathcal{D}$ such that $\{(x, a), (y, b)\}$ is a positive edge in I.

A pattern $P = \langle A_P, \rho_P \rangle$ *occurs* in pattern $Q = \langle A_Q, \rho_Q \rangle$ if there is a mapping f from A_P to A_Q which respects variables, maps negative edges to negative edges and positive edges to positive edges, i.e.

1. $f(x, a) = (u, c)$ and $f(x, b) = (v, d)$ implies that $u = v$.
2. $f(x, a) = (u, c)$, $f(y, b) = (v, d)$ and $\rho_P((x, a), (y, b)) \in \{\text{negative, positive}\}$ implies that $u \neq v$ and $\rho_P((x, a), (y, b)) = \rho_Q((u, c), (v, d))$.

We use the notation $P \rightarrow Q$ to denote that P *occurs* in pattern Q (and $P \nrightarrow Q$ if it does not). It is easy to see from its definition that occurrence is transitive: $P \rightarrow Q$ and $Q \rightarrow R$ implies $P \rightarrow R$. We consider two patterns P, Q to be equivalent if $P \rightarrow Q$ and $Q \rightarrow P$: we write $P \approx Q$. For example, patterns $P1$ and $P2$ in Fig. 1 are equivalent; we notably have $P1 \rightarrow P2$ since (x, a), (y, b) can both map to (z, c). Clearly, we have $P2 \rightarrow P3$, and then, by transitivity, $P1 \rightarrow P3$. For simplicity of presentation, throughout this paper, we will talk about patterns rather than equivalence classes of patterns.

Each pattern P defines a corresponding set of instances in which P does not occur. For example, the pattern $P3$ of Fig. 1 defines a set of instances which includes all binary CSP instances with Boolean domains, since if $P3 \rightarrow I$ then the points (v, d), (v, e), (v, f) must map to three distinct values for the same variable in I, due to the positive and negative edges in $P3$.

Note that in previous work, it has sometimes been convenient to assume that when P occurs in Q, distinct variables of P map to distinct variables of Q [11,15,19]. However, to establish a Galois connection for flat patterns, we require a looser definition of occurrence in which two or more variables of P may map to the same variable in Q. To impose the stricter definition of occurrence (inducing an injective mapping of variables of P), it suffices, for each pair of distinct variables x, y, to add two new points (x, a), (y, b) to A_P and an extra dummy positive edge between points (x, a), (y, b) in P; this prevents x, y mapping to the same variable in Q (and only changes the semantics of P in a trivial way). A more elegant solution (in order to impose an injective mapping of variables) is to augment the patterns with a not-equal-to relation between variables which is possible in the framework of augmented patterns discussed in Sect. 6.

We consider sets S of patterns. These sets will usually be finite, indeed, often a singleton. When forbidden, a set S of patterns defines a set of instances (those sets of instances in which none of the patterns in S occurs). Such sets T of instances are hereditary in the sense that $(I \in T) \wedge (I' \subseteq I) \implies (I' \in T)$, where $I' \subseteq I$ means $(A_{I'} \subseteq A_I) \wedge (\rho_{I'} = \rho_I|_{A_{I'}})$. Many, but not all, classes of interest are hereditary. For example, for any k, the set of instances whose tree-width is bounded by k is hereditary. On the other hand, the set of instances which is arc-consistent is not hereditary, since a value which has a support at another variable in an instance I will not necessarily have a support in $I' \subset I$. Thus forbidden flat patterns alone cannot express any class of instances which requires arc consistency (or a higher level of consistency) [36]. Nevertheless, we will see in Sect. 6 how a combination of augmented patterns and filters on instances provides a very expressive language in which to define classes on instances, allowing us to express such classes of instances.

In order to obtain a Galois connection we consider sets of generic instances, where a generic instance can be viewed as a partially-specified instance and is, in fact, again just a pattern. However, the lattice structure on sets of patterns is different depending on whether we view these patterns as partially-specified instances or as forbidden sub-instances. When defining tractability of sets of generic instances we filter instances keeping only those that are completely specified.

Definition 1. *A set T of generic instances is* tractable *if there is a polynomial-time algorithm which decides all completely-specified instances in T. A set S of forbidden patterns is tractable if the corresponding set of instances in which none of the patterns in S occur is tractable.*

To define lattices of (sets of) instances and (sets of) patterns, we also require the following operation on patterns: if P, Q are patterns, then $P + Q$ is a single pattern consisting of (copies of) the two patterns P and Q (without any common points and without any edges between P and Q). We call this the *juxtaposition* of the two patterns P and Q. Observe that $P + P \approx P$ (since $P + P \to P$ follows from the definition of occurrence which allows us to map the two copies of P to P). If S_1, S_2 are sets of patterns, then $S_1 + S_2$ is the set of patterns $\{P + Q \mid P \in S_1 \wedge Q \in S_2\}$.

We also require another operation on pairs of patterns, which can be seen as the greatest lower bound of the two patterns. If P, Q are patterns, then $P \times Q$ is a single pattern built by forming the juxtaposition of all patterns R such that $(R \to P) \wedge (R \to Q)$. We say that such patterns R are *common factors* of P and Q. We only include patterns R which are maximal in the sense that there is no $R' \not\approx R$ such that $R \to R'$ and $(R' \to P) \wedge (R' \to Q)$. Observe that including only maximal R, ensures that we have $P \times P \approx P$. The operation $\times$ is illustrated in Fig. 2. In this example, the patterns P and Q have only two maximal common

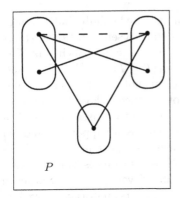

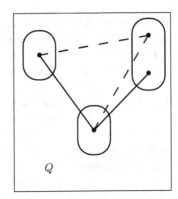

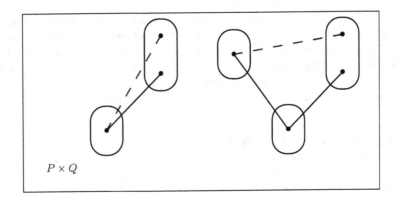

Fig. 2. The operation $P \times Q$.

factors (modulo the equivalence relation $\approx$) and $P \times Q$ is the juxtaposition of these two common factors. Note that $P1$ and $P2$ (shown in Fig. 1) are both common factors of P and Q, but since $P1 \approx P2$ we only need to include one of these patterns in $P \times Q$. If S_1, S_2 are sets of patterns, then $S_1 \times S_2$ is the set of patterns $\{P \times Q \mid P \in S_1 \wedge Q \in S_2\}$.

The following lemmas provide a logical interpretation of the $+$ and $\times$ operations on patterns.

Lemma 1. *For all patterns P_1, P_2, I, we have $P_1 + P_2 \nrightarrow I$ if and only if $(P_1 \nrightarrow I \vee P_2 \nrightarrow I)$*

Proof. For all patterns P_1, P_2, I, $P_1 + P_2 \rightarrow I$ if and only if $(P_1 \rightarrow I \wedge P_2 \rightarrow I)$ by the definition of $P_1 + P_2$. By contraposition, for all patterns P_1, P_2, I, $P_1 + P_2 \nrightarrow I$ if and only if $(P_1 \nrightarrow I \vee P_2 \nrightarrow I)$.

Lemma 2. *For all patterns P, I_1, I_2, $P \nrightarrow I_1 \times I_2$ if and only if $(P \nrightarrow I_1 \vee P \nrightarrow I_2)$.*

Proof. By contraposition, it suffices to show that $P \to I_1 \times I_2$ if and only if $P \to I_1 \land P \to I_2$. If $P \to I_1 \land P \to I_2$, then P is a common factor of I_1 and I_2 and hence $P \to I_1 \times I_2$. On the other hand, if $P \to I_1 \times I_2$, then, due to the lack of edges between the connected components of $I_1 \times I_2$, P must be the juxtaposition of patterns $P_1, \ldots, P_r$ where for each $i = 1, \ldots, r$, $P_i \to R_i$ for some R_i which is one of the connected components of $I_1 \times I_2$. Each connected component R_i of $I_1 \times I_2$ satisfies $R_i \to R_i'$ for some common factor R_i' of I_1 and I_2. By transitivity of the occurrence relation and by definition of $I_1 \times I_2$, we have $P_i \to I_1$ and $P_i \to I_2$ (for $i = 1, \ldots, r$) and hence $P \to I_1$ and $P \to I_2$.

3   The Two Lattices

Let $\mathcal{P}$ be the set of all patterns and $\mathcal{I}$ be the set of all generic instances. Let $\mathcal{T}$ be the set of all subsets of $\mathcal{I}$. Let $\mathcal{S}$ be the set of all subsets of $\mathcal{P}$. In this section we show that $\mathcal{S}$ and $\mathcal{T}$ have lattice structures with partial orders based on notions of occurrence. Although $\mathcal{P} = \mathcal{I}$, $\mathcal{S}$ and $\mathcal{T}$ are distinct since they do not have the same partial order.

We require two different definitions of occurrence of one set of patterns in another, depending on whether the sets of patterns are considered as forbidden patterns or sets of generic instances. For $S_1, S_2 \in \mathcal{S}$, we write $S_1 \twoheadrightarrow S_2$ to mean that $\forall Q \in S_2$, $\exists P \in S_1$ such that $P \to Q$. We write $S_1 \twoheadleftrightarrow S_2$ if $S_1 \twoheadrightarrow S_2$ and $S_2 \twoheadrightarrow S_1$. For $T_1, T_2 \in \mathcal{T}$, we write $T_1 \mapsto T_2$ to mean $\forall P \in T_1$, $\exists Q \in T_2$ such that $P \to Q$. We write $T_1 \leftrightarrow T_2$ if $T_1 \mapsto T_2$ and $T_2 \mapsto T_1$. It follows directly from their definitions that $\twoheadleftrightarrow$ and $\leftrightarrow$ are equivalence relations.

Let $\overline{\mathcal{T}}$ be the set of all equivalence classes (according to $\leftrightarrow$) of sets of generic instances. Let $\overline{\mathcal{S}}$ be the set of all equivalence classes (according to $\twoheadleftrightarrow$) of sets of forbidden patterns.

It is not difficult to see that $\mapsto$ is a partial order on $\overline{\mathcal{T}}$ and that $\twoheadrightarrow$ is a partial order on $\overline{\mathcal{S}}$. It follows that $\overline{\mathcal{T}}$ and $\overline{\mathcal{S}}$ both have a lattice structure [2,21]. The following proposition shows that the set $\overline{\mathcal{T}}$ has a lattice structure with meet and join operations $\times$ and $\cup$, whereas the set $\overline{\mathcal{S}}$ has a lattice structure with meet and join operations $+$ and $\cup$.

Proposition 1. *For all $S_1, S_2 \in \mathcal{S}$, (1) $S_2 \twoheadrightarrow S_1 \Leftrightarrow S_1 + S_2 \twoheadleftrightarrow S_1$ and (2) $S_2 \twoheadrightarrow S_1 \Leftrightarrow S_1 \cup S_2 \twoheadleftrightarrow S_2$. For all $T_1, T_2 \in \mathcal{T}$, (3) $T_1 \mapsto T_2 \Leftrightarrow T_1 \times T_2 \leftrightarrow T_1$ and (4) $T_1 \mapsto T_2 \Leftrightarrow T_1 \cup T_2 \leftrightarrow T_2$.*

Proof. (1) $\Rightarrow$: $S_2 \twoheadrightarrow S_1$ means $\forall P \in S_1$, $\exists Q \in S_2$ such that $Q \to P$ and hence $P + Q \to P$. Thus $S_1 + S_2 \twoheadrightarrow S_1$. Clearly $S_1 \twoheadrightarrow S_1 + S_2$.
(1) $\Leftarrow$: $S_1 + S_2 \twoheadrightarrow S_1$ means $\forall P \in S_1$, $\exists R + Q \in S_1 + S_2$ such that $R + Q \to P$ which implies $Q \to P$. Hence $S_2 \twoheadrightarrow S_1$.
(2) $\Rightarrow$: $S_2 \twoheadrightarrow S_1$ means $\forall P \in S_1$, $\exists Q \in S_2$ such that $Q \to P$. Now, since $\forall Q$, $Q \to Q$, we have $\forall R \in S_1 \cup S_2$, $\exists Q \in S_2$ such that $Q \to R$. Hence $S_2 \twoheadrightarrow S_1 \cup S_2$. Clearly $S_1 \cup S_2 \twoheadrightarrow S_2$.
(2) $\Leftarrow$: $S_2 \twoheadrightarrow S_1 \cup S_2$ implies that $\forall P \in S_1$, $\exists Q \in S_2$ such that $Q \to P$ and so $S_2 \twoheadrightarrow S_1$.

(3) $T_1 \mapsto T_2$ means that $\forall I \in T_1, \exists J \in T_2$ such that $I \to J$, so I is a common factor of I and J and hence $I \to I \times J$. Thus $T_1 \mapsto T_1 \times T_2$. Thus, by definition of $\times$, $T_1 \times T_2 \mapsto T_1$.

(3) $\Leftarrow$: $T_1 \mapsto T_1 \times T_2$ means that $\forall I \in T_1, \exists I \times J \in T_1 \times T_2$ such that each connected component of I occurs in a common factor of I and J, and hence each connected component of I occurs in J and so $I \to J$. Thus $T_1 \mapsto T_2$.

(4) $\Rightarrow$: $T_1 \mapsto T_2$ means $\forall I \in T_1, \exists J \in T_2$ such that $I \to J$. Thus $T_1 \cup T_2 \mapsto T_2$. Clearly $T_2 \mapsto T_1 \cup T_2$.

(4) $\Leftarrow$: $T_1 \cup T_2 \to T_2$ implies $\forall I \in T_1, \exists J \in T_2$ such that $I \to J$ which is exactly $T_1 \mapsto T_2$.

The following lemmas are not essential for the lattice structure of $\overline{S}$ and $\overline{T}$, but will be useful later.

Lemma 3. *If $S_1 \supseteq S_2$ then $S_1 \twoheadrightarrow S_2$. If $T_1 \subseteq T_2$ then $T_1 \mapsto T_2$.*

Proof. If $S_1 \supseteq S_2$ then $\forall Q \in S_2, \exists P = Q \in S_1$ such that $P \to Q$. If $T_1 \subseteq T_2$ then $\forall P \in T_1, \exists Q = P \in T_2$ such that $P \to Q$.

Lemma 4. *For all sets of patterns S_1, S_2, $S_1 + S_2 \twoheadrightarrow S_1 \cap S_2$ and $S_1 \cap S_2 \mapsto S_1 \times S_2$.*

Proof. We have $\forall P \in S_1 \cap S_2, P \leftrightarrowtwoheadrightarrow P + P \in S_1 + S_2$. Hence $S_1 + S_2 \twoheadrightarrow S_1 \cap S_2$. Also $\forall I \in S_1 \cap S_2, I \leftrightarrow I \times \in S_1 \times S_2$. Hence $S_1 \cap S_2 \mapsto S_1 \times S_2$.

If we consider that $S_1 \leq S_2$ if $S_2 \twoheadrightarrow S_1$, then the minimal element in the lattice $\overline{S}$ is the empty set of patterns and the maximal element is $\{P_\emptyset\}$ where $P_\emptyset$ is the pattern containing no points or edges. If we consider that $T_1 \leq T_2$ if $T_1 \mapsto T_2$ then the minimal element of $\overline{T}$ is the empty set of patterns and the maximal element is the set of all patterns.

The two lattices $\overline{S}$ and $\overline{T}$ are both distributive, as shown by the following proposition.

Proposition 2. *For all $S_1, S_2, S_3 \in S$, we have $S_1 + (S_2 \cup S_3) \leftrightarrowtwoheadrightarrow (S_1 + S_2) \cup (S_1 + S_3)$ and for all $T_1, T_2, T_3 \in T$, we have $T_1 \cup (T_2 \times T_3) \leftrightarrow (T_1 \times T_2) \cup (T_1 \times T_3)$.*

Proof. These follow immediately from the definitions.

4   The Galois Connection

The Galois connection is based on two functions $f : S \to T$ and $g : T \to S$, defined as follows.

$$f(S) = \{I \in \mathcal{I} \mid \forall P \in S, P \nrightarrow I\}$$
$$g(T) = \{P \in \mathcal{P} \mid \forall I \in T, P \nrightarrow I\}$$

Theorem 1. *There is an antitone Galois connection between $\overline{S}$ and $\overline{T}$.*

Proof. The functions f, g, applied to equivalence classes of $\mathcal{S}$ and $\mathcal{T}$ define a Galois connection between $\overline{\mathcal{S}}$ and $\overline{\mathcal{T}}$ if $\forall S \in \mathcal{S}, \forall T \in \mathcal{T}, T \leq f(S) \Leftrightarrow S \leq g(T)$. This corresponds to $(T \mapsto f(S)) \Leftrightarrow (g(T) \twoheadrightarrow S)$, which holds because $(T \mapsto f(S))$ and $(g(T) \twoheadrightarrow S)$ are both equivalent to $\forall P \in S, \forall I \in T, P \not\rightarrow I$. We therefore have a Galois connection between $\overline{\mathcal{S}}$ and $\overline{\mathcal{T}}$.

We now study this Galois connection in more detail.

Proposition 3. *For all $S_1, S_2 \in \mathcal{S}$, if $S_1 \twoheadrightarrow S_2$ then $f(S_1) \subseteq f(S_2)$. For all $T_1, T_2 \in \mathcal{T}$, if $T_1 \mapsto T_2$ then $g(T_2) \subseteq g(T_1)$.*

Proof. Suppose $S_1 \twoheadrightarrow S_2$. Then $\forall P_2 \in S_2, \exists P_1 \in S_1$ such that $P_1 \twoheadrightarrow P_2$. Consider $I \in f(S_1)$. By definition of f, $\forall P_1 \in S_1, P_1 \not\rightarrow I$. It follows that $I \in f(S_2)$ since otherwise we would have some $P_2 \in S_2$ such that $P_2 \rightarrow I$ and some $P_1 \in S_1$ with $P_1 \rightarrow P_2 \rightarrow I$ which contradicts $P_1 \not\rightarrow I$.

Suppose $T_1 \mapsto T_2$. Then $\forall I_1 \in T_1, \exists I_2 \in T_2$ such that $I_1 \rightarrow I_2$. Consider $P \in f(T_2)$. By definition of g, $\forall I_2 \in T_2, P \not\rightarrow I_2$. It follows that $P \in g(T_1)$ since otherwise we would have some $I_1 \in T_1$ such that $P \rightarrow I_1$ and some $I_2 \in T_2$ such that $P \rightarrow I_1 \rightarrow I_2$ which contradicts $P \not\rightarrow I_2$.

We immediately have the following corollary.

Corollary 1. *For all $S_1, S_2 \in \mathcal{S}$, $S_1 \twoheadrightarrow S_2 \Rightarrow f(S_1) \mapsto f(S_2)$. For all $T_1, T_2 \in \mathcal{T}$, $T_1 \mapsto T_2 \Rightarrow g(T_1) \twoheadrightarrow g(T_2)$.*

Proposition 4. *For any patterns S_1, S_2, $f(S_1) = f(S_2)$ if and only if $S_1 \longleftrightarrow S_2$.*

Proof. Suppose $f(S_1) = f(S_2)$. Then $\forall I, (\forall P \in S_1, P \not\rightarrow I) \Leftrightarrow (\forall P \in S_2, P \not\rightarrow I)$. This is equivalent to $\forall I, (\exists P \in S_1, P \rightarrow I) \Leftrightarrow (\exists P \in S_2, P \rightarrow I)$. It follows, by setting $I = P \in S_2$, that $\forall P \in S_2, \exists P' \in S_1$ such that $P' \rightarrow P$, and hence $S_1 \twoheadrightarrow S_2$. By setting $I = P \in S_1$, by a symmetrical argument, we obtain $S_2 \twoheadrightarrow S_1$, and hence $S_1 \longleftrightarrow S_2$.

Now suppose that $S_1 \longleftrightarrow S_2$. Then, by Proposition 3, we can deduce that $f(S_1) = f(S_2)$.

It is important to observe that $\mathcal{T}$ includes sets of partially-specified instances. If we considered only sets of completely-specified instances in $\mathcal{T}$, then Proposition 4 would not hold. For example, consider S_1 and S_2 shown in Fig. 3. It is easy to see that we do not have $S_1 \twoheadrightarrow S_2$, even though S_1 and S_2 define the same set of completely-specified instances when forbidden, namely those instances which have only positive edges or only negative edges. They do not define the same set of *generic instances*, since, for example, the single pattern $Q \in S_2$ is in $f(S_1)$ but not $f(S_2)$.

Proposition 5. *For any patterns T_1, T_2, $g(T_1) = g(T_2)$ if and only if $T_1 \leftrightarrow T_2$.*

Proof. Suppose $g(T_1) = g(T_2)$. Then $\forall P, (\forall I \in T_1, P \not\rightarrow I) \Leftrightarrow (\forall I \in T_2, P \not\rightarrow I)$. This is equivalent to $\forall P, (\exists I \in T_1, P \rightarrow I) \Leftrightarrow (\exists I \in T_2, P \rightarrow I))$. Setting $P = I \in T_1$, we obtain $\forall I \in T_1, \exists I' \in T_2$ such that $I \rightarrow I'$, and hence $T_1 \mapsto T_2$.

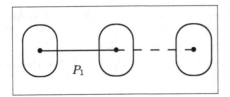

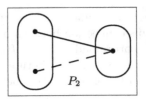

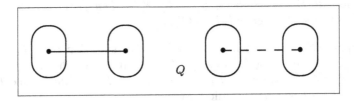

Fig. 3. The sets of patterns $S_1 = \{P_1, P_2\}$ and $S_2 = \{Q\}$ define the same set of completely specified instances when forbidden, but $f(S_1) \neq f(S_2)$.

Setting $P = I \in T_2$, by a symmetrical argument, we obtain $T_2 \mapsto T_1$, and hence $T_1 \leftrightarrow T_2$.

Now suppose that $T_1 \leftrightarrow T_2$. By Proposition 3, we can deduce that $g(T_1) = g(T_2)$.

We now show to what extent the lattice structure of S and T is preserved via the mappings f and g.

Theorem 2. $\forall S_1, S_2 \in S, \ f(S_1) \cup f(S_2) = f(S_1 + S_2)$.

Proof. For $i = 1, 2$, $f(S_i) = \{I \mid \forall P \in S_i, P \nrightarrow I\}$. So $f(S_1) \cup f(S_2) = \{I \mid (\forall P \in S_1, P \nrightarrow I) \vee (\forall P \in S_2, P \nrightarrow I)\} = \{I \mid \forall P_1 \in S_1, \forall P_2 \in S_2(P_1 \nrightarrow I \vee P_2 \nrightarrow I)\}$. Thus, by Lemma 1, $f(S_1) \cup f(S_2) = \{I \mid (\forall P_1 \in S_1, \forall P_2 \in S_2(P_1 + P_2 \nrightarrow I)\} = \{I \mid \forall P_1 + P_2 \in S_1 + S_2(P_1 + P_2 \nrightarrow I)\} = f(S_1 + S_2)$.

Theorem 3. $\forall S_1, S_2 \in S, \ f(S_1) \cap f(S_2) = f(S_1 \cup S_2)$.

Proof. $f(S_1 \cup S_2) = \{I \mid \forall P \in S_1 \cup S_2, P \nrightarrow I\} = \{I \mid \forall P_1 \in S_1, P \nrightarrow I\} \cap \{I \mid \forall P_2 \in S_2, P \nrightarrow I\} = f(S_1) \cap f(S_2)$.

The lattice structure and Theorems 2 and 3 are illustrated in Fig. 4.

Theorem 4. $\forall T_1, T_2 \in T, \ g(T_1) \cap g(T_2) = g(T_1 \cup T_2)$.

Proof. $g(T_1 \cup T_2) = \{P \mid \forall I \in T_1 \cup T_2, P \nrightarrow I\} = \{P_1 \mid \forall I \in T_1, P_1 \nrightarrow I\} \cap \{P_2 \mid \forall I \in T_2, P_2 \nrightarrow I\} = g(T_1) \cap g(T_2)$

Theorem 5. $\forall T_1, T_2 \in T, \ g(T_1) \cup g(T_2) = g(T_1 \times T_2)$.

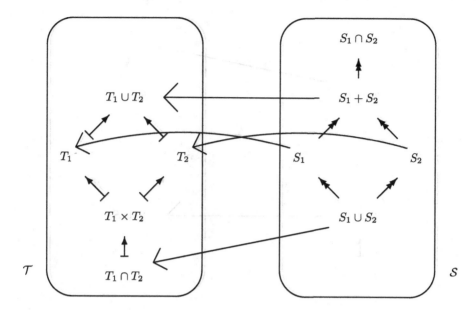

Fig. 4. The function f from S to T

Proof. $g(T_1 \times T_2) = \{P \mid \forall I \in T_1 \times T_2, P \not\twoheadrightarrow I\} = \{P \mid \forall I_1 \in T_1, \forall I_2 \in T_2, P \not\twoheadrightarrow I_1 \times I_2\}$. By Lemma 2, this is equal to $\{P \mid \forall I_1 \in T_1, \forall I_2 \in T_2, (P \not\twoheadrightarrow I_1 \vee P \not\twoheadrightarrow I_2)\}$ $= \{P \mid \forall I_1 \in T_1, P \not\twoheadrightarrow I_1\} \cup \{P \mid \forall I_2 \in T_2, P \not\twoheadrightarrow I_2\} = g(T_1) \cup g(T_2)$.

Theorems 4 and 5 are illustrated in Fig. 5.

Definition 2. *A set T of patterns is* downward-closed *if for all patterns P, Q, $(P \to Q) \wedge (Q \in T) \Rightarrow (P \in T)$. A set of patterns S is* upward-closed *if for all patterns P, Q, $(P \to Q) \wedge (P \in S) \Rightarrow (Q \in S)$.*

In the case of upward-closed sets of forbidden patterns and/or downward-closed sets of generic instances, the lattices, and the corresponding Galois connection, become simpler as the following proposition shows. In this case the two lattices become lattices of sets with meet and join operations $\cap$ and $\cup$. In practice, however, we are generally interested in small sets of forbidden patterns which cannot be upward-closed (otherwise they would be infinite).

Proposition 6. *If S_1, S_2 are upward-closed, then $S_1 + S_2 \longleftrightarrow\!\!\!\twoheadrightarrow S_1 \cap S_2$. If T_1, T_2 are downward-closed, then $T_1 \cap T_2 \leftrightarrow T_1 \times T_2$.*

Proof. $\forall P + Q \in S_1 + S_2$, we have $P \to P + Q$ and $Q \to P + Q$. By the upward closedness of both S_1 and S_2, it follows that $P + Q \in S_1 \cap S_2$. Thus $S_1 \cap S_2 \twoheadrightarrow S_1 + S_2$. By Lemma 4, we have $S_1 + S_2 \longleftrightarrow\!\!\!\twoheadrightarrow S_1 \cap S_2$.

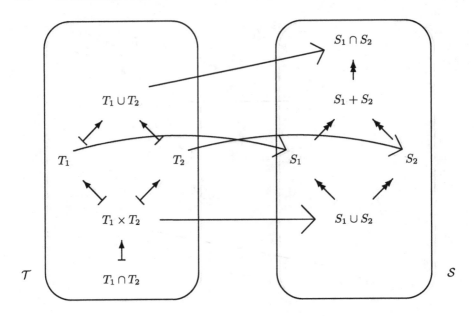

Fig. 5. The function g from $\mathcal{T}$ to $\mathcal{S}$

$\forall P \times Q \in T_1 \times T_2$, $P \times Q \to P$ and $P \times Q \to Q$. If T_1, T_2 are downward-closed, then $P \times Q \in T_1 \cap T_2$. Thus $T_1 \times T_2 \mapsto T_1 \cap T_2$. By Lemma 4, we have $T_1 \cap T_2 \leftrightarrow T_1 \times T_2$.

5 Tractability Consequences of the Galois Connection

In this section we show that tractable sets of patterns form a sublattice of $\overline{\mathcal{S}}$.

Recall that we say that $T \in \mathcal{T}$ is tractable if there is a polynomial-time algorithm to decide all completely-specified instances in T. We consider that incompletely-specified instances (i.e. generic instances with at least one pair of points not joined by a (positive or negative) edge) can be recognised as such in polynomial time and hence do not affect the tractability of T. A consequence of this is that it is not true that $T_1 \mapsto T_2 \wedge (T_2 \text{ tractable}) \Rightarrow T_1$ tractable. For example, T_2 could be trivially tractable because it contains no completely-specified instance even when T_1 is the set of all binary CSP instances. However, we have the following important result.

Proposition 7. If $T_1 = f(S_1)$ and $T_2 = f(S_2)$, then $(T_1 \mapsto T_2 \wedge (T_2 \text{ tractable})) \Rightarrow T_1$ tractable.

Proof. Let $T_1 = f(S_1)$ and $T_2 = f(S_2)$, where $T_1 \mapsto T_2$. By Proposition 3, we have $g(T_2) \subseteq g(T_1)$ and so by Lemma 3, $g(T_1) \twoheadrightarrow g(T_2)$. By definition of the functions f and g, we have $f(g(f(S))) = f(S)$ for all S, and so $f(g(T_1)) = f(S_1)$ and $f(g(T_2)) = f(S_2)$. It follows from Proposition 4 that $S_1 \leftrightarrow\!\!\!\rightarrow g(T_1)$ and $S_2 \leftrightarrow\!\!\!\rightarrow g(T_2)$. Thus $S_1 \leftrightarrow\!\!\!\rightarrow g(T_1) \twoheadrightarrow g(T_2) \leftrightarrow\!\!\!\rightarrow S_2$. By transitivity of $\twoheadrightarrow$, we have $S_1 \twoheadrightarrow S_2$ and, by Proposition 3, $T_1 = f(S_1) \subseteq f(S_2) = T_2$. It follows that if T_2 is tractable, then so is T_1.

This means that it may be possible to classify the complexity of all classes $f(S)$ for all finite sets $S \in \mathcal{S}$. Indeed we conjecture that there is a P/NP-complete dichotomy. This has already been proved for sets of patterns containing only negative edges [9].

The following proposition tells us that the tractable sets of patterns form a sub-lattice of $\overline{\mathcal{S}}$.

Proposition 8. *If S_1, S_2 are tractable sets of patterns, then so are $S_1 \cup S_2$ and $S_1 + S_2$.*

Proof. $f(S_1 + S_2) = f(S_1) \cup f(S_2)$ and hence can be solved in polynomial time if $f(S_1)$ and $f(S_2)$ can be. A similar remark holds for $f(S_1 \cup S_2) = f(S_1) \cap f(S_2)$.

We can observe that the finite sets of $\mathcal{S}$ form a sublattice of $\mathcal{S}$ since $S_1 + S_2$ and $S_1 \cup S_2$ are finite if S_1, S_2 are finite. It follows that the finite tractable sets of $\mathcal{S}$ form a sublattice. We are particularly interested in finite sets of patterns, since detecting the absence of finite sets of patterns can be achieved in polynomial time, whereas testing the absence of an infinite set of patterns may not even by computable. We can observe that there are infinite sets of patterns S such that $f(S)$ is tractable but for no finite subset S' of S is $f(S')$ tractable, e.g. acyclic instances that can be defined by forbidding cycles of all lengths but by no finite set of flat patterns [11].

6   Augmented Patterns: Motivation

We can make the language of patterns much richer by adding relations to patterns (and possibly quantifying over these relations). A *flat* pattern (the kind of pattern we have studied up to now in this paper) has only the binary relations of compatibility between points (positive edges), incompatibility between points (negative edges) and the equivalence relation between points corresponding to assignments to the same variable (represented in figures by ovals representing its equivalence classes). Suppose that we add a new relation, such as an ordering or a colouring of the points of the pattern. We call this an *augmented pattern*. In this section, we motivate the study of augmented patterns by showing that they can be used to define interesting tractable classes that cannot be defined using flat patterns. Examples of such augmented patterns are a pattern in which we add an ordering between points (the new relation is binary) or a colouring of points (in which case the new relation is unary). For these new relations to be meaningful, they must satisfy the basic properties of, for example, orderings or colourings. To impose this we can replace a single pattern P by a set of patterns, one being the augmented pattern P and the others designed in such a way as to impose the required properties of the new relation.

Consider a binary relation $R_<$. Each of the following three statements can be seen as an augmented pattern involving only the relation $R_<$:

$$R_<(a, a) \tag{1}$$
$$R_<(a, b) \wedge R_<(b, a) \tag{2}$$
$$R_<(a, b) \wedge R_<(b, c) \wedge R_<(c, a) \tag{3}$$

By forbidding these three patterns, we impose that $R_<$ is an irreflexive, anti-symmetric relation with no length-3 cycles. In the following we only consider instances in which $R_<$ is total in the sense that for all distinct a, b, we have $R_<(a, b)$ or $R_<(b, a)$. It is easy to see that this implies that $R_<$ is a strict total order (since, in particular, forbidding pattern (3) corresponds to transitivity). From now on, for notational convenience, we use the operator $<$ instead of the relation $R_<$, i.e. we write $a < b$ instead of $R_<(a, b)$. If we also forbid the augmented pattern shown in Fig. 6(a), then we not only impose an order on the points of an instance, but we also impose that there is a corresponding order on the variables which is consistent with this order on the points.

If we also forbid the augmented pattern in Fig. 6(b), then we are saying that there is a total ordering of the variables of the instance such that each variable is constrained by at most one previous variable in this order. The set of completely-specified instances with a total ordering on its points in which none of these five augmented patterns occurs corresponds exactly to the set of instances whose constraint graph is acyclic. It is well known that this class of binary CSP instances is tractable since it is solved by arc consistency [22]. Recall that no finite set of forbidden *flat* patterns defines the set of acyclic instances [11]. This example demonstrates the power of augmented patterns compared to flat patterns, since acyclicity can be defined by forbidding a set of just five augmented patterns.

In fact, for any fixed $k \geq 1$, we can define the class of instances with tree-width bounded by k using a finite set of augmented patterns. We saw above that the patterns (1), (2), (3) together with the pattern shown in Fig. 6(a) effectively allows us to impose an order on variables. Apart from this variable-order relation, we also introduce another binary relation IE (for Induced Edge between two variables in the constraint graph) which, using the same idea as in Fig. 6(a), is also effectively a relation on variables. For simplicity of presentation, in the following, we apply $<$ and IE to variables rather than points. We also require the relation $\overline{IE}$ and we will consider only those instances in which IE and $\overline{IE}$ cover all pairs of variables. To ensure that $\overline{IE}$ is the complement of IE we forbid the augmented pattern

$$IE(x, y) \wedge \overline{IE}(x, y)$$

The semantics of the induced-edge relation IE is given by the following rules:

1. IE is symmetric.
2. If there is a negative edge between variables x and y, then $IE(x, y)$.

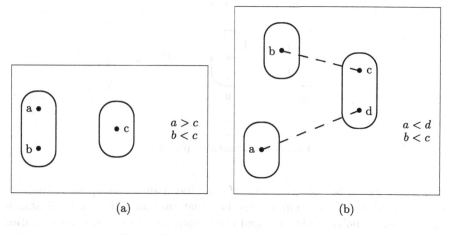

Fig. 6. Examples of augmented patterns.

3. If $x < z$, $y < z$, $IE(x, z)$ and $IE(y, z)$, then $IE(x, y)$.

These rules can easily be coded using forbidden augmented patterns involving $<$, IE and $\overline{IE}$. Symmetry is coded by the forbidden pattern

$$IE(x, y) \wedge \overline{IE}(y, x)$$

Rule 2, above, can be imposed by forbidding the augmented pattern shown in Fig. 7. Rule 3 can be coded by the forbidden pattern:

$$(x < z) \wedge (y < z) \wedge IE(x, z) \wedge IE(y, z) \wedge \overline{IE}(x, y)$$

In order to impose a bound of k on the tree-width of the constraint graph, there must exist a total variable order and relations IE, $\overline{IE}(x, y)$ (that cover all pairs of variables) such that the following augmented pattern does not occur:

$$(x_1 < z) \wedge \ldots \wedge (x_{k+1} < z) \wedge IE(x_1, z) \wedge \ldots \wedge IE(x_{k+1}, z)$$

This corresponds to a well-known characterisation of graphs with bounded tree-width as subgraphs of k-trees [22,24]. This example illustrates the fact that we need to apply a filter to the set of instances I defined by forbidding a set of augmented patterns. In this case, the filter is that I is completely specified, $<$ is a total order on variables and IE, $\overline{IE}$ form a cover. When defining tractability of augmented patterns, we are only concerned in deciding instances satisfying the filter.

Another example which motivates the use of augmented patterns is the study of tractable languages. All known tractable constraint languages are defined by the existence of a polymorphism (a pointwise closure operation) which guarantees tractability [27]. Indeed, tractability is guaranteed by the identities satisfied by the polymorphism [4]. The existence of a polymorphism satisfying any given

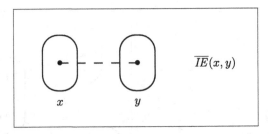

Fig. 7. An augmented pattern.

set of identities can be stated in terms of a forbidden augmented pattern. Indeed, an augmented pattern can enforce the fact that the constraints of the instance must all have a polymorphism f and other patterns can enforce the identities that f must satisfy. By existentially quantifying over f we can then define the class of all instances whose constraints all have some majority polymorphism f, for example, or all of whose constraints have a Siggers polymorphism [39].

We illustrate this for weak near-unanimity polymorphisms, given their importance in the characterisation of tractable languages [3, 41]. A binary CSP instance I has the k-ary polymorphism $f : \mathcal{D}^k \to \mathcal{D}$ if for all binary relations R of I we have $\forall (a_1, b_1), \ldots, (a_k, b_k) \in R$, $(f(a_1, \ldots, a_k), f(b_1, \ldots, b_k)) \in R$. The first step to expressing the fact that a binary CSP instance has the k-ary polymorphism f is to forbid the augmented pattern $\mathrm{POLY}_k(f)$ shown in Fig. 8 for the case $k = 4$. A weak near-unanimity operation is a function $f : \mathcal{D}^k \to \mathcal{D}$ satisfying the identities $f(b, a, \ldots, a) = f(a, b, a, \ldots, a) = \ldots = f(a, \ldots, a, b)$. These identities are equivalent to forbidding each of the following augmented patterns

$$(f(b, a, \ldots, a) = c) \wedge (f(a, b, a, \ldots, a) = d) \wedge (c \neq d)$$
$$(f(b, a, \ldots, a) = c) \wedge (f(a, a, b, a, \ldots, a) = d) \wedge (c \neq d)$$
$$\vdots$$
$$(f(b, a, \ldots, a) = c) \wedge (f(a, \ldots, a, b) = d) \wedge (c \neq d)$$

For some fixed k, after forbidding these augmented patterns (the polymorphism pattern $\mathrm{POLY}_k(f)$ as illustrated in Fig. 8 together with the above patterns corresponding to the identities of a weak near-unanimity polymorphism of arity k), we obtain a set of instances. We then have to apply a filter so that we only keep those instances $I = \langle A_I, \rho_I \rangle$ in which f is a total function and such that all domains are closed under f, i.e. for all $x \in \mathcal{X}$ and for all $a_1, \ldots, a_k \in \mathcal{D}$ such that $(x, a_i) \in A_I$ $(i = 1, \ldots, k)$, we have $(x, f(a_1, \ldots, a_k)) \in A_I$. This example again illustrates the fact that tractability of augmented patterns depends on the existence of a polynomial-time algorithm to decide instances satisfying the corresponding filter.

Another motivating example involves a colouring of points. Suppose that both S_1 and S_2 are tractable sets of flat patterns. Then we know that $S_1 + S_2$ defines the tractable class of instances in which either S_1 does not occur or S_2

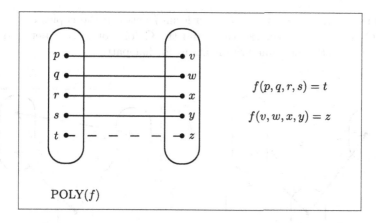

$$f(p, q, r, s) = t$$

$$f(v, w, x, y) = z$$

POLY(f)

Fig. 8. Polymorphisms can be defined by forbidding augmented patterns, as illustrated for this arity-4 polymorphism f.

does not occur. The number of patterns in $S_1 + S_2$ is (in the worst case) quadratic in the size of S_1 and S_2. We can give a set of augmented patterns which is linear in the size of S_1 and S_2 as follows. We augment each pattern in S_1 by colouring all its points red and each pattern in S_2 by colouring all its points green. We then add a pattern consisting of two points, one red and the other green. The set of instances for which there is a 2-colouring of its points in which none of these augmented patterns occurs is exactly the set of instances in $f(S_1) \cup f(S_2)$.

7   Augmented Patterns: Definitions

An *augmented pattern* is simply a flat pattern together with a conjunction of atomic formulas such as $R_i(p_1, \ldots, p_{a_i})$ where each R_i is a relation (of arity a_i) and $p_1, \ldots, p_{a_i}$ are points. An augmented pattern P occurs in another augmented pattern Q if there is a mapping from P to Q which corresponds to the occurrence of the flat version of P in the flat version of Q and which also preserves the new relation(s) R_i. The new relation(s) R_i may, for example, correspond to an order. As an example, the augmented pattern in Fig. 9(a) does not occur in the augmented pattern in Fig. 9(b) since the variable order is not preserved. On the other hand, the pattern $P1$ in Fig. 1 does occur in Fig. 9(b) since there is no variable order in $P1$ to preserve.

    As a starting point, we can consider instances augmented with one or more new relation(s). In other words we consider structured instances (e.g. instances with an order on the variables). As usual, in order to establish a Galois connection, we have to consider the lattice of all generic instances including partially-specified instances (partial in the sense that certain pairs of points are joined by neither a negative nor a positive edge *or* the new relations do not form a cover, e.g. the variable order is only partial). The operations $\times$ and $+$ and the functions f and g are defined as for sets of flat patterns. In particular, in $P + Q$

there is no relation (e.g. no variable ordering) between the copies of P and Q in $P + Q$. The two lattice structures and the Galois connection between them follow from exactly the same arguments as for flat patterns.

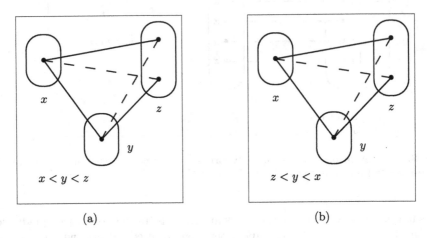

Fig. 9. (a) The broken-triangle pattern (BTP). (b) An alternative pattern which defines the same class.

However, our aim is to consider the existential quantification of the relations (variable ordering, polymorphism, colouring) associated with a (set of) augmented pattern(s). As an example of an augmented pattern, consider the broken-triangle pattern (BTP) [16] shown in Fig. 9(a). We associate with this pattern all instances for which there is some variable ordering for which BTP does not occur. It turns out that, in the case of BTP, it is decidable in polynomial time whether such a variable ordering exists [16]. In general, each structured instance (e.g. an instance with new relations such as a variable ordering) has a corresponding flat version in which the new relations are forgotten, and our aim is to establish a Galois connection between sets of *flat* instances and augmented patterns.

We would like to establish a Galois connection between the set of sets of flat generic instances T and the set of sets of augmented patterns which we denote by S_A. However, this does not seem possible. Instead we present in Sect. 8 a Galois connection between T and Σ_A the set of sets of sets of augmented patterns. Each $\sigma \in \Sigma_A$ is a set of the form $\{S_1, S_2, \ldots\}$ where each $S_i \in S_A$ is a set of patterns. Observe that since every element S of S_A has a corresponding singleton element $\{S\}$ in Σ_A, we can consider Σ_A as an extension of S_A. We extend our definition of $\twoheadrightarrow$ from S_A to Σ_A as follows: $\sigma_1 \twoheadrightarrow \sigma_2$ if $\forall S_2 \in \sigma_2$, $\exists S_1 \in \sigma_1$ such that $S_1 \twoheadrightarrow S_2$. We define $\overline{\Sigma}_A$ to be the set of equivalence classes with respect to the equivalence relation $\twoheadleftarrow\twoheadrightarrow$ in Σ_A.

We first have to understand the lattice structure of $\langle \overline{\Sigma}_A, \leq \rangle$, where $\sigma_1 \leq \sigma_2$ if and only if $\sigma_2 \twoheadrightarrow \sigma_1$. The meet and join operations of this lattice are the operations $+$ and $\cup$. This follows from the following lemmas.

Lemma 5. *For $\sigma, \sigma_1, \sigma_2 \in \overline{\Sigma}_A$, if $\sigma_1 \twoheadrightarrow \sigma$ and $\sigma_2 \twoheadrightarrow \sigma$ then $(\sigma_1 + \sigma_2) \twoheadrightarrow \sigma$.*

Proof. Suppose that $\sigma_1 \twoheadrightarrow \sigma$ and $\sigma_2 \twoheadrightarrow \sigma$ and consider any $S \in \sigma$. We have $\exists S_i \in \sigma_i$ such that $S_i \twoheadrightarrow S$ $(i = 1, 2)$. So $\forall P \in S, \exists P_i \in S_i$ such that $P_i \rightarrow P$ $(i = 1, 2)$. Thus $P_1 + P_2 \rightarrow P$ and hence $S_1 + S_2 \twoheadrightarrow S$. It follows that $(\sigma_1 + \sigma_2) \twoheadrightarrow \sigma$.

Lemma 6. *For $\sigma, \sigma_1, \sigma_2 \in \overline{\Sigma}_A$, if $\sigma \twoheadrightarrow \sigma_1$ and $\sigma \twoheadrightarrow \sigma_2$ then $\sigma \twoheadrightarrow (\sigma_1 \cup \sigma_2)$.*

Proof. If $\sigma \twoheadrightarrow \sigma_1$ and $\sigma \twoheadrightarrow \sigma_2$, then $\forall S_i \in \sigma_i, \exists S \in \sigma$ such that $S \twoheadrightarrow S_i$ $(i = 1, 2)$. Hence, $\sigma \twoheadrightarrow (\sigma_1 \cup \sigma_2)$.

We fix a relational signature. Indeed, for simplicity of presentation, in the following we assume that there is a single new relation Rel of a fixed arity a (which could be the cartesian product of several relations). We denote by $\mathcal{REL}$ the set of all possible functions from the set of (flat) instances to the set of relations of arity a. Thus, given a flat instance $I \in \mathcal{I}$ and a function $Rel \in \mathcal{REL}$, $\langle I, Rel(I) \rangle$ is an augmented version of I (e.g. the instance I with an ordering on its variables). We can now define occurrence of a set $S \in \mathcal{S}_A$ of augmented patterns in an instance $I \in \mathcal{I}$ as $\forall Rel \in \mathcal{REL}, \exists P_A \in S$ such that $P_A \rightarrow \langle I, Rel(I) \rangle$. Hence, S does not occur in I if

$$\exists Rel \in \mathcal{REL} \text{ such that } \forall P_A \in S, \ P_A \not\rightarrow \langle I, Rel(I) \rangle.$$

Thus occurrence of a *set* S of augmented patterns depends on a single quantification over $\mathcal{REL}$. This is the reason why we need to consider sets of sets of augmented patterns to obtain a Galois connection.

8   A Galois Connection for Augmented Patterns

In order to establish a Galois connection between $\overline{\Sigma}_A$ and $\overline{\mathcal{T}}$, we require the following functions $F : \Sigma_A \rightarrow \mathcal{T}$ and $G : \mathcal{T} \rightarrow \Sigma_A$.

$$F(\sigma) = \{I \in \mathcal{I} \mid \forall S \in \sigma, \exists Rel \in \mathcal{REL} \text{ such that } \forall P \in S, P \not\rightarrow \langle I, Rel(I) \rangle\}$$
$$G(T) = \{S \in \mathcal{S}_A \mid \forall I \in T, \exists Rel \in \mathcal{REL} \text{ such that } \forall P \in S, P \not\rightarrow \langle I, Rel(I) \rangle\}$$

To give a concrete example to illustrate the definition of F, if S contains patterns which when forbidden impose that Rel is a partial order on the variables, then $F(\{S\})$ only contains instances equipped with a partial order on their variables. As in the case of BTP, we may want to impose a total order on the variables. $F(\{S\})$ contains many instances which are either incompletely specified or for which Rel is not total; such instances can be recognised (and filtered out) in polynomial time and thus are irrelevant for deciding whether S is tractable or not, but are essential for the Galois connection. This is analogous to the Galois connection for flat pattern where $f(S)$ included incompletely-specified instances.

Given a set of instances T, there may be more than one way of describing T using forbidden augmented patterns. For example, let S_1 be the set of augmented patterns imposing a partial order on variables (as described in Sect. 6) together with the pattern BTP shown in Fig. 9(a), and let S_2 be identical to S_1 except that BTP is replaced by the pattern in Fig. 9(b). It is easy to see that $F(\{S_1\}) = F(\{S_2\})$. Hence, if $T = F(\{S_1\})$, then $S_1, S_2 \in G(T)$.

Theorem 6. *The functions F and G define an antitone Galois connection between $\overline{\Sigma}_A$ and $\overline{\mathcal{T}}$.*

Proof. To show that we have an antitone Galois connection between $\overline{\Sigma}_A$ and $\overline{\mathcal{T}}$, it suffices to show that $\forall \sigma \in \Sigma_A, \forall T \in \mathcal{T}, T \leq F(\sigma) \Leftrightarrow \sigma \leq G(T)$. This corresponds to $(T \mapsto F(\sigma)) \Leftrightarrow (G(T) \twoheadrightarrow \sigma)$.

By definition, $T \mapsto F(\sigma)$ if and only if $\forall I_T \in T, \exists I \in \mathcal{I}$ with $I_T \to I$ and such that $\forall S \in \sigma, \exists Rel \in \mathcal{REL}$ such that $\forall P \in S, P \nrightarrow \langle I, Rel(I)\rangle$. Thus $T \mapsto F(S)$ if and only if $\forall I_T \in T, \forall S \in \sigma, \exists Rel \in \mathcal{REL}$ such that $\forall P \in S, P \nrightarrow \langle I, Rel(I)\rangle$.

On the other hand, $G(T) \twoheadrightarrow \sigma$ if and only if $\forall S \in \sigma, \exists S' \in \mathcal{S}_A$ with $S' \twoheadrightarrow S$ and such that $\forall I \in T, \exists Rel \in \mathcal{REL}$ such that $\forall P' \in S', P' \nrightarrow \langle I, Rel(I)\rangle$. Thus $G(T) \twoheadrightarrow \sigma$ if and only if $\forall S \in \sigma, \forall I \in T, \exists Rel \in \mathcal{REL}$ such that $\forall P \in S, P \nrightarrow \langle I, Rel(I)\rangle$.

We therefore have $(T \mapsto F(\sigma)) \Leftrightarrow (G(T) \twoheadrightarrow \sigma)$ which completes the proof.

The Galois connection is similar to the Galois connection between $\overline{\mathcal{T}}$ and $\overline{\mathcal{S}}$, as demonstrated by the following results.

Theorem 7. *For all $\sigma_1, \sigma_2 \in \overline{\Sigma}_A$, $F(\sigma_1 + \sigma_2) = F(\sigma_1) \cup F(\sigma_2)$.*

Proof. $F(\sigma_1 + \sigma_2) = \{I \in \mathcal{I} \mid \forall S \in \sigma_1 + \sigma_2, \exists Rel \in \mathcal{REL}$ such that $\forall P \in S, P \nrightarrow \langle I, Rel(I)\rangle\} = \{I \in \mathcal{I} \mid \forall S_1 \in \sigma_1, \forall S_2 \in \sigma_2, \exists Rel \in \mathcal{REL}$ such that $\forall P_1 \in S_1, \forall P_2 \in S_2, P_1 + P_2 \nrightarrow \langle I, Rel(I)\rangle\}$. But $P_1 + P_2 \nrightarrow \langle I, Rel(I)\rangle$ if and only if $P_1 \nrightarrow \langle I, Rel(I)\rangle$ or $P_2 \nrightarrow \langle I, Rel(I)\rangle$ (by an immediate generalisation of Lemma 1 to augmented patterns). Furthermore, $\forall P_1 \in S_1, \forall P_2 \in S_2, P_1 \nrightarrow \langle I, Rel(I)\rangle$ or $P_2 \nrightarrow \langle I, Rel(I)\rangle$ if and only if $\forall P_1 \in S_1, P_1 \nrightarrow \langle I, Rel(I)\rangle$ or $\forall P_2 \in S_2, P_2 \nrightarrow \langle I, Rel(I)\rangle$. From all this, it follows that $F(\sigma_1 + \sigma_2) = \{I \in \mathcal{I} \mid \forall S_1 \in \sigma_1, \exists Rel \in \mathcal{REL}$ such that $\forall P \in S_1, P \nrightarrow \langle I, Rel(I)\rangle\} \cup \{I \in \mathcal{I} \mid \forall S_2 \in \sigma_2, \exists Rel \in \mathcal{REL}$ such that $\forall P \in S_2, P \nrightarrow \langle I, Rel(I)\rangle\} = F(\sigma_1) \cup F(\sigma_2)$.

Theorem 8. *For all $\sigma_1, \sigma_2 \in \overline{\Sigma}_A$, $F(\sigma_1 \cup \sigma_2) = F(\sigma_1) \cap F(\sigma_2)$.*

Proof. $F(\sigma_1 \cup \sigma_2) = \{I \in \mathcal{I} \mid \forall S \in \sigma_1 \cup \sigma_2, \exists Rel \in \mathcal{REL}$ such that $P \nrightarrow \langle I, Rel(I)\rangle\} = \{I \in \mathcal{I} \mid \forall S \in \sigma_1, \exists Rel \in \mathcal{REL}$ such that $\forall P \in S, P \nrightarrow \langle I, Rel(I)\rangle\} \cap \{I \in \mathcal{I} \mid \forall S \in \sigma_2, \exists Rel \in \mathcal{REL}$ such that $\forall P \in S, P \nrightarrow \langle I, Rel(I)\rangle\} = F(\sigma_1) \cap F(\sigma_2)$.

The lattice structure of Σ_A and Theorems 7 and 8 are illustrated in Fig. 10.

Theorem 9. *For all $T_1, T_2 \in \overline{\mathcal{T}}$, $G(T_1 \cup T_2) = G(T_1) \cap G(T_2)$.*

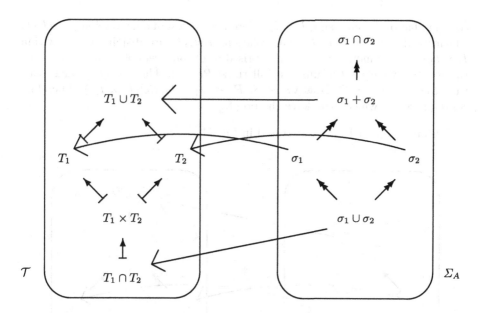

Fig. 10. The function F from Σ_A to $\mathcal{T}$

Proof. $G(T_1 \cup T_2) = \{S \in \mathcal{S}_A \mid \forall I \in T_1 \cup T_2, \exists Rel \in \mathcal{REL} \text{ such that } \forall P \in S,$ $P \nrightarrow \langle I, Rel(I) \rangle\} = \{S \in \mathcal{S}_A \mid \forall I \in T_1, \exists Rel \in \mathcal{REL} \text{ such that } \forall P \in S,$ $P \nrightarrow \langle I, Rel(I) \rangle\} \cap \{S \in \mathcal{S}_A \mid \forall I \in T_2, \exists Rel \in \mathcal{REL} \text{ such that } \forall P \in S,$ $P \nrightarrow \langle I, Rel(I) \rangle\} = G(T_1) \cap G(T_2).$

Theorem 10. *For all* $T_1, T_2 \in \overline{\mathcal{T}}$, $G(T_1 \times T_2) = G(T_1) \cup G(T_2)$.

Proof. $G(T_1 \times T_2) = \{S \in \mathcal{S}_A \mid \forall I \in T_1 \times T_2, \exists Rel \in \mathcal{REL} \text{ such that } \forall P \in S,$ $P \nrightarrow \langle I, Rel(I) \rangle\} = \{S \in \mathcal{S}_A \mid \forall I_1 \in T_1, \forall I_2 \in T_2, \exists Rel \in \mathcal{REL} \text{ such that }$ $\forall P \in S, P \nrightarrow \langle I_1 \times I_2, Rel(I_1 \times I_2) \rangle\}$. Now, for any $Rel \in \mathcal{REL}$, $\langle I_1, Rel(I_1) \rangle$ $\times \langle I_2, Rel(I_2) \rangle \rightarrow \langle I_1 \times I_2, Rel(I_1 \times I_2) \rangle$. Thus $P \nrightarrow \langle I_1 \times I_2, Rel(I_1 \times I_2) \rangle$ implies $P \nrightarrow \langle I_1, Rel(I_1) \rangle \times \langle I_2, Rel(I_2) \rangle$ which (by an immediate extension of Lemma 2 to augmented patterns) is equivalent to $(P \nrightarrow \langle I_1, Rel(I_1) \rangle) \vee (P \nrightarrow \langle I_2, Rel(I_2) \rangle)$. It follows from the above that $G(T_1 \times T_2) \subseteq \{S \in \mathcal{S}_A \mid \forall I_1 \in T_1,$ $\forall I_2 \in T_2, \exists Rel \in \mathcal{REL} \text{ such that } (P \nrightarrow \langle I_1, Rel(I_1) \rangle) \vee (P \nrightarrow \langle I_2, Rel(I_2) \rangle)\}$. But, the latter is equal to $\{S \in \mathcal{S}_A \mid (\forall I_1 \in T_1, \exists Rel \in \mathcal{REL} \text{ such that } (P \nrightarrow$ $\langle I_1, Rel(I_1) \rangle)) \vee (\forall I_1 \in T_2, \exists Rel \in \mathcal{REL} \text{ such that } P \nrightarrow \langle I_2, Rel(I_2) \rangle)\} =$ $G(T_1) \cup G(T_2)$. Thus $G(T_1 \times T_2) \subseteq G(T_1) \cup G(T_2)$.

In order to show $G(T_1) \cup G(T_2) \subseteq G(T_1 \times T_2)$, and hence to complete the proof, without loss of generality, we only need to show $G(T_1) \subseteq G(T_1 \times T_2)$. Consider $S \in G(T_1)$. We have $\forall I_1 \in T_1, \exists Rel_1 \in \mathcal{REL}$ such that $\forall P \in S,$ $P \nrightarrow \langle I_1, Rel_1(I_1) \rangle$. Therefore, for all common factors I of I_1 and $I_2, \exists Rel \in \mathcal{REL}$ such that $\forall P \in S, P \nrightarrow \langle I, Rel(I) \rangle$. Indeed, we can clearly choose $Rel = Rel_1$ for each such I. Now $I_1 \times I_2$ is the juxtaposition of copies of such common factors I. These copies are comprised of disjoint sets of points. For each such copy of a common factor I composing $I_1 \times I_2$, there is a corresponding version of $Rel_1(I)$ which we denote by $Rel_I(I)$. The relations $Rel_I(I)$ are disjoint (since within $I_1 \times I_2$ each common factor I is comprised of disjoint sets of points). Let R be the relation which is the union of all these $Rel_I(I)$. Then $\exists Rel \in \mathcal{REL}$ such that $Rel(I_1 \times I_2) = R$. Now $\forall P \in S$, $P \nrightarrow \langle I_1 \times I_2, Rel(I_1 \times I_2) \rangle$. Therefore $S \in G(T_1 \times T_2)$ which completes the proof.

Theorems 9 and 10 are illustrated in Fig. 11.

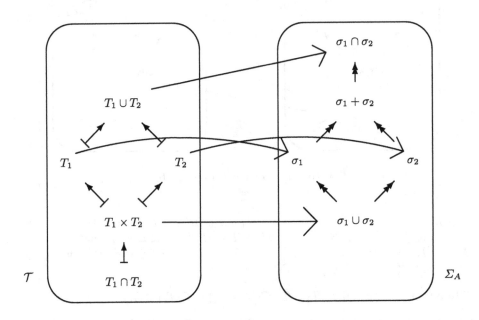

Fig. 11. The function G from $\mathcal{T}$ to Σ_A

In order to define tractability of sets of augmented patterns we must apply a filter to instances so that we only consider completely-specified instances with a certain property. Examples of filters include the property that an ordering relation is total or that two relations (such as the relations IE and $\overline{IE}$ that we introduced in Sect. 6) form a cover of all pairs of assignments to distinct variables. For example, in the case of BTP, we are only interested in instances equipped with a total ordering on the variables, since the pattern shown in Fig. 9(a) trivially does not occur on variables which are not ordered. This leads to the following definition of tractability.

Definition 3. *Let $\mathcal{F}$ be a property of instances $I \in \mathcal{I}$ that can be verified in polynomial time. We say that $\sigma \in \Sigma_A$ is tractable (with respect to the filter $\mathcal{F}$) if there is a polynomial-time algorithm to decide the set of completely-specified instances in $F(\sigma)$ (which satisfy the filter $\mathcal{F}$). In particular, we say that $S \in \mathcal{S}_A$ is tractable (w.r.t. $\mathcal{F}$) if $\{S\}$ is tractable (w.r.t. $\mathcal{F}$).*

Proposition 9. *The tractable elements of $\overline{\Sigma}_A$ form a sublattice. Furthermore, the tractable sets of augmented patterns form a join semi-lattice of $\mathcal{S}_A$.*

Proof. If $\sigma_1, \sigma_2 \in \overline{\Sigma}_A$ are tractable, then so are $\sigma_1 + \sigma_2$ and $\sigma_1 \cup \sigma_2$. This follows immediately from the fact that $F(\sigma_1 + \sigma_2) = F(\sigma_2) \cup F(\sigma_2)$ and $F(\sigma_1 \cup \sigma_2) = F(\sigma_2) \cap F(\sigma_2)$. The tractable sets of augmented patterns form a join semi-lattice, since S_1, S_2 tractable implies that $S_1 + S_2$ is tractable.

9   Discussion and Conclusion

In this paper we have initiated the study of the Galois connection between lattices of sets of forbidden patterns and sets of instances. The consequences of this Galois connection for expressibility and tractability questions remains largely unexplored. However, we have shown that the tractable sets of patterns form a sub-lattice.

Augmented patterns provide a rich language in which we can define many interesting classes of instances in a concise form, notably by adding an order on the variables or the values. We have seen that both bounded treewidth and the existence of a polymorphism satisfying a set of identities can be expressed using augmented patterns (together with a filter on the set of instances). This leads to an orthogonal question of the tractability of the recognition of classes defined by augmented patterns. For example, given a binary CSP instance, it is NP-hard to determine whether there exists an ordering of the values under which all relations are max-closed [25]. On the other hand, it is tractable to decide whether the relations have a conservative Mal'tsev polymorphism [6]. Determining the tractability frontier of this meta-problem is an open question for augmented patterns. As we have pointed out, the recognition problem is always tractable for finite sets of flat patterns.

It is natural to ask whether the Feder-Vardi dichotomy [23] (for classes of CSP instances defined by finite languages of constraint relations) generalises to classes of CSP instances defined by augmented patterns. However, we know that no such P/NP-hard dichotomy can exist by the work on lifted patterns by Kun and Nešetřil [33] and by Ladner's theorem [34]. It is an open question whether classes of CSP instances defined by forbidding *flat* patterns exhibit a dichotomy in the following sense: all finite sets of patterns are either tractable or NP-complete. We conjecture that this is true.

References

1. Barto, L., Krokhin, A.A., Willard, R.: Polymorphisms, and how to use them. In: Krokhin, A., Živný, S. (eds.) [32], pp. 1–44. https://doi.org/10.4230/DFU.Vol7. 15301.1
2. Birkhoff, G.: Lattice Theory, vol. 25, 3rd edn. AMS Colloquium Publications, American Mathematical Society, New York (1967)

148   D. A. Cohen et al.

3. Bulatov, A.A.: A dichotomy theorem for nonuniform CSPs. In: Umans, C. (ed.) 58th IEEE Annual Symposium on Foundations of Computer Science, FOCS 2017, Berkeley, CA, USA, 15–17 October 2017, pp. 319–330. IEEE Computer Society (2017). https://doi.org/10.1109/FOCS.2017.37
4. Bulatov, A.A., Jeavons, P., Krokhin, A.A.: Classifying the complexity of constraints using finite algebras. SIAM J. Comput. **34**(3), 720–742 (2005). https://doi.org/10.1137/S0097539700376676
5. Bulin, J., Delic, D., Jackson, M., Niven, T.: A finer reduction of constraint problems to digraphs. Log. Methods Comput. Sci. **11**(4), 1–33 (2015). https://doi.org/10.2168/LMCS-11(4:18)2015
6. Carbonnel, C.: The dichotomy for conservative constraint satisfaction is polynomially decidable. In: Rueher, M. (ed.) CP 2016. LNCS, vol. 9892, pp. 130–146. Springer, Cham (2016). https://doi.org/10.1007/978-3-319-44953-1_9
7. Carbonnel, C., Cohen, D.A., Cooper, M.C., Živný, S.: On singleton arc consistency for CSPs defined by monotone patterns. Algorithmica **81**(4), 1699–1727 (2019). https://doi.org/10.1007/s00453-018-0498-2
8. Carbonnel, C., Cooper, M.C.: Tractability in constraint satisfaction problems: a survey. Constraints **21**(2), 115–144 (2016). https://doi.org/10.1007/s10601-015-9198-6
9. Cohen, D.A., Cooper, M.C., Creed, P., Marx, D., Salamon, A.Z.: The tractability of CSP classes defined by forbidden patterns. J. Artif. Intell. Res. (JAIR) **45**, 47–78 (2012). https://doi.org/10.1613/jair.3651
10. Cohen, D.A., Cooper, M.C., Jeavons, P.G., Krokhin, A.A., Powell, R., Živný, S.: Binarisation for valued constraint satisfaction problems. SIAM J. Discret. Math. **31**(4), 2279–2300 (2017). https://doi.org/10.1137/16M1088107
11. Cohen, D.A., Cooper, M.C., Jeavons, P.G., Živný, S.: Binary constraint satisfaction problems defined by excluded topological minors. Inf. Comput. **264**, 12–31 (2019). https://doi.org/10.1016/j.ic.2018.09.013
12. Cooper, M.C.: Beyond consistency and substitutability. In: O'Sullivan, B. (ed.) CP 2014. LNCS, vol. 8656, pp. 256–271. Springer, Cham (2014). https://doi.org/10.1007/978-3-319-10428-7_20
13. Cooper, M.C., Cohen, D.A., Jeavons, P.: Characterising tractable constraints. Artif. Intell. **65**(2), 347–361 (1994). https://doi.org/10.1016/0004-3702(94)90021-3
14. Cooper, M.C., Duchein, A., Mouelhi, A.E., Escamocher, G., Terrioux, C., Zanuttini, B.: Broken triangles: from value merging to a tractable class of general-arity constraint satisfaction problems. Artif. Intell. **234**, 196–218 (2016). https://doi.org/10.1016/j.artint.2016.02.001
15. Cooper, M.C., Escamocher, G.: Characterising the complexity of constraint satisfaction problems defined by 2-constraint forbidden patterns. Discrete Appl. Math. **184**, 89–113 (2015). https://doi.org/10.1016/j.dam.2014.10.035
16. Cooper, M.C., Jeavons, P.G., Salamon, A.Z.: Generalizing constraint satisfaction on trees: hybrid tractability and variable elimination. Artif. Intell. **174**(9–10), 570–584 (2010). https://doi.org/10.1016/j.artint.2010.03.002
17. Cooper, M.C., Živný, S.: Hybrid tractability of valued constraint problems. Artif. Intell. **175**(9–10), 1555–1569 (2011). https://doi.org/10.1016/j.artint.2011.02.003
18. Cooper, M.C., Živný, S.: Hybrid tractable classes of constraint problems. In: Krokhin, A., Živný, S. (eds.) [32], pp. 113–135. https://doi.org/10.4230/DFU.Vol7.15301.4
19. Cooper, M.C., Živný, S.: The power of arc consistency for CSPs defined by partially-ordered forbidden patterns. Log. Methods Comput. Sci. **13**(4) (2017). https://doi.org/10.23638/LMCS-13(4:26)2017

20. Courcelle, B., Mosbah, M.: Monadic second-order evaluations on tree-decomposable graphs. Theor. Comput. Sci. **109**(1&2), 49–82 (1993). https://doi.org/10.1016/0304-3975(93)90064-Z

21. Davey, B.A., Priestley, H.A.: Introduction to Lattices and Order, 2nd edn. Cambridge University Press, Cambridge (2002)

22. Dechter, R., Pearl, J.: Tree clustering for constraint networks. Artif. Intell. **38**(3), 353–366 (1989). https://doi.org/10.1016/0004-3702(89)90037-4

23. Feder, T., Vardi, M.Y.: The computational structure of monotone monadic SNP and constraint satisfaction: a study through datalog and group theory. SIAM J. Comput. **28**(1), 57–104 (1998). https://doi.org/10.1137/S0097539794266766

24. Freuder, E.C.: A sufficient condition for backtrack-bounded search. J. ACM **32**(4), 755–761 (1985). https://doi.org/10.1145/4221.4225

25. Green, M.J., Cohen, D.A.: Domain permutation reduction for constraint satisfaction problems. Artif. Intell. **172**(8–9), 1094–1118 (2008). https://doi.org/10.1016/j.artint.2007.12.001

26. Grohe, M.: The complexity of homomorphism and constraint satisfaction problems seen from the other side. J. ACM **54**(1), 1:1–1:24 (2007). https://doi.org/10.1145/1206035.1206036

27. Jeavons, P.: On the algebraic structure of combinatorial problems. Theor. Comput. Sci. **200**(1–2), 185–204 (1998). https://doi.org/10.1016/S0304-3975(97)00230-2

28. Jeavons, P., Cohen, D.A., Gyssens, M.: Closure properties of constraints. J. ACM **44**(4), 527–548 (1997). https://doi.org/10.1145/263867.263489

29. Jeavons, P., Cooper, M.C.: Tractable constraints on ordered domains. Artif. Intell. **79**(2), 327–339 (1995). https://doi.org/10.1016/0004-3702(95)00107-7

30. Jégou, P.: Decomposition of domains based on the micro-structure of finite constraint-satisfaction problems. In: Fikes, R., Lehnert, W.G. (eds.) Proceedings of the 11th National Conference on Artificial Intelligence, Washington, DC, USA, pp. 731–736. AAAI Press/The MIT Press (1993). http://www.aaai.org/Library/AAAI/1993/aaai93-109.php

31. Knuth, D.E.: Stable Marriage and Its Relation to Other Combinatorial Problems, CRM Proceedings & Lecture Notes, vol. 10. American Mathematical Society, Providence (1996)

32. Krokhin, A.A., Živný, S. (eds.): The Constraint Satisfaction Problem: Complexity and Approximability, Dagstuhl Follow-Ups, vol. 7. Schloss Dagstuhl - Leibniz-Zentrum fuer Informatik (2017). http://www.dagstuhl.de/dagpub/978-3-95977-003-3

33. Kun, G., Nešetřil, J.: Forbidden lifts (NP and CSP for combinatorialists). Eur. J. Comb. **29**(4), 930–945 (2008). https://doi.org/10.1016/j.ejc.2007.11.027

34. Ladner, R.E.: On the structure of polynomial time reducibility. J. ACM **22**(1), 155–171 (1975). https://doi.org/10.1145/321864.321877

35. Mouelhi, A.E.: Tractable classes for CSPs of arbitrary arity: from theory to practice. Constraints **22**(1), 97–98 (2017). https://doi.org/10.1007/s10601-016-9262-x

36. Naanaa, W.: Unifying and extending hybrid tractable classes of CSPs. J. Exp. Theor. Artif. Intell. **25**(4), 407–424 (2013). https://doi.org/10.1080/0952813X.2012.721138

37. Naanaa, W.: Extending the broken triangle property tractable class of binary CSPs. In: Bassiliades, N., Bikakis, A., Vrakas, D., Vlahavas, I.P., Vouros, G.A. (eds.) Proceedings of the 9th Hellenic Conference on Artificial Intelligence, SETN 2016, Thessaloniki, Greece, pp. 3:1–3:6. ACM (2016). https://doi.org/10.1145/2903220.2903230

38. Régin, J.: A filtering algorithm for constraints of difference in CSPs. In: Hayes-Roth, B., Korf, R.E. (eds.) Proceedings of the 12th National Conference on Artificial Intelligence, vol. 1, pp. 362–367. AAAI Press/The MIT Press (1994). http://www.aaai.org/Library/AAAI/1994/aaai94-055.php
39. Siggers, M.H.: A strong Mal'cev condition for locally finite varieties omitting the unary type. Algebra Univers. **64**(1–2), 15–20 (2010)
40. Stergiou, K., Samaras, N.: Binary encodings of non-binary constraint satisfaction problems: algorithms and experimental results. J. Artif. Intell. Res. (JAIR) **24**, 641–684 (2005). https://doi.org/10.1613/jair.1776
41. Zhuk, D.: A proof of the CSP dichotomy conjecture. J. ACM **67**(5), 30:1–30:78 (2020). https://doi.org/10.1145/3402029

Author Index

Printed in the United States
by Baker & Taylor Publisher Services